TACTICAL REALITY

Louis Awerbuck

TACTICAL REALITY

An Uncommon Look at Common-Sense Firearms Training and Tactics

Tactical Reality: An Uncommon Look at Common-Sense Firearms Training and Tactics
by Louis Awerbuck

Copyright © 1999 by Louis Awerbuck

ISBN 1-58160-051-8
Printed in the United States of America

Published by Paladin Press, a division of
Paladin Enterprises, Inc., P.O. Box 1307,
Boulder, Colorado 80306, USA.
(303) 443-7250

Direct inquiries and/or orders to the above address.

The chapters from "The Gunfighting Mind-Set" through
"The Drawstroke" are reprinted with permission from Omega
Group Publishers, publishers of *Soldier of Fortune* and
Fighting Firearms magazines. All other chapters are reprinted
with permission from the "Tactics and Training" column of
S.W.A.T. magazine.

Visit our Web site at: www.paladin-press.com

Table of Contents

Foreword

Louis Awerbuck is an old friend and respected shooting master of long standing. If there were such a thing as a doctorate in small arms, Louis would be one of a half-dozen people I think qualified for the title. In the great days of Orange Gunsite, Louis was one of our most valued range-masters with pistol, rifle, carbine, and shotgun. He is not only a master marksman with all four weapons but he is a particularly good instructor, combining complete mastery of subject matter with outstanding teaching technique. He is notably expert in explaining to a student not only what he should do but also why he should do it, so that his pupils are in a sense teaching themselves.

A great shooting master must know not only the theory of his subject but its demonstrated practice, together with the ability to impart confidence and enthusiasm into people who may undertake training without either of those necessary attributes.

Louis' students are always impressed by his unusual degree of patience, which is sometimes lacking in other coaches. He is, above all, dedicated to the achievement of his students, rather than demonstrating his own abilities. Anyone signing up with Louis Awerbuck for training has made a very wise choice. He is a certified master of the art.

—Jeff Cooper, Gunsite, 1999

For my Five Horsemen:

Died March 7, 1982
Died September 16, 1982
Died July 14, 1986
Died August 28, 1991
Died August 11, 1992

. . . and for Mr. Ewin, last shot fired May 7, 1999

Foreword

The pen is mightier than the sword—until war is declared. This book is not for the person who believes otherwise. It is not for the man who would sacrifice honor and integrity for anything. It is not for the man who looks for trouble where he could have avoided it. It is not for the man who shuns cover and takes an unnecessary bullet. It is not for the squeamish or those who aren't prepared to defend themselves. And last, but not least, it's not for those who won't read the writing on the wall and recognize that history is about to repeat itself one more time.

The contents are a compilation of previously published magazine articles spanning a decade of comments and personal commentary on subjects ranging from target systems and ideas to firearms marksmanship and manipulation techniques to defensive survival of a deadly-force encounter.

But above all the book is intended to promote thought on winning and surviving a fight in an increasingly deteriorating society. Without a fighting brain, tactics, and common sense the soldier becomes a non sequitur—the weaponry is almost irrelevant. And, finally, it's a payment of debt to the mentors of my life, many of whom are deceased—and in their passing showed me *how it should be done*.

Louis Awerbuck
Arizona, 1999

Warning

*F*irearms are potentially dangerous and must be handled responsibly by individual trainees and experienced shooters alike. The technical information presented here on firearms handling, training, and shooting inevitably reflects the author's beliefs and experience with particular firearms and training techniques under specific circumstances that the reader cannot duplicate exactly. Therefore, the information in this book is presented *for academic study only* and should be approached with great caution. This book is not intended to serve as a replacement for professional instruction under a qualified instructor.

Introduction

The sword is more important than the shield, and skill is more important than either. The final weapon is the brain. All else is supplemental.

—John Steinbeck

John Steinbeck, better than any other writer since Sun Tzu with his classic *The Art of War* (500 B.C.), summed up the definition of fighting expertise in a nutshell. The secret to successful fighting, especially that of a defensive nature, is that the weapon is merely the means to an end.

Certainly, marksmanship is a vitally important aspect of self-preservation, but without competent, reflexive gun-handling and a tactical mind, all is lost. If you don't hit what you're shooting at, you may or may not get a second chance; but if you don't see your opponent until it's too late, there will definitely not be another opportunity.

Situation:
Joe Shootist pours round after round into the X-ring every Saturday afternoon at the local shooting range. Come Saturday night, the Cookie Monster appears from the bushes. Our hero, forced to shoot to defend himself, fires 10 rounds at a distance of seven feet.

Result:
One bullet lodges in the baddie's foot, one creases his arm, and eight end up in the schoolyard a half a mile down the street.
If you think 20-percent peripheral hits is impossibly bad, it's time to start checking some past documented situations.

What went wrong? Joe S. didn't train for the realities of a defensive encounter, that's what. We've already established that he's a proficient marksman, as evidenced by his 50-yard, perfect 300 score on a paper target. The underlying problem reverts back to Steinbeck—the brain is the key. To train on unrealistic, forgiving, stationary targets under

Utopian conditions is not the answer; in fact, it could very well leave you with a false sense of security.

Thinking that you are capable of handling a deadly-force situation when you aren't is probably worse than underestimating your ability.

It's all very well to quote such clichés as "What you practice you will do for real," or "Keep it simple stupid." The underlying problem is this: Why does a proficient 50-yard marksman miss 80 percent at seven feet?

The answer, unfortunately, is complex, to say the least. It's not as easy as saying, "Just tune out the fear and do what you did on the shooting range."

Firstly, most of us aren't exactly the personifacation of courage when it gets down to the wire, though we proclaim that we are to whoever is stupid enough to believe it. Secondly, and possibly more importantly, the fertilizer impacting the oscillator bears not the slightest resemblance to the carefully planned drills you performed at close range.

In these chapters, we'll stage some hypothetical confrontations and then analyze why they did or didn't come to a successful conclusion. All situations can be regarded from the perspective of a firearm being discharged because other possible means of resolving conflict had been exhausted. Often a competent tactitian/shooter can solve a situation *without* shooting simply because he has the ability to control the situation.

We'll try to cover everything from the basics of marksmanship to mental control tactics to gunhandling with various small arms.

At first glance some of these future articles may appear to be hogwash, but when competent marksmen are continually missing their targets in deadly-force confrontations, something is wrong somewhere with the current training techniques. The bad guys aren't winning a shootout because they're better brained—we're losing because we're beating ourselves. Range training techniques simply are not adequate preparation for potential street situations.

The root causes are unrealistic range targets and a tendency for instructors to force students into clone positions—with body positions, firing grips, and tactics conveniently packaged in a gospel that states everything must be just so.

Unfortunately, the criminal isn't always standing belt buckle to belt buckle, he isn't always where he should be, and he doesn't always react like the textbook promised he would.

Consequently, the first subjects to be covered will be ideas for practical target training systems and the suspected pitfalls of cloning shooters into regimented robots.

Obviously Joe S. needs remedial training when his 50-yard, two-inch groups enlarge to 10 inches merely because he's facing a live target.

"The final weapon is the brain; all else is supplemental."

You Are What You Practice

*I*n the introduction we met Joe Shootist—expert marksman, but he took second place in a two-man gunfight.

PLAY 1

Scene 1:
A prospective big-game hunter practices marksmanship on a life-size mock-up of a lion, the cat standing broadside to the shooter.

Scene 2:
Out in the African bush, the hunter is charged by an angry lion.

Scene 3:
We leave the lion quietly burpin' over the specialty of the house— hunter fillets.

PLAY 2

Scene 1:
Joe Shootist practices marksmanship on a life-sized, human-shaped target. The target is standing straight on to the shooter, belt buckle to belt buckle.

Scene 2:
Out in the street, the trainee is attacked by a crazed hop-head.

Scene 3:
The coroner's wagon leaves the scene with our hero and two innocent bystanders on board. The junkie is nowhere to be found.

This target is good for numerical marksmanship qualification score but little else. An eight-ring hit on this target would miss a side-on human torso.

It's not surprising if you didn't spot the difference between the two scenarios. There isn't any. Both victims practiced marksmanship on unrealistic targets. While this did wonders for *marksmanship*, it did little for their ability to deal *reflexively* with a deadly-force situation, with the inevitable result.

The shooting range is the place to find out that the lion's head is mostly mane, that the skull is surprisingly small and slopes at an alarming angle, that the cat can cover 25 feet in a single bound, and that in a frontal charge the huge body is now tucked behind the head—which is mostly mane, surrounding a surprisingly small skull, which slopes at an . . .

In other words, practice the worst-case scenarios you can imagine on the range. The street is not the place to find out about the rudiments of Murphy's Law.

While this series of articles consists of personal opinion and conjecture, there are two inviolables: (a) targets are used on a training range, and (b) what you practice on the range you will revert to in the street.

What this means, in essence, is if you revert to range training on the street and your range training didn't simulate street conditions, you're probably in trouble. Similarly, if the shooting range targets didn't emulate street targets, it's going to be time to wash the walls again.

While there are many facets to the art of missing—most of which (it is hoped) will be covered in ensuing articles—this edition is devoted to the use of range targets to simulate deadly-force problems. Again, while the mechanics and psychology will be analyzed at a later date, the premise is that Joe Shootist is already an expert marksman and can control his emotions under pressure.

There are many paper targets currently on the market—some good, some bad, and some ugly. Unfortunately, the value derived from the targets is not only in their inherent design, but in *how* you utilize them.

Typical "option-shaped" targets vary by optics (camouflage, coloring, etc.)

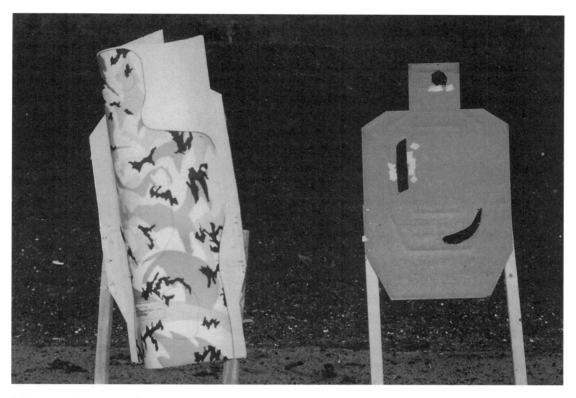

This target is more realistic. A curved, angled target combined with a negative target, forcing the shooter to think each time he fires during training.

and by the shape and size of the hit areas. Some are better than others. For example, some have no aiming point—such as a convenient dark patch in the X-ring—and in some the vital zones are indistinct and can't be distinguished at average fighting distances. Both of these situations force the trainee to aim at the center of mass of an overall picture: the ideal training regimen.

The downside of this situation is the fact that once the shooter becomes accustomed to the graphics, he's back to square one—a 30 x 18-inch target. Many of the targets currently available have an A, B, C, or D zone with corresponding point values. The problem with this is that a hit outside the A zone just *isn't good enough for the street*.

Although it *may* be good enough (depending on the bullet recipient's state of mind), it *probably* won't be. You have to go on the assumption that a hit that isn't in the vital area on a target range wouldn't have done the job for real. Also, there are no guarantees that even a perfectly placed hit will stop the adversary.

Summing up, if the small, bobbing skull on the lion is all you have to shoot at, you'd better be able to hit it.

A common, conveniently forgotten aspect of defensive shooting is the fact that we are morally, ethically, and legally responsible for the *terminal* resting place of each projectile. Not only do you have to stop the opponent, you cannot afford stray rounds in the schoolyard. Thus, anything not in the vital zone is a potential problem one way or another.

How do you confine the trainee to this during practice? Design a target like Rick Miller's Paladin System, whereby, to put it in a nutshell, only hits count. The alternative is to modify any of the other targets to make the problem more difficult. Merely restricting overall time frames is not enough for serious defensive training.

Fold over corners on the target to block off portions of the torso, head, and X-rings. Any vital hits outside the remaining visible portions of the vital areas don't cut it. Hits in the folded-over portions should be heavily penalized.

Tilt the target at varying angles and set it at different elevations. Anything can be accomplished with repetition, but different angles and elevations force the trainee to use time-tested basics—or he won't hit what he's shooting at.

Scenario:

The Cookie Monster starts his charge from halfway up a flight of stairs, dressed in a trench coat. In a split second, you have a problem literally descending on you at varying elevations, bobbing and weaving with an extremely difficult-to-discern vital hit zone. You're back in the bush with the lion, and all of a sudden it's not fair because they didn't explain this to you on the range. Result? Hunter fillets or the menu again.

This leads us to the next stage: graphic human-shaped targets. A word of warning: Trainees tend to shoot at what triggers their mind. If you use poorly designed targets that simulate the baddie standing and facing you and shooting from chest level, obviously the baddie's gun will be depicted in the center of his chest area. You shoot at his gun and get center hits. Amazing. Use human-shaped targets depicting *different body angles* and *various vital zone sizes and angles*.

So now you're gonna go out and buy a $3 million moving-target system, right? Wrong. When was the last time you saw somebody running sideways smoothly at 40 miles per hour? The real problem is a target, probably 10 to 30 feet distant, bobbing and weaving. If you want to shoot clay pigeons, shoot clay pigeons. You need a simple system to simulate a real problem, not a sporting target that can be "gamed" by leading or missing. A little ingenuity and a few dollars can build an extremely beneficial training aid.

Here is where you find that the "always shoot twice" syndrome doesn't always apply. The target may not be there after the first shot. The head may be too difficult to hit under specific scenarios, or you may have to fire four or five times at the body because that's all that is available to you tactically, etc. As far as *always* firing twice at the body and then once at the head—good luck. Steel targets have become popular training aids since the inception of John Pepper's "Poppers."

Again, don't make it any easier on yourself than it might be on the street. Steel that is calibrated to fall over with a center chest hit will fall over with a bullet impacting the top of the skull. Mediocre shooting at best. Don't lose sight of your primary objective—hitting the adversary in the vital area.

Reactive steel is easier to hit than paper if you don't lose front-sight focus, merely because a hit virtually anywhere is a hit, whereas psychologically we are always trying to shoot neat groups on paper. If you use steel follow the manufacturer's safety suggestions and *inspect your hits* after the target goes down.

The last phase is (usually) expensive video simulators. These, however, are a little beyond the average wallet, though they are excellent training aids once the trainee is an accomplished marksman/tactician.

Once you've tried some of these ideas and found out how difficult the real world is, don't go home and kick the dog. It's better finding out on the range and then practicing, rather than having Mutley waiting at home next to an empty food bowl because you learned the hard way on the street, as so many others have.

If you followed some of the target suggestions in the previous article, some basic differences probably materialized between your normal shot groups and those on the "modified" targets.

The reason for this is that even though it was a piece of steel or paper, the overall problem was more street-comparative than the regular generic target shape or height. Using the suggested and varied target ideas forces the trainee to change his *tactical* approach to delivering the shot, much as it is forced upon you for real.

We would do well to repeat at this stage that we are legally, morally, and ethically responsible for the *terminal* resting place of the projectile(s). In other words, hits outside the desired hit area *don't cut it*, one way or another.

What follows is an attempted analysis of the cause and effect of the difference between the two target problems.

Always fire twice at the body with a handgun. Well, that's fine and dandy if you have the *availability*. While it does increase the probability of stopping the

fight compared to a single strike, it also, in all reality, usually results in the shooter using a "hammer" (first round sighted, second unsighted) in the frantic rush to "always fire twice," especially when shooting on the move.

Joe Shootist (remember him?), who can fire "hammers" all day long on a normal target, now has a hard-to-discern, moving target. Being a great marksman, he can keep both shots within two inches of each other. Unfortunately, in the situation forced upon him, he misses his desired mark by four lousy inches—*twice*. The better the marksman, the closer he can keep the second point of impact to the first—but when the first one missed, guess where the second one went? Perhaps firing sighted rounds, one at a time, is a surer *real* answer.

If you tried the bobbing target idea, this may have proven painfully evident. The subgun with a good two-round burst technique will mechanically take care of the "fire twice" syndrome on its own, hence its superiority over the handgun. But if you fire twice with the handgun, why not with the rifle or shotgun? Ballistically they may be superior, but B-52 bombers they aren't.

Shifting to the head after two quick body shots—the Automatic Failure Drill—is a good way to go if forced to, as long as you have the availability and, as always, can guarantee the hit.

As far as the "if two quick body shots don't stop him, another 10 won't" theory is concerned, tactically *you may not have a choice*. You will have been forced into a shooting you didn't want and will have to continue delivering *accurate* fire until the assailant ceases to resist, or you're going home in a box.

Extending the situation to multiple assailants, which is becoming increasingly common, we are now thrown into a scenario of three moving "bad guys," all different heights and all having different oblique body angles. How does that compare to an El Presidente range drill? Let's face it—*it doesn't*. Here again, seven-second El Presidente Joe Shootist blows it in the street because there was no correlation between the range drill and street reality.

Folding over portions of three paper targets to blot out a small section of the X-rings and placing the targets at varying heights reduces El Presidente to a humbling exercise and far better simulates reality.

If you buy the theories so far and have been following the game plan, you will have noticed one of two things on folded-over targets: The projectiles will have, for the most part, impacted to one side of the X-ring, or they hit the folded-over portion. There are two reasons for this. The first is the shooter's not concentrating on the job at hand and, in an attempt to make sure the "hostage/barricade" simulation portion of the target is not hit, the shooter's holding off too far to the opposite side and not getting hits in the center of what's left of the vital zone. The second is that the shooter tightens up to such an extent that he strangles the gun and slams on the trigger, impacting the target in the one place he couldn't afford.

Remember, you have a twofold problem: to deliver accurate fire to a vital zone and to *not* hit the "good guy" hostage, barricade, etc. Impacting the

assailant in the Y-ring on the range may get you three points—on the street it gets you nothing but an escalating situation. The projectile must enter the desired vital zone and nowhere else.

Bear in mind, too, that while angles don't have to be taken into consideration on single-dimensional paper targets—in reality they do.

For example, shooting from an oblique right-to-left angle at a paper target, a hit in the humanoid target's right cheekbone scores points. In the street you would need the bullet to enter the left cheekbone/eye socket area to have the desired entry/exit wound channel for a brain shot.

Taking this a step further, by using a multiprojectile shotgun from an oblique angle, it can be seen how the simple hold-off technique for the paper-range hostage scenario becomes a nightmare on live three-dimensional human beings. Definitely the time to use a slug or transition to a single-projectile weapon!

To work on stress control, a superb street-simulation drill was evolved by Colonel Jeff Cooper, to whom so many owe so much. It is the man-on-man competition, whereby two trainees face off against a mirror image, knock-down steel target problem. The first shooter to complete his part of the drill wins. It's not as easy as it looks!

The bottom line here, as in the street, is, to quote Ross Seyfried, "You can't miss fast enough to catch up."

Making Your
Training Realistic

Delusion: A false belief regarding the self that persists despite the facts and is common in psychotic states.

—*Webster's Dictionary*

You can't have a cure if you don't know what the problem is, and most times a street confrontation doesn't correlate to last week's range problem. Last week's range situation consisted, among other things, of a known target shape, a known distance, a target on the same elevation as the shooter, and an "expected" time frame on an unchanging, unmoving scenario. Ergo, if you base your street training on unrepresentative range drills, the result is inevitable—you lose.

Taking the above ingredients in order:

A. *Known target shape and distances.*

If you repeatedly train on the same target and merely progressively extend the distance, all you are doing is honing your sight picture and trigger control skills. In the street, a six-foot situation is often more difficult to control than a 25-yard range problem because you have to react to a threat, *identify the vital zone,* and then hit it.

On the commonly used, generic, option-shaped target, you know in advance where the vital zone is; it's in the center of mass of a square-edged, rectangular target. You don't have to expend time finding it before you can shoot, unlike reality where the irregularly shaped target is invariably moving and angled to the shooter.

Inflate several party balloons to different sizes, suspend them all individually from cotton thread at five yards, wait for a light breeze, and then commence firing. This will bring home the problems of tracking down the ever changing vital zone you will encounter for real.

As discussed previously, it's not fair and it's not easy, but it is better than deluding yourself.

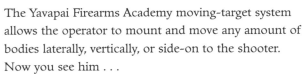

The Yavapai Firearms Academy moving-target system allows the operator to mount and move any amount of bodies laterally, vertically, or side-on to the shooter. Now you see him . . .

. . . Now you don't.

B. *Differing elevations.*

It's 3 A.M. and you are forced into shooting to defend yourself in your home. Mr. X is rapidly descending the stairs to your lounge—distance from you: 12 to 15 feet.

In the space of a couple of seconds his elevation, relative to yours, has changed about four feet. He is dressed in a three-quarter-length coat, which is flapping wildly about his body. You prudently didn't switch on any lights, so you now have an extremely difficult-to-

discern vital hit zone on a moving, angled target, albeit at "only" four to five yards.

Let's face it. What you have is a problem much more difficult to solve than your broad daylight range problem at 50 yards on a nonmoving, belt buckle to belt buckle option target, where, as should be increasingly apparent by now, all you accomplished were marksmanship and manipulation.

The range drill did nothing to get the job done, and it won't until your range scenarios and basic target scenarios simulate the street or until you accept the fact that basic range drills are just that: basic range drills.

C. *"Expected" time frames.*

If you "Pavlov's Dog" two rounds at five yards in two seconds with a handgun on the range, you will pull the same pooch performance on the 3 A.M. intruder in a frantic effort to revert to what you have mechanically practiced.

Obviously, the target situation is constantly changing, and, obviously, you aren't going to crank off two mechanical rounds like a vegetable, because for sure the second bullet will miss under these circumstances. Equally obvious is the fact that all the mechanically executed range drills based on a stopwatch and static distances have come to naught.

The answer boils down to finding the vital zone(s) and hitting it/them repeatedly and as quickly as possible. This will be different every single time and will be dictated by the tactical circumstances.

The projectiles have to be delivered quickly, of course, but if you don't hit a vital area, you're lost. Maybe a solid hit doesn't do the job, and you'll have to shoot again until he stops. The bottom line is, fast and inaccurate fire will definitely not accomplish anything. The objective is to shoot as fast as you can and still maintain accuracy. This will be dependent upon the tactical situation, not on a stopwatch and prescribed range distances.

Two things to think about:

1. Anybody can throw a 50-yard touchdown pass on Monday morning. Very few can do it on Sunday with a nose-tackle spitting in their face.
2. Recently I was observing one of the very few who really has "been and done" practicing on the range. I overheard an armchair quarterback commenting on how he didn't know how the man in question had survived, shooting as "slow" as he did. What the observer didn't understand is that the Ark was designed by Amateurs; the Titanic was designed by Experts.

The Monday Morning Quarterback and the Self-Proclaimed Expert

Reference was made in the previous column to two hypothetical people who are probably the curse of modern defensive shooting: the Monday morning quarterback and the self-proclaimed expert.

The quarterback conveniently solves every gunfight after it's over, comfortably seated in front of his fireplace like a ballistic Sherlock Holmes. In his omniscient euphoria he laboriously gathers what he assumes to be all the facts and, presto, four days later he comes up with the solution to what "those jerks" should have done.

A classic example is the infamous FBI shoot-out in Dade County, Florida. Certainly, there were some tactical blunders, but there always are. The major problem was that the "good guys" ran into someone who was very good at what he did and who refused to succumb to his wounds.

An annoying upshot of the situation are the droves of quarterbacks who claim to all and sundry, "Boy, if I'd been there it would have been all over in five seconds with half a dozen rounds fired."

Well, maybe it would have, and maybe it wouldn't. The point is, they *weren't* there and they didn't have to *immediately react* to a situation.

Feast your eyes on this one from *About Face* by Colonel David H. Hackworth:

> *The second problem with war stories is that they have their genesis in the fog of war. In battle, your perception is often only as wide as your battle sights. Five participants in the same action, fighting side by side, will often tell different stories of what happened, even within hours of the fight. The story each man tells might be virtually unrecognizable to the others. But that does not make it any less true.*

The essence of Colonel Hackworth's observation is that no matter how well a fight is documented, all the facts are not brought to light.

Unperturbed, the Monday morning quarterback charges head on into

1,500 pounds of defense in a ludicrous attempt to score a self-glorifying touchdown. If he'd had the courtesy to pass the ball to his unmarked wide receiver, the team would have a touchdown.

The moral of the story? Debriefing and documentation are intended to hopefully prevent the same mistakes from recurring. To, hopefully, just once, give the good guys an edge.

To sit on the sidelines and pass snotty comments after the fact, especially when all the facts aren't available, gets nobody anywhere. Unless he has *constructive* criticism that will help some unfortunate, all the quarterback is doing is taking a cheap shot, and an inaccurate one at that.

The "instant expert" is a different kettle of rotten fish. He lives in a different hallucinatory world, but at least has the decency not to put down other people.

He deceives his audience, not always intentionally, by baldly stating that "my way is the only way." The unfortunate situation is that he is usually a two-day sergeant who has read three books and had a vision while he was sleeping. The next day he waltzes onto the firing range and proclaims to everyone that "this is the only system that works." His captive audience runs into trouble in the street, and guess where he finds out that the wonderful system doesn't work?

Even when utilizing tactics and techniques that have worked in the past, there are no guarantees. Using an instant-expert technique in the street will buy you nothing but trouble.

The underlying theme of this "Training and Tactics" series is to forewarn against the pitfalls of self-delusion—thinking that the street is as easy as the range. Hand in hand with this goes the potential of assuming that the "expert" knows better than you. He may very well not. You know your personal circumstances better than anyone else and may just have a more applicable answer to your situation than the resident expert.

Stay with instructors who can justify everything they do on the range relative to the street. Clint Smith of ITC is a good example of someone who does realistic, no-ego training.

One of the oft-asked questions is, "Do I need advanced training?" It's a matter of semantics. Basic training is just that: implanting the basics. Advanced training broadens your ability to fight, without necessarily getting into fancy, esoteric range drills. What does it help if you can shoot a four-inch group with a handgun at 30 yards, but can't hit a bobbing, angled target at six feet?

The bottom line is that every street fight is an advanced drill. You can't be half pregnant, and it doesn't matter if the L.A. traffic is moving at only 10 miles per hour—you're still pregnant and you're still in L.A. traffic.

Single-Handed Operation

*I*t's pointless wearing a safety belt on a 500-mile road trip and not buckling up for a two-mile drive to the convenience store. One-handed shooting is like wearing a safety belt; if you need it, you need it in the worst way.

There are various reasons for firing defensive small arms one-handed, but they all stem from one root cause: you're in deep trouble. Small arms are utilized one-handed out of necessity, not out of choice.

The most obvious reason for one-handed shooting is to continue the fight after receiving an incapacitating wound in an arm or hand, but there are other tactical considerations as well. You may, for example, be "caught" in the middle of a reload while covering a downed subject with a shotgun.

Whatever the unfortunate circumstances, it is imperative for successful self-preservation that you are competent not only in one-handed marksmanship, but that you also have the ability to mechanically operate the weapon with one hand.

A common training drill runs thus:

Draw the handgun, fire six rounds strong-handed only, reload using *both* hands, transfer the pistol to the weak hand, and fire another six rounds weak hand only.

Question: If you had the use of both hands for the reload, why were you relegated to only one hand for the shooting stage? Conversely, if one of your hands was out of commission for the shooting, how did it magically heal itself for the reload?

What we're coming down to is the same old problem of range training bearing no similarity to the street. While the drill admittedly makes for a safe range (and range safety is paramount), if the man on the firing line is so uncoordinated that he can't be trusted with "for real" training drills, he shouldn't be let loose on society with a gun, because, when it goes down for real, without training he'll try to improvise in the middle of a fight, with the inevitable result.

Another facet of this type of training drill is the assumption that the good guy will take a hit only after the fight has started. Too many people have been hit before they cleared leather for that theory to hold water.

The trick is to practice the draw-stroke with either hand and from a variety of body positions. Obviously, seated in a vehicle, most people can't access a strong-side hip holster with their weak hand traversing behind their back. Ergo, work on a system whereby you can clear leather weak-handed by moving your weak hand past your abdomen to access your weapon.

From the "what it's worth" department, a reliable system is to reach across and unsnap any existing retaining devices. Now, raise the weapon straight up, but not clear of the holster. Rotate the weapon so the gun butt is facing your weak side, attain a firing grip, and then—and only then—remove the weapon from the holster.

It is well to remember that you'll be working with your "stupid" hand. Keep your finger off the trigger until you are on target and have committed to shoot!

The next stage in single-handed operation is the ability to reload and clear malfunctions. If you have a backup gun, now's the time, but bear in mind you will be drawing it from a different place on your body than you did your primary weapon.

Reloading can be accomplished relatively easily with a semiauto. A revolver requires more dexterity and a thorough knowledge of the fact that north is up and south is down. You won't be the first person to try and insert cartridges into the front of a revolver cylinder when limited to one hand.

The most common system in use

As severely wounded as this, you have no choice but to fire one-handed.

for one-handed revolver reloads and semiauto malfunction clearances is to "use the old duty belt." But keep in mind that you won't have a belt on at home (and in bed) at 3 A.M., unless you're decidedly weird.

You will, however, have both your knees to clamp the weapon while reloading, clearing malfunctions, etc. If you drop into a double-kneeling position (both knees on the ground) you will also have the use of either foot's heel to cycle a semiauto, left- or right-handed. Again, *finger off the trigger*!

Use walls, sidewalks, car doors, or

15

your dog's ear to help, but you must be able to perform these emergency drills before you run into the necessity for real.

Shotguns, rifles, and subguns are longer and heavier than handguns and as a result are more difficult to operate one-handed than pistols. The bottom line, however, is the same: use your head and train with as simple a system as possible that will fill your individual needs. Depending on your tactical problem, it may or may not be the time to transition to a handgun at this stage, subject to its availability.

As far as marksmanship goes, if you have the luxury of a barricade, use it! Most long guns, when dead-rested on the fore-end (not the barrel), won't change the point of bullet impact as much as you may have heard.

Similarly, a couple of "tips" to try with the handgun: step into the target, much like a bull's-eye shooter, before firing. Also, try shooting with the top of the receiver canted over toward your body centerline. The shooting arm should be straight. Experiment with a mixture of these techniques with each hand. They work for some people, not for others.

A primary tactical reason for shooting the handgun one-handed is to keep it away from a close assailant. While the technique is not discussed here, it is probably one of the most important facets of defensive handgunning, because of the extremely close nature of personal attacks, especially for law enforcement personnel.

A final problem with one-handed small-arms operation is the "loss" of your tactical flashlight/laser. If you have one of the excellent Laser Products systems mounted on the weapon, as opposed to an independent light normally operated with the non-shooting hand, you might think about utilizing Laser Products remote pressure switch. Commonly secured in one position on the gun by means of Velcro, under emergency conditions it can be repositioned and manipulated by the shooting hand.

When all is said and done, it all comes down to the basic, "Forewarned is forearmed" syndrome. If you take a hit and go on, you may or may not win. If you take a hit or run into a tactical situation where you don't know how to continue, you lose.

The Test of Skill

The *Webster's Dictionary* definition of training is, in part, "so as to be fitted, qualified, or proficient; to make prepared for a test of skill." Ergo, it follows that if one does not undergo training, one will not be qualified, proficient, or prepared for the "test of skill."

Unfortunately, in small-arms conflicts, second place in the "test of skills" results in—at best—an undesirable loss of blood. Bill Jordan said it all: "There is no second-place winner in a gunfight."

If a situation has deteriorated to such a degree that gunplay becomes necessary, you can survive on a large dose of reflexive ability mixed with a small helping of Lady Luck, because it is nothing you haven't seen before. (This based on the assumption that your training has been realistic and relative to the real world "test of skill.")

If, on the other hand, no training has been conducted prior to the gunfight, you will need a titanic slice of luck to get you through the ordeal, because you have nothing else.

The above-mentioned situation is based on the premise that gunplay could not be avoided. The beauty of good defensive small arms training is that it often results in no gunfire simply because the "winner" had the mechanical ability to perform the shooting, but didn't have to resort to it because of superior mental control, tactics, and command presence.

Unfortunately, the good guys are almost always at a disadvantage, having to react to a threat, as opposed to initiating the action. This results in a one-half to three-fifths-of-a-second delay before the White Knight begins to respond to his brain commands. It is a mental diversion forced on him, much the same as a flash-bang works in his favor against his opponents.

In half a second an assailant can cover almost 10 feet in distance. Obviously, you won't have time to consciously think under these circumstances, and, equally as obvious, if you don't react reflexively and immediately, you lose the skill test and probably a large amount of blood.

So it all comes full circle. The only chance you have (unless blessed with more luck than you deserve) is to partake of realistic training, which will put you in a physical and mental condition capable of reacting reflexively to a threat. As always, the key word is "realistic."

It's no use bleeding into the gutter, complaining to your white corpuscles that "this isn't the same as the shooting range." Firstly, they won't listen; they have their own problems. And, secondly, guess what? They don't even care.

The answer is not to whine after the fact. The trick is to prepare as best you can beforehand, finding ways to eliminate or at least reduce the disadvantages forced upon you. Complaining doesn't seal bullet holes; training can prevent them.

Many people regard defensive small-arms training as merely the ability to hit a paper target on a shooting range. It is much more than that.

The gun is but the medium. Good defensive training instills the ability to hit a vital area of a target under field conditions—on demand. In other words, unless extremely unlucky, you don't get to choose the battlefield or the circumstances. The target dictates the scenario. If the situation can be solved without resorting to gunfire, so much the better.

What you must have, however, is the mental, physical, and mechanical wherewithal to reflexively sum up a problem and deal with it, either with brain cells or bullets or both.

SITUATION A

John Smith, Olympic relay track star, can't find the entrance to the stadium. The entire team loses the event.

SITUATION B

John Smith, Olympic relay track star, drops the baton. The entire team loses the event.

SITUATION C

John Smith, Olympic relay track star, tries to sprint 200 meters as fast as two other men sprint 100 meters each. The entire team loses the event.

The moral of the story? You must practice—and possess—the complete package to win. The greatest sprinter in the world can't win if he can't find the stadium door.

If you don't train for years for that one potential 10-second race, you haven't a chance of making it onto the team. It then becomes a matter of semantics whether you can find the door or won't drop the baton. It's too late and it doesn't matter and you won't even have the chance to try.

Defensive small-arms training requires dedication and mental control, above all else. A fully loaded pistol is no use to the man who has an empty magazine between his ears.

On second thought, Bill Jordan was wrong. There are second-place winners; graveyards are full of them.

Blaming the Weapon
for Operator Error

*L*et's face it—if it walks like a duck and it looks like a duck, it probably isn't the goose that lays the golden egg. Handguns, probably because they are more prolific in urban use than the other small arms, have increasingly raised contentious issues over past decades. It has now reached the stage of having gone from the sublime to the ridiculous.

Everybody is looking for the better handgun mousetrap, and, in itself, that is a fine pursuit. Progress is always admirable. The problem is, when it comes down to the bald facts (i.e., the gunfights), except for a small percentage of the law-abiding population, results are increasingly poor.

No, not because of the ballistics or ammunition capacity, but because of the projectile recipient's state of mind and *shot placement*. It doesn't matter if you have the latest hot-dog caliber; a miss is a miss is a miss.

While an off-center hit with a .45 ACP is undoubtedly better than one with a .38 Special, that's like saying one flat tire is better than two flat tires. You still have to get the *hit*, even if it is off center.

Handguns are utilized for only two reasons in preference to other small arms: (1) convenience and (2) tactical considerations.

Nobody in their right mind would use a pistol out of choice, unless they had a portability or tactical reason for not selecting a more powerful weapon. So, as with everything else, we try to kill two birds with one stone. We try to make a handgun as efficient as a rifle, shotgun, etc. How do we do it? By trying to improve ballistics.

Where did we get that idea? Well uh . . . you know, with that Philippine thing with them Indian fellers . . . in, you know, 1911 I think it was. There's only one fallacy to this whole deal: *The .45 didn't work any better than the .38s.* Sure, legend says that it worked better, but authentic documentation says it didn't. For the most part, it's legend, lore, and pure drivel. The .45 is undoubtedly ballistically more efficient than the .38, but is it *that* much better? The answer is probably no.

There are very, very few people who can shoot anywhere near their weapon's potential, especially a handgun. What we have done is lost the ability to operate the machinery, save for that small minority who have persevered to hone their physical and mental skills. We have become a race of distorted statistics believers and "first kid on the block" wannabes.

The latest "Instant Magic Kit" is wrapped up in a 10mm pistol cartridge. Of two gentlemen who purchased the ranch via that cartridge, number one was a suicide, so it worked—a CB cap would also have done the job. Number two was struck in the center of his chest twice from a distance of three feet. He thereupon *ran* 80 yards before shuffling off his mortal coil and apparently did a fair amount of shuffling before the coil fell off.

Now enters the .40 Smith & Wesson. Who knows?

The point is that no matter what you do with the ballistics, you can't transform a pumpkin handgun into a Cinderella rifle. What you *can* get is an edge, but this is not going to be anywhere near enough to make up for a lack of operator performance.

Reverting to the subject of statistics: people write statistics to prove a point, and most of the time it is biased, albeit often unintentionally. Usually there is a false premise involved: for example, Ford trucks have four wheels; therefore anything with four wheels is a Ford truck. While you may feel that it is so, the Chevy owner has his bowels in a knot over "that ridiculous statement" and points to the four wheels on his Chevy.

Much of 20th-century handgun design has come about because of political, as opposed to mechanical, reasons. This has, in essence, led to a 90-year firearms Ferris wheel. John Browning, may his soul rest in the Great Armory in the sky, designed a grip safety for his .45 autopistol because it was a contract requirement for all manufacturers wishing to compete in the military trials at the beginning of the century. Come 1935 and he removed it from his high-capacity 9mm Hi-Power, an extremely reliable, efficient pistol. After the 1950s, everybody bought a .45 auto instead of the "puny" 9mm Parabellum. Thirty years later and the same people sell their mighty .45 autos and buy a Glock, a high-capacity 9mm pistol.

Old joke: What's that white stuff in the middle of chicken feces? Answer: More chicken feces.

Admittedly, for law enforcement, the criminal problem has developed into situations that have multiple adversaries, and, granted, there can never be enough ammo. But what are we talking about, ammunition capacity, or ballistics? We'll still be arguing the ballistics until hell freezes over.

Another political decision has been the double/single-action and mechanical/nonmechanical safety catch zoo. Here's the rub: if you don't practice and train to become proficient with the weapon, no amount of mechanical fitting on the gun will improve your performance *or* prevent an accidental discharge.

Two interesting schools of thought are as follows:

1. In South Africa, the Lynx revolver was fitted with a mechanical safety catch to prevent child accidents. An adult still had a lethal weapon immediately available.

2. In the United States, trigger locks are becoming mandatory to prevent child accidents. Nobody can use the weapon.

Personal handgun selection requires a lot of forethought. Study your specific needs and buy the pistol that most closely meets *your* requirements. A handgun ideally suited to a man who is very good in his particular field is not necessarily the best choice for you. The trick is to sort the wheat from the chaff. There is no golden goose.

Don't be misled by advertising, and *do* become proficient with the weapon. Your proficiency will be the number one factor in a life-threatening situation.

The Importance
of Follow-Through

I"I can't believe I missed the target!" Famous last words. Although many causes of the above situation have been covered in previous "Training and Tactics" columns, one of the biggest pitfalls of marksmanship is overlooked time and time again: the lack of follow-through.

You can do everything right with regard to sight picture and trigger control up to the moment of primer ignition, but if you do not follow through after that stage, you will probably miss your mark.

The strong quarterbacks like Joe Montana and John Elway get their power and distance from completing the full passing rotation, even *after* the football leaves their hand. Similarly, the long-yardage golf and baseball hitters complete their swings *after* initial contact with the ball. What does this have to do with shooting? Same problem, same result.

The athlete loses yardage without follow-through; the shooter doesn't lose yardage because the bullet obviously has built-in power. What the shooter *does* lose, however, is accuracy, because without follow-through the sights are not aligned with the desired target area when the bullet exits the gun barrel.

Internal ballistics take only fractions of a second, but the hand is faster than the eye! If the sight picture is altered during the short time it takes the primer to flash, the powder to start burning, and the pressure to build and force the bullet through and out the barrel, the projectile will not impact the target in the desired location.

How many times have you been "positive" of your sight picture, only to realize afterward that you saw a hole appear in the paper target? If you see the impact of the bullet, it will not be where you wanted it to be, because the human eye *cannot* focus on two different focal lengths at the same time. Ergo, if you see the bullet impact, it obviously means that your vision was not focused on the weapon's front sight when the projectile exited the muzzle. This is the single most annoying aspect of marksmanship to cure, because it is extremely difficult to recognize that you are doing it. If, however, you see holes or blood appear

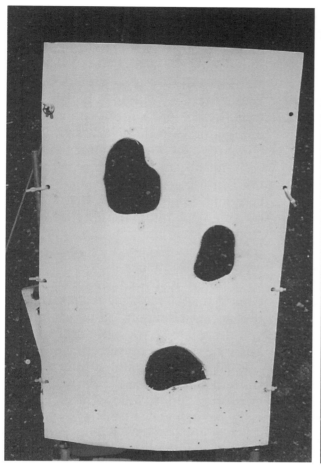
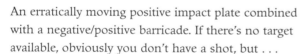
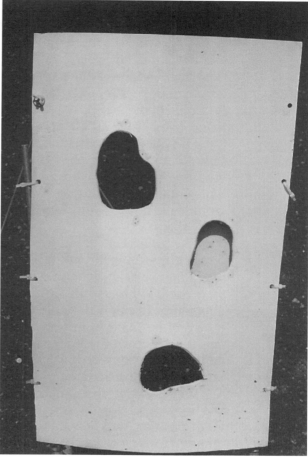

An erratically moving positive impact plate combined with a negative/positive barricade. If there's no target available, obviously you don't have a shot, but . . .

. . . when the target momentarily appears while moving behind one of the negative portholes, the shot must be fired instantly. If this doesn't reinforce the principles of follow-through on a moving target, nothing will.

immediately after firing, rest assured that that is your problem.

The *only* way to cure/avoid this problem is to make sure that you have sight alignment, with the front sight in sharp focus, ready for another shot after firing. (Obviously, the second round of a "hammer" or close-in weapon retention drills are the exception to this rule.)

Why the long spiel about what may seem to be an unimportant issue?

Street practicality.

On a shooting range, either you or your instructor designates in advance how many rounds are to be fired in a specific drill. In a street situation, you do not know in advance how many times you will have to fire.

If you decide to fire two rounds from your handgun at your assailant's torso and then stand around to admire your handiwork, you will have one of two situations: (A) the two rounds will achieve the desired result and your opponent will be subdued, or (B) the tactic will fail, and you're now out of time, luck, and breathing space. If you are justified in shooting to stop a deadly-force encounter, you are justified in firing once, twice, or 50 times!

The point of the matter is, if your target is still a threat, the only way to stop the threat is to continue shooting. This entails recovering the weapon's front sight in focus until the deadly-force threat stops.

The individual situation will be different every time. Situation X may dictate a failure drill (switching to the head after the body hits), but *for real* head shots are extremely difficult. Situation Y may require firing continuous rounds to available parts of the body, if the head cannot *immediately* be engaged and the attacker is still a threat.

Whatever the situation, firing two to the body, observing the results from a low ready position, and only then attempting a head shot as a matter of course on a bobbing, weaving, insane human is asking for trouble, This is known as the Mozambique drill. The problem is, if the body hits didn't work *for real*, there's no time to do anything else.

In these troubled times, when coke is white powder and not dark liquid, handgun bullets are less and less achieving desired one- or two-shot stops to a deadly-force situation. While everybody and his cousin are trying to solve the problem by developing a new magic pistol cartridge (and some are *slightly* better than others), nothing dictates the result more than shot placement and the bullet recipient's state of mind. If you're conducting your range training for serious street defense, make sure you are ready to shoot again after completing *every* firing sequence.

If you're instructing, allow the student to fix his marksmanship mistake before "switching off." If, for example, you designated a two-shot drill and he knew he screwed up with one of the hits, allow him to automatically put in a third insurance round. This will encourage him to follow through optically and tactically in the street.

The bottom line? Even a perfectly placed shot doesn't guarantee the end of the fight. If the assailant doesn't know that he's been hit, you will probably have to shoot again.

Be ready for it by following through.

Reaction Time

One of the disadvantages of being one of the good guys is that most of the time you have to react to a deadly-force threat, as opposed to having the leeway to initiate the action.

Obviously, if you have to react to somebody else's action, there will be a certain amount of reaction time involved. This time frame, for the average, well-tuned individual, will hover somewhere between two-fifths and three-fifths of a second. This can hurt you in two areas: (A) acquiring the target quickly and (B) hitting the desired target.

Area A is not having the ability to acquire the target quickly—e.g., in the case of a slow drawstroke from the holster, when a handgun is urgently required. Going hand-in-hand with this is the "all-day-long" mounting of a long gun onto the desired target area.

Logically, the presentation of the weapon from carry position onto target should be diligently practiced until it can be performed reflexively in the time frame of a second or (preferably) faster. As a human on the move can cover ground at the rate of seven yards a second, and most deadly-force encounters occur well inside this distance, it is obvious why a fast reflexive gun mount should be deemed an absolute necessity. There is a commonly accepted school of thought that opposes this, proclaiming that if you use the correct tactics you will see the trouble coming and will already have the handgun clutched in your sweaty paws, ready for use.

Area B is also controlled by reaction time, but constitutes hitting the desired target after area A is no longer a problem—i.e., after the drawstroke has already been accomplished. This is where "normal" ideologies may not take everything into account.

If on the firing line of a shooting range, all the shooter has to do is impact a static target within a specific time frame, he will hasten the drawstroke only to give himself more time to shoot.

If on the firing line, the overall score on a multiple target drill is "Comstocked" (score divided by or into the overall time taken for the

SPOT THE FLAWS

1. Law enforcement personnel are often restricted by policy as to when they can and cannot draw a handgun, depending on what constitutes a deadly-force threat.

2. Try strolling across the parking lot behind a stop-and-rob, pistol in hand, and then explaining to a police officer that you "didn't like the look of the three men" lounging around near your truck.

3. Unless you have multidirectional vision like a fly, much of the time in an urban environment you won't see trouble coming until it's almost on top of you. Ergo, there is a very real need to be able to access the gun of your choosing within fractions of a second. This, however, is not as big a problem as it seems. It can be relatively easily achieved with diligent repetitive practice. It goes without saying that the greatest marksman in the world is rendered impotent if he can't access the firearm.

drill), the shooter will fire the rounds irrespective of accuracy, hoping to achieve a good mathematical factor by sacrificing accuracy in the hopes of salvaging the drill by taking less time. This establishes a dangerous precedent for the street where accuracy cannot be sacrificed. What you practice on the range you will do in the street.

The root fallacy of the area B problem in the street is one discussed in prior "Training and Tactics" articles: that of body movement. If the draw-stroke is accomplished, acquiring the target quickly is no longer a problem. Hitting the target is, however, still of paramount concern, and this is where reaction time comes into play.

If your target is not moving (as in the standard, static range target), it's merely a matter of sight picture and trigger control—and away you go. But if the target is displaying typical erratic, irregular, human motion, it's a whole new ballgame.

As he weaves to your left, your mind says "shoot." Only two-fifths to three-fifths of a second later does your trigger pressure begin, due to reaction lag time. If he continues to move in the same direction, no problem—merely "track" him with the sights and put on gradual trigger finger pressure. Ignition will occur while the sights are on the target and the projectile (or projectiles) flies true.

If, however, Mr. Baddie is moving erratically (weaving and bobbing left, right, and up and down), you will fire at a target who is no longer where he was, because he moves faster than you can react. He moves left and right, and you shoot right and left because neither you nor the rangemaster is controlling the game anymore. The target is, and you are always X amount of lag time behind his initiating action. Yes, it's easy to miss by a foot in the street!

In three years of utilizing an erratically moving target we have had few torso hits, even by experienced marksmen, until they have analyzed, and understood, the complexity of a moving human target. Even once this level has been attained, the head shot is more difficult, 10 times over.

Reaction time is an important facet of defensive training and is one more aspect that must be taken into account when training on the range for street realism.

Can You Make Tactical Training Realistic?

Miss on paper, it's only a caper; miss in the street, there's no repeat.

There are only two certainties in life: death and taxes. Of course, the good news about being dead is that you don't have to come up with next year's IRS donation. Equally as obvious is the fact that if you don't seriously envision having to do it for real, all you have to do is continue with banal and mundane range training and look forward to the next paper/steel competition. Competition is an excellent training aid from the perspective of marksmanship and gun handling, but for the most part, the targets and relevant tactics encountered can set up a false sense of security.

While the final say in the street always comes down to the basics of sight picture and trigger control (and, therefore, these must be religiously practiced), it'll be a cold day in hell when you are attacked by a one-dimensional piece of paper or steel of known shape and size, set at a known distance and moving at a known pace.

If you're using competitions or range work to practice for the street, regard a miss as the end of the fight and not merely as a 10-point penalty. Only luck will give you a second chance in the street if you miss the first time around. On the range, there are third-, fourth-, and fifth-place trophies. In a gunfight, there's first and second place only—and it doesn't take a NASA employee to figure out which one you don't want to be.

The inherent problem with competition target situations is the same as with law enforcement qualification courses: there has to be standardization of drills, distances, and targets to get a mean, documentable numerical figure. Street confrontations are different every time and often require angled hits, both vertical (as through open windows or gaps in barricades) and lateral (i.e., shooting at a human whose position is momentarily quartered to the shooter).

If, as a matter of course, you always shoot center of mass of a target with clean, straight outlines, you know in advance where the vital zone

This adverary is dark and partially obscured and doesn't resemble a standard training target in the least.

is. In a fight, the vital zone is constantly changing with body movement, and you are forced to first find it before you can even think of impacting it. You are thus forced to put quick hits onto a human target over whom you have no control, because the target is dictating the situation, unlike on the range.

You may not have the tactical leeway to "step off to the side" or change your position to give yourself an easier shot because of time constraints, terrain, layout, etc. In the street, you have to maintain accuracy. This is why range "gospel" drills, for the most part, fall apart in the street. The target is invariably different from that offered on the range, and the tactical delivery of projectiles has to be reflexively modified accordingly.

For example, if you were trying to stop an assailant from repeatedly stabbing a third party, you would have a constantly moving, erratic target, changing every millisecond. The target picture would be continuously changing with the swing of his clothing. What the shooter is faced with here is a situation of putting in projectiles until the attack stops. Changes in lighting, distance, terrain, and weaponry would all contribute to changing the tactical shooting every time. To merely mechanically shoot a predetermined number of rounds at the center of mass of the overall target, as is constantly practiced on the shooting range, will possibly result in bullet holes through the assailant's clothing only and none through his torso. This may help explain why good range shooters miss the mark at close distances in the street.

Angles have to be taken into consideration. If you shoot from a 45-degree angle at a one-dimensional paper target, you are "required" to impact it in the center of the X-ring to gain a full range score—be it competition or qualification. If you do this in the street in this situation, you will not achieve an incapacitating wound, because of the entry/exit wound channel path. For real, the bullet would have needed to be placed in the paper "B" zone, which obviously costs points on the range.

To clarify: this column is designed to promote thinking about "for real" tactical shooting, where the shooter has already qualified for score on the range but wishes to progress further.

It is hard to split the difference between A and B zone hits when you're under duress. On the range, we're programmed to always shoot for the A zone, but because of obvious range safety problems, the tactical and "med-

Although this officer has delivered a perfect head shot on her own on a moving three-dimensional target system (note the dust on the backstop) . . .

. . . the same problem becomes much easier to handle with more manpower. The hostage taker runs out of angle options, and reaction time becomes his enemy and no longer his friend.

ical" benefits of angled shots aren't taken into consideration, and training is done from the "hit the belt buckle to belt buckle, nonmoving target in the A zone" perspective.

That's great for marksmanship and gun handling, but it leaves a lot of good guys bewildered and confused in the middle of a life-threatening situation.

I'd rather have no trophies and no grave marker than a wall full of trophies and one tombstone.

There's Nothing New

*O*nce you have a wheel, you can build it stronger or lighter or to fit a better-performing tire, but the race still depends on the ability of the car driver.

While there are many fine firearms-related accouterments available on the market today, most of them were around 40, 50, and even 100 years ago. And although equipment can help a 90-percent shooter become a 95-percent shooter, it will not magically give a 50-percent performer 90-percent ability.

A *competent* fighter with good equipment will beat a *competent* fighter with poor equipment, but a second-rate fighting man is nothing, irrespective of his equipment. To give, for example, a Robar 60 or 90 Series sniper rifle to a man who can shoot only a 10-inch group at 100 yards is like casting pearls before swine. On the other hand, put the same rifle in the hands of a Carlos Hathcock and you have a shooting machine.

The difference is that a Hathcock can do just fine, thank you very much, without top-of-the-line equipment. He has ability, which is complemented by top-class equipment.

It was humiliating for me to stand at Gettysburg, work out positions of shooters and shootees, and have to admit to myself that I couldn't have made half of the sniper shots taken by 15-year-old kids with ratty equipment.

My sole consolation is that there aren't many out there these days who can make those shots either. It did, however, teach me a bitter lesson: to stop relying on trick equipment and to get back to the basics of shooting.

I also realized that I'd listened too long to modern authorities, instead of paying more attention to the tried and tested systems of yesteryear.

My first big shocker came while reading an old Fairbairn-Sykes manual—and realizing the brilliant "new" techniques taught to me a dozen years ago had been lifted almost verbatim from 40-year-old text.

The more "old" books I read, the more interesting—and amus-

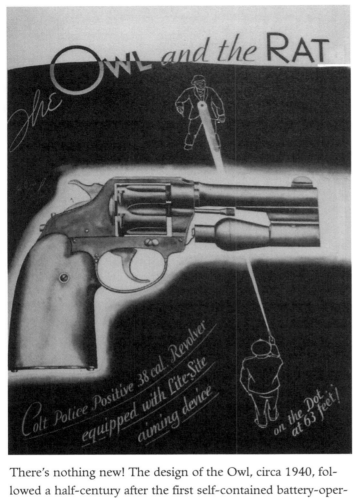

There's nothing new! The design of the Owl, circa 1940, followed a half-century after the first self-contained battery-operated flashlight.

ing—it became. These manuals regurgitated "modern" inventions so often, it was almost monotonous. The truth of the matter is that, for the most part, there are *no* new inventions, merely rediscoveries—usually in about 40- to 50-year cycles.

Some examples?

• How about a miniflashlight attached to a handgun, complete with remote pressure switch? (The Owl, 1942)

• Or the venerable ghost ring rear sight? (Montgomery Ward catalog, 1896)

• Interested in "120-year-old" ammunition-carrying systems for your rifle or shotgun, or maybe a "new" three-position rifle sling from 1916?

The point is not to denigrate the efforts and products of current manufacturers or authorities, but let's face it: today there are only a handful of Hathcocks. Virtually every 15-year-old a hundred years ago was an accomplished marksman under field and battle conditions.

Why? *Because he had to be.* If Sonnyboy went out foraging with the family Brown Bess and one cartridge, he was expected to come home with lunch draped over his shoulder. Today's solution? Buy a microwave oven on the never-never plan.

These days the training range is often regarded as a nonserious gathering place to do some nonrepresentative drills and show off the latest "first-kid-on-the-block" gadgets (which are usually five-year-old ideas). Strange how the guys with the most toys never seem to be able to hit anything.

A training range is just that—an area where shooting can be conducted to represent as closely as possible a potential future (or past) deadly-force encounter.

No amount of mechanical junk on a firearm will make you a better fighter. What some of the equipment can do is improve your overall performance by giving you an edge tactically (e.g., throwing light on the target and helping to silhouette the sights, making ammunition readily accessible to your hand).

Give one of the good ones like Ross Seyfried a strange, standard handgun and he'll still shoot a 95-percent score. Somebody who managed to duplicate one of John Satterwhite's shotgun circus tricks says he's now "as good as Satterwhite." No you aren't. All you've done is repeat one trick of a master's repertoire. Ed McGivern used a double-action revolver in each hand—and on and on.

Keep it simple; rely on equipment that's worked for a hundred years; and practice, practice, practice. You can kid yourself all day long that the way to fix a flat is to jack up the car and rotate the flat part of the tire to the top, but when you "pay the piper" in the street, you pay in blood.

Equipment for Poor-Light Conditions

As a large percentage of urban shootings occur during inclement light conditions, serious attention should surely be paid to this problem during training.

Normally, a disproportionate amount of range time is devoted to poor-light training techniques and equipment. While normal daylight street shooting is difficult, adverse light conditions compound the situation because (A) target identification is more difficult, and (B) the elements of sight alignment and sight picture require that much more concentration.

In this type of situation, optional/additional weaponry equipment becomes almost essential, at least until such time as the naked eye becomes capable not only of seeing in the dark but also of focusing on two or three different focal lengths simultaneously.

Target identification is essential both in law enforcement and the civilian fields. Usually this must be established optically, though there is the rare exception where audio can be used for target ID. While most military operations are not as stringent about individual shooter responsibility for terminal shot placement, the civilian and law enforcement shooter is ultimately and totally responsible for every round launched downrange.

While there is at least one excellent technique for operating a handgun in unison with a flashlight controlled by the nonshooting hand, as well as several other systems that may or may not work in the street, a remote flashlight is not always immediately at hand, especially to an armed civilian caught flat-footed when not at home. There are very few halfway feasible techniques for shooting a shoulder weapon while simultaneously operating a remote flashlight—a last resort at best.

If the added nightmare of losing the use of an arm is taken into consideration, it can be seen that, for once, the fitting of a mechanical illumination device to the basic weapon could be an asset, as opposed to gimmickry—especially for the armed professional going into a known-in-advance dim-light situation.

Of the many companies producing flashlight attachments for small

Mike Harries' pistol-flashlight technique.

arms, Laser Products (18300 Mt. Baldy Circle, Fountain Valley, CA 92708) has been the longtime forerunner in the "modern" field. (I say "modern" because the initial concept was created in the 1940s.)

Other companies have produced light-emitting units as well, but Laser has been around for a long time, and its units have proven extremely reliable in action. It also offers the user several alternatives, such as either a unit-construction on/off pressure switch embedded in shoulder weapon fore-ends or a unit supplied with a remote pressure switch. The latter obviously negates the one-handed operational problem mentioned above, because the pressure switch can be instantly repositioned on the weapon.

Probably the sole downside to Laser Products' tactical lights was the use of nonrechargeable batteries. However, this problem was overcome in January 1991 by a modification to the base light, which incorporates an adapter. This adapter allows the user to retrofit any of the first-generation lights to have rechargeable capacity, with the added bonus of a 20-percent increase in power.

The other aspect of dim-light shooting is encountered when the target is identifiable without the requirement of additional mechanical illumination. This situation involves both good news and bad news. Good news, because additional light is not necessary to effect target identification; bad news because, often under these circumstances, a satisfactory sight picture cannot be acquired.

This, in poor ambient light conditions, often becomes guesswork with standard small-arms sights, because more often than not, the sights are "lost" against the background. An invaluable aid in these circumstances is the availability of tritium inserts in both the front and rear sights on the weapon, allowing the shooter to acquire both sight alignment and sight picture.

While most of the Top Guns known to this writer are using a single horizontal bar rear sight with a dot front sight on handguns, Innovative Weaponry also offers a three-dot system and a twin-bar/single-dot configuration. Obviously on shoulder weapons, because of the sighting plane, a different combination is required.

If you are in the unenviable situation of foreseeing potential gunplay or merely want that extra insurance policy, either a light-emitting unit or a self-luminous set of tritium inserts could prove invaluable.

Both systems are especially useful indoors, where ambient light is often unsatisfactory, even during daylight hours.

The Pros and Cons of Two Common Training Techniques

Often, what seem to be logical small-arms defensive training drills turn out to be unsuccessful and impossible to execute during a real ballistic swap meet. What follows is a two-sided look at some common training techniques: the pros and cons. This article, as always, is personal opinion and is in no way intended to be construed as criticism of anybody's training systems, techniques, or philosophies.

THE HEAD SHOT

This is usually the most difficult shot to accomplish, because it is often the only time when absolute accuracy is required. It is usually taken for one of two reasons:

1. Prior torso shots didn't achieve the desired result.
2. The head was the only available target.

Whereas two inches' leeway in accuracy on an assailant's torso will probably still net a reasonably solid strike, a couple of inches off on a head produces a large zero in desired results. Even if a capable performer can consistently place center hits on the head of a one-dimensional, straight-on range target, it becomes a whole new ballgame on an angled, three-dimensional human head, especially if it's moving, even slightly.

If you have one inch of target movement and split the two rounds of a full-auto pair by an inch, you're already looking at a projectile (the second) that can potentially be off target and out in the street. Worst case scenario here, of course, is that the suspect hasn't been hit centrally, plus there're 147 grains of lead floating down the boulevard.

Automatic Failure Drill

A popular handgun technique is the automatic failure drill: two torso shots plus an immediate follow-up shot to the head, if required

Intended to simulate a 50-yard head-shot problem (though obviously photographed at close distance), the steel target is intentionally merged into the background and half-obscured. A broken clay pigeon or dust impact gives instant training feedback on misses.

(subguns, 4+2). This drill is a vast improvement on, and evolved from, the Mozambique drill. The Mozambique requires the same amount of rounds fired, but differs in that there is a pause after the torso hits to admire your handiwork and see if the desired result has been obtained.

Again, as stated in prior columns, if the body shots did the job, the head shot becomes superfluous. If, however, the primary shots didn't stop your opponent's aggression, kiss your derrière *buenas noches*, because you're out of time to do anything else. This is probably what cost an officer his life in Flagstaff, Arizona, several years ago.

Another popular technique with the MP5 submachine gun at close distances is to "hold" on the assailant's hairline. This is to compensate for low strikes at contact distances with a weapon that has a high sightline/low bore line ratio. If you tried this on the street and missed on a moving, raving maniac, this paragraph is a large clue—*you can't hit what you can't see*. If you have to "chase" an aiming point for two or three seconds at contact distance, you're gone.

Fortunately for those who still believe in honor and apple pie, the baddie is often in a stationary mode, frozen from a diversion, and the extra fraction of a second can be taken to pinpoint the aim zone. This, however, will not be the case for the Alamo-type shoot-outs that are becoming more and more prevalent as time goes by.

So what to do? If the head is not immediately available as a target, go back to the torso or pelvis, both of which are invariably easier to hit. The pelvis is the biggest bone in the body, and hits will probably break his transmission, preventing further locomotion. Pelvic strikes, however, will not prevent actuation of a trigger finger. They are designed to buy time. They may, if you're lucky, also lead to the antagonist's surrender or cessation of aggression.

In answer to the bland statement "Well, the first couple of body shots didn't stop him, so another couple won't," what else are you going to do? Sling a bunch of projectiles in the general vicinity of his head, hoping to get "lucky"? First, you won't get lucky—the Good Guys never do. Second, unless there's a 101-percent safe backstop behind the suspect, one of the projectiles in that swarm is going to hit an innocent party.

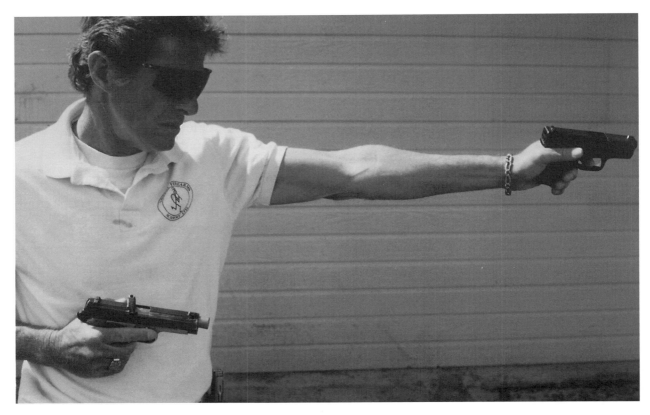

When Old Faithful malfunctions, the backup pistol is immediately drawn and fired. Note that the shooter's right-hand trigger finger is straight and the wrist maintains contact with the body to tactilely maintain a safe muzzle distance.

RELOADING/MALFUNCTIONS

Probably the most divergent opinions among firearms instructors occur on the subjects of reloading and malfunction clearances during a shoot-out. The bottom line with either of these situations, if you are still in the act of engaging an adversary, is to transition to a second or tertiary weapon. It is faster, more positive, and less stressful on whatever brain cells are still in operation at this stage of the proceedings.

The nitty-gritty is that the situation will dictate your tactics. It doesn't take a NASA employee to work out that trying to clear a double feed in the middle of a room while someone is shooting at you isn't going to classify you with Einstein—or Methuselah.

On the other hand, this operation could be safely conducted if you had the availability of solid cover. In other words, speed reloads and malfunction clearances should probably be executed in direct proportion to your immediate personal safety situation (or that of others). Otherwise, transition to another weapon. Tactical reloading should be done as a matter of course upon completion and containment of each individual scenario of an operation, but when there is obviously no immediate threat.

Often, people are taught to drop to a kneeling position automatically during reloading or malfunction situations. While this is a good idea in itself to lower your target line, bear in mind that law enforcement personnel often work both alone and in team mode on both dynamic and stealth operations. Automatically kneeling could have dire consequences on a dynamic team entry.

Range training should represent street problems and, as such, should always take in a certain amount of elasticity to allow for adaptability to differing tactical circumstances.

What Do You Do After the Hit?

*I*t's amusing to watch a cocker spaniel chasing a bus, because you know it won't know what to do with the bus when it catches it. It's not so amusing if you are the spaniel and the bus is someone you've been forced to shoot. Where's the corollary? What's the point?

The point is that very few take this into consideration during training. Most training scenarios culminate in the shooter's reholstering a handgun or reslinging a shoulder weapon immediately after the bullets have been launched downrange.

"So," you say, "what's the problem? I've got two hits in the X-ring, haven't I?" The problem is that the two center hits demonstrate marksmanship and not much else. It is highly unlikely that the cardboard target will rise from the ashes and proceed to assault you with a baseball bat.

With today's escalation of drug use, combined with the preponderance of criminals sporting armor (and a mental attitude of immortality), there is an increasing likelihood of having to go into round two before hostilities can be curtailed. This obviously means that you are forced to fire more rounds, but that's not the spaniel problem. This merely means that you've chased the bus farther down the road to the next bus stop. Chew on the tires long enough and sooner or later, with four flat tires, the bus will lose its ability to be steered, and it will crash.

Here's where we have to analyze the "cocker crisis." Why did we chase the bus? To stop its locomotion or switch off the motor? If we don't turn off the motor, the bus can still run, *even with four flat tires*. The fact that it crashed doesn't mean it can't start up the entire debacle all over again.

X-ring hits are the same as flat tires—they may not be enough. The show isn't over until your assailant's hands are handcuffed or his wrists are bound together—i.e., the spaniel scenario ends when the ignition key is pulled from the bus.

We would do well, at this stage, to emphasize the fact that we are looking at *terminating any further potential hostility on the part of the assailant* and not implying that he should be *killed*. If no shots need to be fired, we are still faced with the original problem: what to do with the bus?

Here's the scoop: if you reholster in a flash after shooting cardboard and steel targets on a firing range, don't be surprised if you get caught with your tail under a bus wheel in the street.

Most cockers have docked tails, either done in advance or because it had to be done after being mangled by a bus. Docking your tail in advance means "covering-down" on targets after the shooting, until such time as backup arrives to complete the handcuffing phase. If the assailant has died as a result of the confrontation, cuff him anyway. Gruesome as this may sound, you won't be yet another person to be shot or stabbed by a "dead" man.

Operating on a multiple-target range scenario? Check the hits on targets before walking by them to the next stage. Walking up on targets is not real

bright. Use a cover man or whatever, but anything behind you in the street and it's tail-mangling time again. If you're on your own, you have two choices: (1) wait for backup or (2) approach the target.

Obviously option one is no problem, but option two almost forces tunnel vision on you, laying you open to a potential threat from a third party because you've been forced into tactical directional movement you would not "normally" take. One thing is for sure: being back-shot is not a good way to go out.

Moral of the story? "Cover-down" on targets on the range *each and every time* you practice. Make it a reflexive part of your shooting regimen and you won't have to think about it in the street.

Speed is essential from holster to target, but there's no rush to reholster a pistol or resling a shoulder weapon. Dock your tail before it is trapped under a bus.

It Ain't Over 'til It's Over

*I*n the last chapter, the situations of covering-down and containing a target scenario were emphasized. To recap: reacting to a deadly-force threat, the good guy is forced to shoot. Down goes Mr. Baddie, condition unverified. Problem: do you holster your pistol immediately and ride off into the setting sun, or do you approach the target to verify that hostilities have unquestionably ceased?

Although this may seem a simple tactical decision, let's extend the problem. What if there's another baddie down the road? Can you afford to march cheerfully past the downed assailant, hoping he's out of the race?

Because if he isn't, you're in deep trouble, front and back. The gist of these two chapters is this: if you don't cover and contain a downed opponent, you're stacking up even more potential odds against yourself further into the scenario.

The reason so much printer's ink is being expended on this single problem is that it is hardly ever approached during training. You can either pretend that the problem doesn't exist, or you can recognize it for the serious potential situation that could arise.

If you ignore it, your training stays the same as it is. If you accept that shooting people isn't the same as shooting cardboard or steel, many facets of your defensive training could change. For example, during handgun flashlight training, most trainers advocate switching off the flashlight beam immediately after firing, closely followed by lateral foot movement "so your opponent won't return fire at the light source and hit you."

This sounds wonderful, but let's think it all the way through. Once you kill the light, you have no idea what you are dealing with. And guess what? Sooner or later you're going to have to turn on the light source again to see what you're dealing with in round two.

If you didn't win round one, guess what happens when you turn on the light the second time? Now you have to react to his action (i.e., gunfire) all over again, aligning the flashlight, sights, and target. So what have you gained by killing the light and sidestepping? Probably nothing. In fact, it's probably going to cost you.

So maybe you have nothing to lose by leaving the light on target and containing the situation with the opponent illuminated. Of course, if there were multiple assailants it might behoove you to switch off the light and move laterally. As stated before, the tactical scenario is different every time. So maybe your flashlight training tactics could stand a second look.

Back to daylight, and reloading raises its ugly head. Most paper/steel-shooting instructors recommend keeping the gun trained on the target during the reloading process. Again, let's think it all the way through. If the subject hasn't yet been ascertained as no longer hostile, why are you reloading? If he's still continuing his aggression, you'd better be shooting and not reloading.

What needs a closer look is the definition of the word "target." If it's paper or steel, there is no danger to the shooter. If on the other hand, the "target" is human, the tactical fallacy appears. Covering-down on the "target" in this case usually means keeping the gun pointed in at a human chest. Unfortunately, this invariably means losing sight of the assailant's hands, and they are the threat—the threat that will decide whether you shoot again.

Therefore, if you are forced to reload, maybe you want the gun in a low ready position, below the threat level and not pointed in at the so-called target.

So maybe the theory of being able to fire your one remaining round while calmly reloading "on target" isn't valid. Of course, if there were one documented case of this ever having been done for real, it would help substantiate the theory. Maybe your reloading tactics could stand a second look.

Covering-down and containing a situation are vitally important to the successful conclusion of a shooting incident. During practice, make sure you cover-down after firing, reacquiring sight picture, and putting in more insurance rounds if poor hits are observed on the range target, before reholstering or slinging the weapon.

During a tactical scenario that requires stealth, force yourself to at least check the hits on each target before moving on, even if it means altering your tactical movement direction. If a "target" that has not been contained gets behind you in the street, you lose.

If you are forced into a shooting, make sure you follow through tactically after the initial gunfire. Incorporate this facet into your training, and it will become second nature in the street.

It ain't over 'til it's over.

A Silent Partner:
Your Backup Weapon

Who needs a backup gun? Probably everyone who carries a gun for self-defense.

Although the subject is nothing new, perhaps the logic behind the necessity for a backup weapon could stand a second going-over.

The first comment you'll encounter from most associates and acquaintances when discussing the subject will incorporate such words as *paranoid, crazy,* or *neurotic.* It's amazing the number of people who think carrying one gun is fine but assume you're bordering on lunacy if you carry two. So the first order of the day is to not broadcast the fact that you are carrying a second gun, for a variety of reasons:

1. By the nature of its mission, most of the time the backup weapon will have to be concealed.
2. It gives you an edge, under certain tactical circumstances, if it is concealed.
3. Today's friend is often tomorrow's enemy—why tip him off to the fact that you have an ace in the hole? You don't advertise your personal bank account holdings, and you certainly don't need to advertise something more life-sustaining than money.

If, on the other hand, you're a member of an entry team or professionally engaged in a situation where a shoulder weapon is primary, then there's obviously no state secret about your secondary gun.

But on to the various reasons for toting a backup. If you're already carrying a gun, you're presumed to be in fear of a deadly-force threat. If this is the case, it follows that you are earnest about self-preservation. Why should it therefore seem paranoid to some to consider hedging an insurance policy with a second gun? If you need the primary weapon, you need it desperately, and if it doesn't do the job, you'll need the backup in the worst way.

Most nonentry personnel carry one sidearm, usually with about 4 million spare rounds of ammunition. Let's face it—there's never enough ammo, especially with today's criminals and with handguns not having the required ballistic effect. But in all honesty, how many times do you think you can reload in the middle of a gunfight before you are hit?

People are trained to reload like crazy on the practice range, which is a fine (and necessary) pursuit in itself. The problem is the continuity of fire by means of reloading becomes less proficient as the stress rises proportionately. A practiced handgun draw-stroke, however, is with you for eternity. (The operative word is *practiced*, as is the case with all facets of firearms manipulation.)

REASONS FOR CARRYING A BACKUP WEAPON

There are three main reasons for considering the presence of a backup gun, and for the purpose of this text it will be assumed the weapon in question is a handgun.

1. You may lose possession of your primary weapon.
2. There may be a mechanical malfunction or a lack of ammo with or for your primary weapon.
3. You may be unable to access your primary weapon because of a tactical situation or injury.

Let's take the three above conditions in order of sequence.

Losing Your Primary Weapon
Deadly-force policy being what it is, escalation for situations like "domestic" calls often start with a fist fight and also often end with the officer staring down the wrong end of his own pistol barrel.

Solution? An easily accessed backup gun.

Experiencing Mechanical Malfunction
Like reloads, mechanical malfunctions are practiced to destruction on the range—and so they should be. But somehow, in a street fight the malfunction takes on a peculiar twist: Murphy's Law extends it to a jam, and you're out of business.

If you don't have cover, deluding yourself into thinking that you're going to fix this puppy at contact distance, on the move . . . well, there's this soggy property I have for sale in Florida, if you're interested.

Time yourself to see how long it takes to clear even the most basic of malfunctions, put it up against how much happens in a real fight in that time and—guaranteed perspiration.

Solution? An easily accessed backup gun.

Having Access to Primary Weapon Denied
Lack of access to the primary weapon, whether because of ugly tactical circumstances or injury, raises one of the biggest side issues of backup guns: how or where to position it on your body. The first and most common answer is the ubiquitous ankle holster. Ever tried accessing a gun from one of those suckers using only one hand? Good luck.

The secret of a second gun is that it must be *instantly accessible to either hand.* Otherwise you're just carrying it like Linus' security blanket in the *Peanuts* comic strip.

Granted, backup guns have been pulled by officers knocked down onto

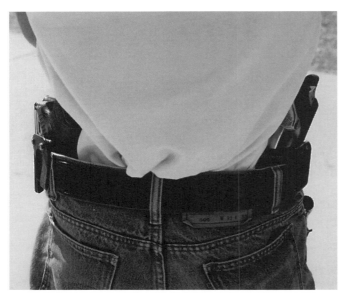

This setup allows fast access to either one of the large-caliber pistols. Where the pistols are carried is largely governed by individual preference, lifestyle, and federal and local firearms laws.

their backs, but, again, in these cases, the officers could access the weapon in this position and, for the most part, with both hands operating.

Solution? An easily accessed backup gun.

In all cases the backup gun *must be accessible*, preferably to either hand.

As with everything else, there is no "golden answer." Differing lifestyles, body builds, physical and societal limitations— they all add up to individualized preferences, requirements, and solutions.

But the sorry fact remains that these days there is room for serious thought about a secondary weapon. It is faster and more positive, in most instances, than trying to resurrect a dead primary gun.

Who needs a backup gun? *Everybody*.

Ballistics:
The Magic Bullet?

"You can't make a silk purse out of a sow's ear." This proverb has been around for a long time and still holds true—especially in the firearms field, where operator ability is becoming increasingly inefficient in direct proportion to so-called advances in weapons technology.

"So-called" because when it comes to ammunition ballistics, primarily handgun, many people seem to think that a handgun can be magically transformed into a shotgun or rifle merely by modifying bullet shape, mass, or diameter. The pistol is used as the topic for this essay because there is more information available on urban conflicts with this weapon than any of the other small arms. There are also more "expert" arguments over handgun ballistics than over other small arms.

ANALYZING A PISTOL'S ABILITY TO STOP DEADLY FORCE

There are several aspects to be considered when analyzing a pistol's ability to stop deadly force, but the following are "guaranteed":

1. There are arguably only two men alive in the United States who truly have the knowledge to discuss ballistics.
2. Reinventing calibers (which didn't work 30 years ago) isn't the answer.
3. A miss with a .44 Magnum is the same as a miss with a .22 Long Rifle.
4. If your attacker hasn't read all the wonderful ballistic information he probably won't cease hostilities because he doesn't know he's supposed to be out of the fight.

Let's take a closer look at the above "guarantees" in chronological order.

1. Unless someone is professionally qualified to discuss ballistics, debate becomes merely a matter of personal opinion, a wrestle to prove one's own point of view. If statistics are to be quoted, all the facts must be included for an honest analysis.

    If you're a proponent of the .45 ACP, for example, face facts: the Thompson/Le Garde/Hatcher theses are based on the shooting of corpses and cattle, and half the reputation attributed to the .45 in the Philippine Insurrection does not conform to the documentation of the conflict.

    On the other hand, a 9mm Parabellum advocate can't discount the considerable success of the .45 in urban U.S. conflicts. Then again, tell the East Coast officer who had 26 stops with a snub-nosed .38 Special that his is an inefficient weapon.

    The editor of *S.W.A.T.* magazine raised an interesting point: several issues back, he suggested that the people who are carrying .45s train harder and as a result chalk up more hits per round fired. Tell the .38 snubbie man he needs a .45 and he'll probably doubt your sanity. Likewise, tell a .45 man who's just witnessed a baddie absorb half a dozen .36-caliber rounds without effect that a 9mm is the answer and he'll probably respond, "I told you so."

    Your chosen caliber is probably better than the other guy's, but handgun calibers are so infinitesimally different in performance, and the lack thereof, that they control only the last few inches of the combat yardstick. Far more important are accuracy, tactics, and the antagonist's state of mind.

2. "New" calibers have once again become all the rage. The 10mm was hailed as the good guy's answer for every situation but then hiccuped and burped as the "mighty" .40 S&W roared its way in. Is anybody out there old enough to remember the .41 Magnum?

    Unless you train with the .40 S&W, .45 ACP, 9mm, or whatever, you won't hit the target, and . . . see 3 below.

3. A miss with a .44 Magnum is the same as a miss with a .22 Long Rifle . . . see 2 above.

4. An assailant will cease hostilities for one (or more) of several reasons: either he has the sanity and clarity of thought to know he is going to lose and elects to bow out gracefully, his central nervous system is shut down, or he receives massive immediate tissue damage, resulting in trauma.

    If it is a matter of inducing trauma, a mortal blow may not necessarily be enough to cause immediate cessation of his deadly force. The point, of course, is to stop his hostility, not to intentionally cause his death.

    If Mr. Baddie has some of the white stuff inserted up his nasal cavities, it's highly unlikely that your magic .45 with its 90-percent one-torso-shot stopping probability (how did they work that one out?) will do that much better than a 9mm. Why? Because Mr. Baddie is now past the stage of stopping unless his central nervous system is shut down or he is subjected to a massive dose of trauma. This will be accomplished by one or more accurate rounds to the central nervous system or by multiple tissue-damaging impacts.

This then becomes a matter of training (or of need for a more effective weapon, such as a rifle, subgun, or a shotgun) and not a matter of minimal ballistic differences.

If you figure caliber is the answer, why are you dropping from a .45 down to .40? If caliber is the answer, why does a 9mm subgun outperform a .45 pistol? If you figure more, smaller bullets are the answer, why are you going to a 10mm or a .40 S&W with less magazine capacity? And, if it's merely the caliber and ballistics, what happened to the .41 Magnum? No, there is no substitute for accuracy. Yes, there is a need for ammunition development.

Better bullets mean better accuracy, better penetration without overpenetration, and more reliable overall performance. But the shooter must be able to deliver the projectile to its mark. Lack of accurate marksmanship won't be compensated for by the latest whizz-bang bullet. It's not too intelligent to rely on hollowpoint bullet expansion at pistol velocities. And if the whizz-bang does expand, explode, or whatever it's supposed to do, you're not going to get requisite penetration, and it's going to blow up on windshields. Besides, when was the last time you were attacked by a wet telephone directory?

The main problem is, as with everything else in the last 20 years, that we're trying to make up for lack of operator competence with technology. There was nothing wrong with the .450 Webley or the 7.63 Mauser at the turn of the century. They solved the problem back then. We've lost the fighting ability. A sow's ear is a sow's ear is a sow's ear . . . and today's pig is tomorrow's bacon.

How to Select the Best Instructor and Training School

Small-arms training should entertain two objectives: the trainee must gain marked improvement in his ability to ballistically handle a deadly-force threat, and, hopefully, he should also, by reason of this increased ability and command presence, often be able to de-escalate a situation by some means other than the use of bullets.

Selection of your instructor and training school could be the most important investment of your life. As in most other aspects of modern society, you often, but not always, get what you pay for. Pay peanuts, you'll probably buy a monkey. On the other hand, there is a very small contingent of carpetbaggers who charge the earth and offer crust.

Obviously, the latter are not limited to the field of firearms training, but it is much more critical in this field, because guess how you find out they've ripped you off? You can always return the lemon car to a disreputable car dealer, but you can't plug up all your bullet wounds.

The following are some obvious guidelines. Stay away from the man who spends half your time with war stories about how many people he killed barehanded in Outer Mongolia. Stay away from the man who insists that "my way is the only way." Stay away from the man who claims he knows it all; the best in the business will readily admit that they don't have half the knowledge they wish they had.

If you have the money and the time, attend every school you can. That way you get a cross-section of opinion. Even if you think the instructor is, in your opinion, a couple of numbers short of a ZIP code, you've learned what not to do. In short, it's still a learning experience.

If, on the hand, you're like the rest of us penniless peasants, you'd probably prefer to forego the pleasure of being ripped off and hopefully get a home run off the first pitch.

The problem with defensive training is that unlike the new car buyer, the trainee often doesn't know what he needs. If people want a Ford, they don't walk into a Chevy dealer. But if they don't know

This officer keeps his cool while delivering rounds to the postitive impact plate on a moving positive/negative target system. It's not as easy as it looks when one considers the bore line-sight line problem, which must be taken into account at close quarters with the weapons system he's using.

whether they need a race car or a pick-up truck, they wind up cruising half a dozen dealers, hopefully finding the ideal vehicle at the first stop.

So what to look for in defensive small arms training?

Instructor: "We'll teach you how to shoot, yessiree Bob."

Trainee: "Shoot what?"

Instructor: "Waddayou mean, *what*?"

Trainee: "Well, my wife's alone at home, and . . ."

Instructor: "No problem. Just buy her a shotgun, point it in the general vicinity of the front door, and blow that sucker away!"

The above example is the epitome of what you can do without. Repugnant, obviously ignorant of his subject matter, and a "Walter Mitty" to boot. What you need is somebody who can improve your latent ability to handle a deadly-force threat and remain within the boundaries of the law. Because if it happens, you'll be the one ultimately responsible and answerable. Mr. Expert Walter Mitty will be at home reading the *TV Guide* when it goes down. Bear in mind, too, that even very good training only improves your odds. There is no such thing as a guarantee.

Training should encompass several aspects of survival, such as marksmanship, tactics, and manipulation of a weapon. If any of these facets are missing from the program, you're starting the race in the last row on the grid.

"What about a nifty class I heard about where I can learn everything I ever wanted to know about 23 weapons in four hours for only $5 million?"

Answer: Your money would be better spent on Iraqi real estate.

"Do I really need to take his basic class? After all, I've been shooting for 635 years."

Answer: Yes, you need the basic class if his class incorporates activities such as moving targets, shooting on the move, dim-light and flashlight sessions, tactics, etc. If you can shoot a one-inch group at 50 yards on a square piece of paper it demonstrates the basics of marksmanship. It does not necessarily mean you're capable of achieving accuracy in a street fight at six feet.

"Well, what distance do you guys go back to in your program?"

Answer: It doesn't mean anything. If you move progressively farther and farther from the same banal paper target (and all you do is increase the shooting time), it does nothing to increase your ability to handle a fight with a maniacal, moving human being. "Basic" training should still incorporate fighting techniques.

"Well, it's going to be close up anyway, so why can't I just shoot him in the knee?"

No answer necessary to that one.

"But I'm not full-time police or military. All I want to accomplish from the class is to be able to load and unload the weapon and to hit an enormous piece of paper at 10 feet. And, uh, maybe win, a teensy-weensy little gunfight."

Answer: You can't have it both ways. If all you want are manipulation and marksmanship, there are some excellent courses on that subject. If you want defensive training, it's a whole different ball game.

For the latter you need instruction from a reputable outfit that specializes in the subject and that can justify and explain every facet of the training on the range. The instructors need to accept the fact that everybody's different and must be able to adapt body positions, firing grips, tactics, and techniques to an individual.

And last, but not least, an instructor must be able to correct problems on the range. To tell somebody how to do something is easy. To be able to correct problems when the desired results are not achieved is the mark of a good instructor. After all, that's what you're laying out the money for.

Defensive small-arms training requires a lot of dedication and forethought. It takes a tremendous amount of effort and investment for a payoff day that may never come. But if the day does arrive, it will be the best insurance policy you can hold.

It's *Not* the Equipment

The accuracy capability that is inherently built into a specific weapon is relative to the shooter's ability.

If the subject under discussion refers either to range or marksmanship, or the one-in-10,000 Carlos Hathcock who could lay in his sniper licks from 500 yards, that's one thing. If, on the other hand, we're talking about "generic" gunfighting, the picture changes.

A good man needs good equipment. If your name does, indeed, happen to be Mr. Hathcock, then you need a rifle and snooper-scope combination that will allow you to place a minute-of-angle assassination shot because you have the mechanical and psychological ability to make a minute-of-angle shot under battle conditions. On the other hand, if you're like the rest of us lesser mortals and are capable of shooting "only" a five- or six-inch group, at best (again, under battle conditions), at 100 yards, what's the point of spending your hard-earned thousands on a rifle that, in your hands, will not produce any better end result than a $150 SKS? Part of it is fashion, part is ego, and part is not understanding the basics of gunfighting.

Being one of the fashionable in-crowd may do wonders for your social life, but it won't elevate your fighting efficiency to that of your great-grandpappy, and he didn't miss when it counted, even though he didn't have a 1992-model wonder gun. The reason he didn't miss is because he knew how to hit. For the overwhelming majority of mano-a-mano fights, "trick" equipment will improve a seasoned professional's performance by only 5 to 10 percent. While this may very well make the difference between success and failure for the one-in-a-million operator who can shoot up to his equipment, it won't make one whit of a difference for anybody else.

The ego problem rears its ugly head with all of us. The saying goes, "If you can't dazzle them with brilliance, baffle them with bull." If all you're trying to do is impress you buddies with your brilliance in a safe environment, that's fine. However, if you're discussing equipment and

A Remington 11-87 backed up by a Para-Ordnance/Colt hybrid. Either will deliver big bullets into a tighter group than most people can shoot.

techniques for deadly-force situations, the techniques and equipment must have a valid basis.

Techniques that haven't been documented and equipment that is nothing but an expensive range toy aren't something to stake your life on in a knockdown, drag-'em-out fight.

Much has been written about the so-called inaccuracy of rifles, such as those in the Kalashnikov family, because they "only shoot into three or four inches at 100 yards." So when's the last time you or your tutor shot into three or four inches when the target was returning fire? Work out how little your enemy has to move for you to miss by a foot; throw in some poor-light conditions, some fear, and all the other ingredients of a fight; and then see if tiny incremental minutes of angle of the rifle's inherent accuracy mean anything.

If you're lying in wait and have the rare luxury of dictating the time and circumstances of the delivery of the shot, then—and only then—is the time for a Hathcock and pinpoint equipment. Any other time an AK will outperform the operator.

The crux of the matter is the difference between target shooting Bambi at your leisure and knocking off a lion in full charge. Unfortunately, some of the people who can shoot into one hole on a target range today were either in Canada or at a university 30 years ago when they had the chance to demonstrate their theories and prowess.

So, yes, sniper equipment is essential for military or police sniper personnel, but true sniping entails much more than the currently used loose definition of the word.

Decided to have your carry handgun accurized? What for, so it will shoot into one inch at 50 yards? It isn't going to happen in a fight!

In fact, you'll be lucky to get the Gospel staccato two rounds into an assailant's torso at five yards for real, let alone within several inches of each other. Tried a for-real head shot at 10 feet lately? No, the problem is training how to fight with the firearm as a medium, not going into a fight with a fancy weapon, gullibility, and little else.

Heresy? Check documented accounts, not unverifiable war stories. If automatic handgun pairs to the body are good, they are good only in the rare Utopian scenario when they are available to the shooter. Most of the time you will have to fire once, twice, maybe half a dozen times at what is available. The problem will not be solved by pursuing a mindless training program that merely consists of regimented cardboard/steel bashing with "accurized" weapons.

Fighting is an art and a science. Shooting nonmoving, square, one-dimensional pieces of paper and steel is a marksmanship aid. No more, no less. If you shoot a one minute-of-angle rifle into two inches at 100 yards, you don't warrant the equipment.

A hundred years ago everybody was a private—battle-hardened and capable, even with ragtag equipment. Today we have droves of two-day sergeants turning out platoons of well-equipped but ill-prepared and gullible combatants.

There are none so blind as those who will not see. Even when they're looking through a $1,000 snooperscope.

"It's Not Fair!"

A common complaint heard on a firing line is the "it's not fair!" wail. (The most common, of course, is the "my gun's sights are off" one.)

Well, life isn't fair, and neither is the fact that I can't win the state lottery, but squealing isn't going to alter the situation. The man who cries "not fair" on a defensive training drill needs to take a long, hard look at his priorities and make an honest appraisal of what he's trying to get from the training exercise. If he's sincerely trying to improve his street-ready capability, the word *unfair* shouldn't exist in his vocabulary, because he's for sure not going to get an even break in a gunfight.

Somebody once commented that shooters are, to a large extent, more concerned about losing on the range in front of witnesses than losing in the street. And he was probably right.

Scenario: The rangemaster sets up a bull's-eye target 10 yards in front of you and allots you a 1 1/2-second time frame to engage said target with your holstered pistol. Cakewalk. On command, you whip out your trusty Scum-Squasher, drill out the center of the target, reholster, and walk off the range with the trophy under one arm and an attitude under the other.

You return to the range the following week, complete with trophy and attitude for all the world to see, but there's a new rangemaster in town. And he has this no-nonsense look on his face.

"Same drill as last week," he says, "but I've added two more targets." Ho-hum. You yawn. More trophies already in the bag. "By the way," says he, "the time frame is the same."

"What the hell is this?" you yell. "Not fair!" (Yup, there's that four-letter F-word again!)

While you whine, the spectators giggle. Your argument, of course, is that you can't hit three targets within such a pressing time period, and you honestly can't, but more on this later.

Mr. Range Rabbit, on the other hand, is trying to prove a point, and a very valid one at that. If, as you claimed last week, you weren't in attendance solely for trophy hunting, but were trying to improve your street-fighting potential, how can you expect to be granted extra time on the range merely because there are additional targets?

Let's get real, folks. You can squeal, whine, and complain until hell freezes over, but you can't seal up the Grand Canyon with a tube of Preparation H.

If you are faced by three armed assailants for real, all three can nail you as quickly as one. They are not going to grant you an extra half-second per enemy merely because your time and motion studies would prefer to start shifting the goalposts.

As you trudge off homeward, you suddenly realize that this is an everyday for-real scenario. But here's the biggie: How do you solve the unsolvable problem? How do you win the battle if the chronometer is so compressed that you cannot deliver enough projectiles in time? You resort to cunning, guile, cheating, and every dirty trick the law will allow, that's how. Face facts: extending time frames on the practice range to conveniently fit the scenario is one of the biggest (and most common) con jobs in evidence today. You will not have that luxury in the street.

Because the logistics won't compute, you will have to resort to plan B: tactics. This will entail judicious, reflexive use of cover, concealment, and a change of body position. In fact, anything that will allow you to stretch the time clock and enable you to set up to where you can deliver the projectiles. No more, no less.

Moving right along, scenario two again has three adversaries, but this time they are staged at different distances. Eeny is 10 yards distant armed with

a shotgun, Meeny is at seven yards brandishing a revolver, and Miney is four feet away, swinging an extremely large pair of clenched fists. Who do you take down first: (A) Eeny, (V) Meeny, (C) Miney, or (D) the most immediate threat on that day?

If you answered D, you're in with a chance. If you go with the normal flow and attempt to deal with the weapons in order of devastation potential (i.e., always the shotgun before the handgun, etc.), Mr. Miney will probably pound your brains to burger before you complete all these rocket scientist thought processes. Of course, then you won't be in the position of having to worry about the shotgun or revolver, either.

This is not to suggest that you always engage the closest threat. It is merely to state, in this author's humble opinion, that the only hope you have is to think fast, settle immediately on what you reflexively feel to be the most dangerous threat (irrespective of weaponry), neutralize it, and then move on.

It seems inconceivable (and again, this is purely personal opinion) that a human brain under these circumstances can be expected to calmly identify weaponry, distances, target definition, etc., and then coolly feed this information to the good guy. Again, as in the first scenario in this chapter, you have precious little time to complete all these brilliant deductions and carry out the appropriate actions. The most dangerous weapon is not always your biggest threat.

Yes, I'm still trying for the lottery. No, I don't think I'll ever win it. Life's not only a bitch, she's also in heat.

Steel Target Design

*T*his is the first of a three-part series on the pros and cons of using steel targets on the firing range. This series has thus been broken down into three main subsections: steel target design, placement of the targets on the range, and criteria governing when the target(s) should be relegated to either long-distance use or the trash dump. This chapter deals with steel target design. The following two chapters deal with target placement and target condition respectively.

Steel targets have two primary advantages over most others used in live-fire training: they are reactionary (as the projectile's impact is recorded either audibly or optically), and they cut training down time to a minimum (for example, time is not wasted taping paper targets).

Although the advantages of incorporating steel targets in range-training scenarios are many, there are certain negative aspects—safety being the most conspicuous. In fact, the overriding factor when determining whether to use steel targets must be the safety aspect. The design of the steel target is as important a factor as target placement and target condition when it comes to the prevention of projectile injury to shooters or bystanders.

Steel targets must also be reliable. Target breakage must be held to a minimum, and repair or replacement time should be a matter of a few minutes, or training will be disrupted. There are two basic elements in steel target design and construction to attain reliability: simplicity and ruggedness.

As with anything else, the objective of the exercise must be studied before the target is designed and built. If, for example, the sole purpose of the steel is to visually register the impact of a .22LR bullet at 100 yards, it could be built of inexpensive mild steel. There is no problem here of ballistic penetration, target destruction, breakage, bullet splash-back, or anything else but the consideration of a safe backstop and ricochets.

(The ricochets in this case are primarily a danger only to a third

Smooth, unblemished, not warped—the best grade armor plate in the business.

party and primarily only in a line left or right of the target or behind it. The angles of projectile rebound will be covered later.)

Thus, in this specific example, the "normal" problems of steel target design and construction don't come into play. If, however, one facet of the intended use of the target is changed, the entire equation changes.

If the .22LR is exchanged for .223, and mild steel is still the material used, there will be no training benefit. Obviously, even though it is still a .22-caliber bullet, the increase in bullet design and velocity will cause the projectile to punch a hole through the mild steel.

Result? No visual impact, no audible impact and target destruction. This comes full circle back to the initial problem: decide what the objective of the training exercise is before building the target.

It is also well to remember that while almost everybody has financial constraints, in the long run it is less expensive to build a good target once than to rebuild a poorly designed target twice. "Measure twice, cut once—measure once, cut twice."

One major question with steel targets has already come to light: can you cut down on expenses by building one target that will get the desired training result using different small arms? The sad answer is this: by and large, it can't be done. There are too many variables, the most important of which are safety and target destruction.

If, for example, we are still operating on the principle of a nonmoving, vertical flat target, a .223 will perforate steel that a softpoint .308 may very well not even dimple. A shotgun slug, on the other hand, may well bow or break the target simply because of its close-range bullet weight and power. A 9mm hardball will pock steel that a .45 ACP softpoint won't, etc.

One of the possible avenues to pursue is the use of frangible bullets, but that's sidetracking the main issue here.

When it comes to visually reacting targets, such as "knockdowns," "swingers," "flippers," etc., the problems are compounded. Again using the .223 as an example, a steel target calibrated to fall on bullet impact at 75 yards will not fall at 200 yards and conversely will sustain severe damage at 25 yards.

Also, a target that reacts by falling, swinging, etc., has to be constructed with a fulcrum (a hinge, pivot point). The heavier the caliber, the heavier the target components and the more difficult it becomes for a small, light bullet to get the desired result.

The only happy medium to halfway

defeating the problem is to go back to the basics: rugged but simple. Geometry is a far better solution than relying on huge globs of weld. By simplifying bracket and support angles, you can keep breakages and weight to a minimum. The idea is to use gravity as a natural aid instead of cluttering up the system with wires, springs, gears, and air compressors, which are inevitably going to break down or run out of fuel in the middle of a training exercise.

Metallurgy plays an important part in the reliability of a steel target. Armor plate can be kept relatively thin and light and still maintain reliability and ruggedness. It is not, however, the magic cure-all and will sustain damage from close, high-velocity bullet impacts. Armor plate comes in varying degrees of hardness. If armor is to be the material used for the target, make sure it is good-quality armor.

One of the negative aspects of armor plate is that it requires an expert welder to attach brackets, pivot points, etc. While welding, if penetration of the armor is not attained, the entire target face will tear off its attachment points on bullet impact after very little range use.

Another area of frequent failure is at the fulcrum of, for example, the commonly used Pepper Popper. If the fulcrum at the bottom of the target is not expertly welded, breakage is common, not so much from bullet impact as from repeated impact when the target hits the ground. Better to attach the bottom fulcrum by bolts for ease of replacement, as sooner or later the fulcrum assembly will break.

Most of the problems associated with steel target design stem from three main problem areas that result from lack of

forethought: (1) safety, (2) breakage and down time, and (3) lack of protection for support mechanism/structure.

Safety, or the lack thereof, is invariably a result of not abiding by the basic rules of target placement and target condition, which will be discussed in parts two and three of this series. Safety can, however, come into play as a result of not studying the angles and fabrication concepts of the support structure of the target.

The assumption should never be made that the trainee is good enough to hit the intended target area. Even if he is, the projectile or fragments may rebound from the target to one of its support elements and from there change direction, angling toward the shooter or bystanders.

The simpler the target system, the less the safety problem and the less the equipment needs to be protected. If a steel target's operation is reliant on gears or spring (in fact, anything remotely removed from the principle of simplicity), it will either break or fail to function as required.

The targets must be weather resistant. While the targets should be checked for function and condition before a training exercise, by nature of their fabrication (usually heavy and inconvenient for portability), in most cases they are left to withstand all weather conditions year round. They must be able to withstand these elements without their performance being affected: another strong case for simple design.

There is the possibility of overkill with steel target design—that is, building them too heavy for the job required. But they must be built to stand at least twice the punishment envisioned for the job they are intended to perform, especially targets that move when hit.

If a target is expected to be impacted 100 times in the vital zone during training, it should be able to withstand 200 impacts over its entire potential hit area.

It must be appropriately sized and shaped to its training use. If a steel target is to be used at 25 yards for rifle training, making it 10 feet high and 6 feet wide is obviously a waste of money and of construction and resource time.

The main objective of using steel targets is invariably to replace paper targets for repetitious use without the dis-

advantage of down time. If the steel does not meet this objective with functional reliability, it has not served its purpose.

The golden rules are as follows:

1. Keep it simple, using good component material.
2. Build it rugged, using geometry and gravity (where possible) to replace excess weight and welding.
3. Protect all parts of the support structure from possible bullet impact.
4. Never underestimate the damage capability bullets have on steel equipment, even armor plating.

The Positioning of Steel Targets

The preceding article covered the general design of steel targets. This chapter will address the positioning of steel targets on the range.

The positioning of steel targets on a firing range is governed by two factors: (1) the marksmanship and tactical requirements of the instructor to attain maximum trainee marksmanship and tactics benefit and (2) range safety.

If the targets used are of paper or cardboard construction and the target frames are made of wood, the sole instructor problems (for the purposes of this text) are a safe backstop and an available arc of fire and complementary backstop appropriate for the training exercise. If, however, the targets are fabricated from steel, or steel target frames are being used, the range safety is immensely compromised.

The six primary factors that control the terminal resting place of the projectiles are as follows:

- Condition of the target
- Distance of the shooter and bystanders from the target
- Angle of the shooter and bystanders relative to the target
- Distance and angle of multiple targets relative to each other
- The ability of the targets to move on bullet impact
- Design of the surrounding support structure of the target

CONDITION OF THE TARGET

For the purpose of this text, the assumption of points two through six is that the steel targets in use are in perfect condition, with no cracks, craters, dimples, or welds of any kind, and that all the target faces are initially vertical and unbowed. However, because target condition is so vital to range safety and because the problems are so many and varied, the subject of steel target condition will be covered in its own article, which follows this one.

The shooter is about to commit range suicide. Note the poor condition of the steel and bad alignment of targets relative to each other and the shooter. If you want realism during training, here's a typical situation where the targets might return fire.

DISTANCE OF THE SHOOTER AND BYSTANDERS FROM THE TARGET

It is important to note that in most cases it is not the shooter who is hit by a refracted projectile, but rather a bystander, instructor, fellow shooter, etc. This is because of the geometric laws of incidence and refraction.

In a recent test it was found that, using smooth, unbowed steel, all projectiles rebound within a 12-degree angle of the point of aim of the main projectile. A natural progression would be to increase stated angle to 20 degrees, to an additional "safety valve" of almost 70 percent.

The main point to bear in mind is the angle of incidence. That is, the angle at which the projectile impacts the steel relative to shooter and his surroundings. If the bullet hits a smooth, flat, vertical surface straight on, it (or portions of it) will refract within a 12-degree arc from the steel surface. The compass direction of this splash-back, however, can be north, south, east, or west.

Obviously, if all else is equal, the closer you are to the steel, the more violent will be the impact when the bullet rebounds.

Many shooters repeatedly ignore manufacturer's minimum shooter-to-target distance recommendations, especially during handgun "competitions." The recommendations are there for a reason.

ANGLE OF THE SHOOTER AND BYSTANDERS RELATIVE TO THE TARGET

If all else remains the same as in the above, except the bullet now impacts the steel from an angle, and therefore at an angle, obviously the rebounding projectile will terminate in a location different than the above. All that has changed is the shooter's body location relative to the target.

The bullet has now impacted the smooth, one-dimensional target at exactly the same point of impact, but at a different angle. The angle of splash-back is still 12 degrees, but it is now a different 12 degrees relative to the target/bystander location. This is why bystanders and fellow shooters often get hit—mainly because they stand off to the side to get a "better" vantage point of the shooting.

Remember that it is virtually mathematically impossible to get a perfect right-angled hit. The bullet will almost certainly always impact the steel at an angle. The given 12 degrees is for a smooth, vertical steel surface impacted by a projectile dead on.

DISTANCE AND ANGLE OF MULTIPLE TARGETS RELATIVE TO EACH OTHER

Steel is often used in multiple form to simulate crowd scenes, multiple assailants, etc. Therefore, one of the prime sources of splash-back is secondary fragmentation or ricochet from a second target or target frame.

The original 12-degree arc of danger remains the same, but under these circumstances the projectile can, after impacting the first target, ricochet laterally to hit a second target. The projectile then rebounds off the second target, again inside a 12-degree arc, but at yet a different angle to the initial ricochet. This is one of the most common causes of "splash" hitting either the shooter or bystanders.

There are two solutions. The first is to place barricades (usually wood) between the targets. This, however, is not always feasible or possible, either physically or from a tactical perspective. If separating barricades are used, do not use rubber. It will probably compound the problem.

The second solution is to study the layout of the targets in relation to each other. Any target within the 12- to 20-degree danger zone of another should be moved to a different location, laterally or vertically.

Obviously, an absolute "never" here is to place targets with impact surfaces at angles to each other. The inevitable result here is an ever-decreasing angle of safety for the shooter/bystanders, with a resultant ever-decreasing margin of safety.

THE ABILITY OF THE TARGETS TO MOVE ON IMPACT

If the target reacts by moving on bullet impact, one important aspect is obvious. Depending on when the target moves, or if it is struck by follow-up shots, its original angle will change. If there are other targets, structures, or people in the vicinity of the target, an immense safety problem becomes apparent. Not only is there an increased safety problem to the shooters, there is now also an increased problem of an unknown angle of ricochet in the direction of the backstop.

The classic example of this is the "Dueling Tree," a stationary target stand with four steel plates that swing independently about the "trunk" when struck by a bullet. Secondary fragmentation and splash off this unit are intense at close distances. Again, the manufacturer stipulates using the target system at a minimum distance of 25 yards for this very reason.

DESIGN OF THE SURROUNDING SUPPORT STRUCTURE OF THE TARGET

Potential secondary fragmentation, ricochet, and bullet splash are again compounded by the amount of structural components supporting the target, which are laterally and vertically in line with the impact surface or forward of it.

Here, the "normal" rules of construction don't necessarily apply. Tubular steel, if hit by a bullet, will normally produce a ricochet at an angle toward the backstop.

However, if the steel pipe is struck on the rebound by a projectile that has already impacted a surface slightly to the rear of it, the projectile will ricochet at a tangent toward the shooter. All support structure, therefore, must be located where it cannot refract secondary projectiles "uprange."

A common example of support structure causing a potential problem is the Pepper Popper. Most people hit by splash from a Pepper Popper are hit by secondary fragments, rebounding from the steel target base. Because shooters often shoot the poppers from a close distance (usually handgunners and, again, usually ignoring distance-to-target warnings), the bullet path is often at a downward angle from gun muzzle to point of impact.

Following the basic 12-degree-angle rule, the bullet splash heads toward the ground but impacts a multifaceted steel target base. Obviously, with a second impact surface of so many angle combinations, it is impossible to gauge where the fragments will terminate.

Mr. Pepper designed a "splash guard" into his target to counteract this, but it is often ignored, with the inevitable result. A large sandbag placed immediately fore of the target face and laid on top of the steel base is a sure and simple cure to this problem.

The Pros and Cons of Steel Targets

*I*n an earlier column, we took a look at the positioning of steel targets on the firing range and how positioning may create a hazard. Now we'll examine how the steel targets themselves may create a safety problem.

Target condition may be a safety problem because all the basic rules of "angle of incidence" and "angle of refraction" change with an alteration in surface area condition.

As long as the rules outlined in the earlier column are taken into account, angles or ricochet and rebound can be safely computed. Deterioration in steel target surfaces, however, leads to guesswork, and guesswork leads to a safety hazard.

Deterioration can be defined as four problem areas:

- Dimpling or cratering
- "Pimple" or convex blemishes
- Concave warpage
- Cracks or joints in the target surface

DIMPLING

Dimpling is invariably caused by using ammunition or calibers not intended for use on that specific target. If the bullet doesn't punch a hole through the steel it leaves an indentation or sometimes a crater similar to those on the moon's surface.

The safety hazard here becomes not the one of secondary splash-back discussed earlier, but rather one of an indeterminate ricochet/rebound angle.

Regardless of the angle's main impact face of the target, the bullet (or fragments) will leave the target surface at an angle relative to the last point of contact.

Atrocious target condition. This steel should be relegated for range drills no closer than 100 yards to shooters or bystanders.

If, for example, the dimple is smooth, caused by a .72-caliber shotgun slug, and a .36-caliber handgun bullet is now fired at the same point of impact, there is no possible way to calculate the angle of splash because the handgun projectile is not impacting a flat surface.

While the 12-degree rule still applies, there is no way in advance to calculate the last point of contact of bullet and steel.

If dimple size and/or bullet size changes, the problem is the same: it can't be calculated in advance. If the bullet impacts partially on the flat surface and partly on the crater, fragmentation will probably occur with fragments coming back toward the shooter at different angles.

Cratering is often caused by a bullet that has bored through the steel but has left a ridged rim behind on the steel surface, looking much like a volcano. This, if anything, is worse than a smooth dimple, because it inevitably causes bullet fragmentation on impact, again with indeterminate angles.

Steel targets used for relatively close range work, and which have one dimple or crater, should be regarded as a hazard. They can be repaired for use by filling the hole with weld and grinding the surface back to its original flat, level texture. A badly scarred target should be put out of commission or relegated to long-range use.

CONVEX BLEMISHES

Convex blemishes, as with dimples, are usually caused by incorrect use of caliber or weaponry on target steel incapable of dealing with that weapon's ballistics.

Commonly found in this field of abuse are mild-steel targets, designed for low-velocity handguns, which have been impacted at relatively long distance by shotgun slugs. This leaves a large (approximately one-inch) pimple on the rear surface of the plate. Not wanting to face the hazards of potentially hitting a "crater," the shooter turns the target about-face 180 degrees. The rear surface of the target now does duty as the impact face.

Though, in theory, this is safer than a concave surface, it should be treated as a hazard and taken out of use or used at long distance only.

CONCAVE WARPAGE

Steel targets sustain concave warp, or bowing, from repeated impact in the same general area. This does not necessarily mean that the surface is damaged, but merely warped overall.

A simple solution is to turn the target about-face 180 degrees to the shooter, as long as the bow is not extreme. If the incidence and refraction angles are taken into account, it can be seen that a convex bow is not much safer than one of concave shape.

Obviously with north-south bowing, the "uprange" safety problem changes, as always, with the angle from which the bullet impacts the target. For example, a severely bowed target may pose a safety problem for a shooter in a kneeling position, but not for a standing shooter who hits the same point of impact. Depending on the point of impact, the opposite may also be true.

CRACKS OR JOINTS

Cracks pose the same potential safety hazard as the craters mentioned above. Usually forming initially at the junction of an irregularly shaped target (i.e., where the "torso" meets the "neck" on a Pepper Popper), cracks are caused by either excessive impacts, a weak structural point, or an "edger" hit that always craters. This crater, if located on the outside edge of the target, often causes a weak point that can lead to cracking.

Joints in the target surface should be carefully mated and are almost always a safety hazard. Joints are commonly used on targets with "flip-away" areas to register bullet zone impact.

These areas are invariably attached on a hinge, or fulcrum system. As long as the bullet impacts either the main target surface or the flip-away surface, there is no problem. If the projectile impacts the cracked area of the joint, the same potential hazards are present as with cratering of the target surface. Here again, the assumption is that the shooter will hit what he is asked to hit, which is often not the case.

The Golden Rule of steel target condition? If there's any doubt, don't use it.

The Bottom Line on Trajectory

Trajectory, simply stated, is the flight curve a bullet describes from gun muzzle to point of impact. It is also a sorely misunderstood subject.

The basic principle of a bullet's flight path is controlled by one unwavering absolute: the force of gravity is constant. This results in the unquestionable fact that a projectile starts to drop toward Mother Earth the instant it exits the gun muzzle. While this may be overstating the obvious to some readers, there is a large percentage of the shooting fraternity that doesn't understand this physics basic.

"Aha!" you say. "Then why does my rifle shoot to a higher point of impact at 100 yards than it does at 25 yards?" Herein lies the crux of this article: If you sighted your 24-inch-barrel rifle to hit point of aim/point of impact at 25 yards, it will indeed shoot to a slightly higher point of impact at 100 yards—not because the bullet "climbs," but because the rifle muzzle is angled above horizontal. In other words, the barrel is not perfectly horizontally in line with the point of impact.

Why not? Because of the relationship of the bore line to the sight line. Here the shooter's eye, the front sight/scope reticle, and the point of desired impact are in a straight line, but the point of impact and muzzle are in a different plane. To compensate for this, adjustments are made to the sighting system of the weapon to collimate the two planes, allowing the weapon to shoot to specific points of impact at specific distances.

If you cut six inches off the barrel, will it shoot to the same point of impact at 500 yards as would the 24-inch barrel? Obviously not. With the velocity loss of the projectile would come a faster "drop-off" in trajectory because of the constant force of gravity.

So what's the big deal? Why all the fancy jargon?

There are three reasons: the sniper, the shotgun slugs, and the average shooter (who, for the most part, can't shoot anywhere near the weapon's inherent capability, especially under battle conditions).

THE SNIPER

The true one-in-ten thousand sniper must be able to deliver absolute precision. A 70-yard head shot that misses its mark by two inches isn't going to solve the problem. Neither will a blown 600-yard body shot that misses by six inches. In other words, the genuine sniper must know to the nth degree exactly where the bullet will impact at specific distances under all conditions—period. This is one reason why top-of-the-line sniper rifles don't have reserve iron sights. They just won't meet the absolute precision requirements of a true sniper situation.

SHOTGUN SLUGS

Knowledge of the specific trajectory and point of impact when shooting slugs through a shotgun is usually more complicated than that required for generic rifle shooting, for several reasons. Although a trained marksman can shoot into five inches at 100 yards with shotgun slugs, sighting systems are often not up to the task and the projectile's trajectory curve is more pronounced, especially past 80 yards. This last, however, is dependent on where the weapon is zeroed.

A shotgun zeroed for point of aim/point of impact at 25 yards will shoot a lot lower at 100 yards than, for example, one zeroed for a 75-yard point of aim/point of impact. Intermediate impact distances will obviously also differ for these respective weapons, especially in the case of shotguns with widely differing barrel lengths.

Again, it is not that a bullet "climbs," but the factor of by how much the shotgun muzzle is elevated above horizontal.

THE AVERAGE SHOOTER

Unfortunately, most of us talk better than we shoot. Most "long" shots are missed by rifle shooters for two reasons—poor marksmanship and lack of knowledge of trajectory. (The word "long" is in quotes because, coupled with the other two problems, is another one—the inability of the average Joe Citizen to estimate range.)

So you trudge off to war, armed with your favorite "25 yards point-of aim/point of impact zeroed" Bambi Basher. Up jumps Freddy Krueger at what looks like about 6,000 yards' distance. The first thing you do is hold about three inches high "to allow for trajectory," and that night you are utterly amazed to hear on the news that a terrorist coincidentally put a .30-caliber hole through a 747 at the same time that you were attempting to deal with Mr. K.

Here's the problem:

1. Freddie was only 80 yards away, not 6,000.
2. Nobody, but nobody, can put them through the same hole in a one-inch group under battle conditions when somebody is moving and returning fire.
3. The reason you "battle-zeroed" your rifle at 25 yards was to allow you to hold dead-on for fighting conditions (with most modern cartridges) out to about 250 meters without messing with hold-over. This stems from an old British artillery term, *point blank*, where the big guns could be

fired up to a specific distance without elevating the gun's barrel.

The great Townsend Whelen stated that only a very good man with a rifle could hit at 300 yards under battle conditions. These days most people can't hold a six-inch group at 100.

So here's the bottom line: zero your rifle/shotgun at a distance that will best suit your potential requirements and know where it will impact at alternate distances. Last, and probably most important, if you can judge three inches on a moving enemy's chest at 300 yards and can shoot a three-inch group in a 15-mile-per-hour wind on a battlefield, then—and only then—should you bother holding over by two inches to allow for trajectory.

If, on the other hand, you're like us lesser mortals, learn where your weapon hits on the range, cut out the fancy crap, and stay with the centuries-old basics of marksmanship, tactics, and fighting.

The Forgotten
Art of Training

Skill with arms is now considered to be a specialty—not an everyday-survival skill.

—Capt. Max Muramoto, U.S. Army

As sad a commentary on current fighting ability as this is, it is also painfully true. So why is it that we can send a man to the moon, yet we have lost the most primitive of abilities?

Two contributory reasons are societal attitudes and unrealistic training. Sections of society insist that firearms are dangerous, that we are about to enter a thousand years of peace, and that you should not defend yourself if attacked. Conveniently, these are the same fine folk who call for the "dogs of war" when their fine oratory bounces off the thick skull of a coke-snorting Neanderthal-like criminal.

Unfortunately, while these dreamers possess admirable viewpoints, there *is* a war going on. There always has been. There probably always will be. Like it or not, the sword is mightier than the pen.

For the purposes of this article, we turn to the person who is of realistic attitude and willing to stand up and be counted. How can he/she improve his/her survival training? Or, more precisely, why is current training (for the most part) ineffective when it comes down to the Real McCoy?

What follows, in the author's humble opinion, is a rundown of several unrealistic and irrelevant aspects of defensive small-arms training:

How about the handgun caliber argument . . . as in, "The 9mm versus the .45—a new look." How many times can the same old subject matter be rehashed, over and over, ad nauseam?

They're the same old arguments, pro and con—only the authors' bylines change as the years roll by. The sorry truth of the matter is that the handgun, regardless of caliber from .36 and larger, is an ineffectual weapon. It does the job most of the time if the shooter places his shot(s) and the person shot is compliant.

The object of defensive shooting is to immediately incapacitate the aggressor. This may or may not lead to death as a secondary result, but the assailant's death is not the prime objective. Similarly, one who does not immediately cease his aggression but dies half an hour later was not satisfactorily "stopped."

So how does a minimally larger, faster, slower, or differently shaped bullet magically down your opponent? It doesn't. It would seem that as time goes by the bullet requirement changes. As of this writing, the argument (from those few who really know) is in favor of caliber and approximately a foot of penetration in correctly monitored ballistic gelatin. Of course, you will have different penetration requirements if you have to punch through the perpetrator's humerus to get to his chest cavity as opposed to having a straight-on torso shot. This is conveniently forgotten.

And, no, I have no more ballistic knowledge than the average person; but I didn't fall off the turnip truck last week, either. It doesn't take an Einstein—or reading 20 minutes of skewed statistics—to work out that perfectly placed torso shots may or may not immediately dispose of an aggressor. Unless he *knows* he's in trouble, he won't quit.

What differing handgun calibers and bullets give you is a minor edge—no more, no less.

Speaking of perfectly placed torso shots, how many gunfights end as a result of two perfect torso strikes? The answer is, very few. These utopian hits are very difficult to achieve in a real fight because of "target" motion, poor-light conditions, etc. If the target is as easy to hit as a normal, banal range target, you are probably not justified in shooting.

So how about a head shot? Same

answer—it's just not that easy to hit for real. If range drills are the perfect answer for a street problem, then why aren't they being executed in the street? Because the target scenario on the range is, for the most part, nonrepresentative of the real problem.

There is a reason why trained, emotionally controlled operators wind up shooting the bad guy in the arms, shoulder, stomach, and other "undesirable" hit areas. In close quarters and under attack you have to go for the easiest, quickest available target—or you lose. If that doesn't work, you'll have to immediately follow up with plan B, C, or whatever else it takes to get the job done. Sometimes the torso or head will be accessible. Sometimes it won't.

The "if the first two torso shots don't work, another two won't work" theory sounds wonderful—until the situation is real and you don't have the time or the target compliance to perform all these magnificent operations. Torso and head are plan A, but you'd better have a plan B standing by.

Well, if I run out of ammo I'll just go ahead with my well-oiled, one-second speed load, right? Sorry, wrong answer. The man hasn't been born who can do a one-second speed load in a gunfight for one reason only: when you are under attack it takes at least a second before you realize that the load is required. The same thing goes with malfunction clearances. More range training can lull one into a false sense of security.

Yes, you should have malfunction clearance and speed-load drills down to a fine art. No, you probably won't have the time to complete them in a fight unless you have a convenient brick wall to use for cover. This is highly unlikely if you're the victim of a car-jacking or on an escalated domestic dispute call. Carry two guns!

As far as being able to deliver quick 50-yard hits with a handgun, it is an admirable proficiency to achieve. However, you'd be better served, in this author's opinion, by spending your limited training time becoming faster and more efficient at closer, more realistic distances with compounded target problems.

The art of training was indeed an art for centuries. Today, bastardization is largely reducing it to a fallacious security blanket. It's a similar situation to the U.S. Army's emasculation of the AR-15. Now the "experts" say the .223 is an inefficient caliber. It wasn't, until the bureaucrats put the cart before the horse.

There's only one way to improve your range training: make it as realistic and difficult as possible.

Also analyze opinions, both verbal and written, before you make a decision as to the tactics and techniques you wish to employ. Don't accept them carte blanche because they were uttered by an "expert." You know your needs, lifestyle, and requirements better than anyone else.

Ultimately, you will be the one making the decisions when the defecation hits the oscillating device—they'd better work.

Tactics for Dealing with Carjackers

Now we're blessed with a new fad—carjacking. Just when it seems the criminal element of society can't sink any lower, up jumps yet another level of degradation. Like any other tactical problem, it is not insurmountable. However, it does require one more chapter of attention in your tactical survival book.

Unfortunately, unlike some tactical situations, there is no distinctive rhyme, reason, or guaranteed physical violence level to the perpetrator's actions. He may be "polite" (if such a word can be used under these circumstances); he may escalate his violence relative to your reactions; or he may merely run a continuous vicious attack from start to finish, regardless of your reactionary behavior.

While "normal" precautions should be taken—such as religiously locking vehicle doors, rolling up windows, and going into "red alert" if rammed while stopped at a traffic signal—circumstances may force you to fight for your survival.

Unfortunately, this means that you have only one choice: immediate, explosive reaction. You have no time to consider a "Mr. Nice Guy" alternative. Time, space, and distance are compressed to such a degree that, literally, a split second of delay or indecision could cost you your life or, at best, severe physical injury.

It's all very well to suggest that the criminal may not harm you and merely cruise off into the setting sun, but the track record seems to indicate that he's going to inflict violent physical damage before he leaves. In short, you can't afford to gamble on not fighting.

WHAT *ARE* YOUR TACTICAL OPTIONS?

The one piece of equipment essential for a gunfight is a gun. Although this may not exactly be earth-shattering news, it will probably entail the carrying of an additional sidearm to the one normally employed unless a cross-draw rig or shoulder holster is your primary carry choice. And even if a shoulder holster or cross-draw rig is your usual choice, it may not be accessible or fast enough in a carjacking situation wherein the driver is seated and strapped into a safety-belt system.

Obviously, if you are standing outside the vehicle when apprehended, the tactical scenario can be handled the same as any other contact distance situation and, for the purposes of this text, is irrelevant to the subject under discussion.

In the United States, most vehicles are left-hand drive and most drivers are right-handed. Most carjackings to date have occurred while the driver is seated and belted into a lap/shoulder combination harness. Access to a strong-side belt holster under these circumstances becomes not only awkward and difficult, but invariably too time consuming to get a handgun into action before the perpetrator can react to your reaction.

The diagonal portion of the vehicle's safety-belt system similarly hampers the smooth withdrawal of a handgun from a shoulder or cross-draw scabbard, but the latter two systems are not quite as restrictive as a right-side belt-level holster because the "strong-side" belt holster requires the driver's upper body to lean forward to allow his shooting elbow to clear the back of the seat.

Access to an ankle holster is also restricted because of safety-belt constraints, and this system also invariably requires the use of both hands to extract the weapon from its retaining receptacle.

There are several other options. One is to carry a handgun cavalry-style (butt facing forward). This is reasonably fast and effective but requires a lot of practice from a belted-in, seated position.

Use your rear-view mirrors. Time to stomp on the gas!

On top of all the preceding bad news is the positioning of the steering wheel, which is one more mechanical device that can dramatically and abruptly interrupt the alignment of your weapon with the target—or the bullet's flight path for that matter. This assumes that your attacker has approached the vehicle on the driver's side, which has been the norm to date.

So what's a viable way out of this nightmare? There are a couple. When driving into or out of the problem area, avoidance is obviously your first choice. Bear in mind that a V-8 Chevy beats a .45 Colt any day of the week. Equally as obvious is the fact that if you choose to drive into the problem you are potentially setting yourself up for a vehicular manslaughter charge. (For this reason, and by reason of any other information contained in this article, neither the author nor the publisher will accept any responsibility, implied or assumed, for any of the techniques later used by the reader in a defensive situation.)

There is one more choice, and this is possibly the more effective. This entails carrying an additional weapon securely attached to the vehicle that will be immediately accessible under the above-mentioned circumstances. This may not be legal in your residential jurisdiction, but if it is, it's the most logical solution to the carjacking situation.

One final cautionary note: If push comes to shove, and you are forced into a shooting situation while strapped into the driver's seat (regardless of whether you have one or multiple attackers on the driver's side, passenger side, front, or rear of your vehicle), you will proba-

bly have to shoot through glass or metal. You stand a good chance of rupturing your eardrums and sustaining injuries (possibly even death or blindness) from refracted bullet fragments and glass. Last, but not least, you will not have absolute control over bullet direction if the projectile has to pass through metal or glass.

While "you pays your money and you takes your chances," and anything is better than dying, avoiding the situation is always your best choice. Use rearview mirrors continuously and keep abreast of the latest carjacking confidence tricks.

Remember, the best gunfighter in the business is the one who can avoid a fight.

How to Avoid Being Terminated While Clearing an Area

It's late at night and you hear a noise downstairs. You grab the family howitzer and take on the *Terminator* role. You're stupid, and you die. Harsh words? Not really.

The sorry truth is that if you attempt a house-clearing exercise on your own, all you're doing is rolling the dice, with your life as the table stakes. No matter how much tactical training you undergo, without at least one backup partner, you're in deep trouble.

Alone, you can reduce the odds against you from 100-to-1 to about 90-to-1, but that's about it. While tactics can be practiced until hell freezes over, there is one bottom line: unless you are a chameleon or a fly, you cannot look in two directions at once. And without that ability, you're doing nothing short of walking into a death trap.

Certainly, there are specific lifesavers you can utilize, such as steering wide of corners, not silhouetting yourself on doorjambs, and knowing which way doors open by observing the hinge pins. These may be the deciding factors if you do, indeed, absolutely have to go looking for the bogeyman (such as a situation where a family member is in trouble). But these few straws will probably not be enough to stop the drowning.

This article may be written from a negative perspective, but at least it's honest.

First, you need to analyze why you are setting off on the "hunt." Anger is good . . . losing your temper is not. If you're setting out to war because you think somebody may be stealing your $100 VCR, it may be the most nonsensical reason you can die for. Panic a penny-ante burglar and he may well kill you just to avoid identification in a police lineup on a minor burglary charge.

Well, you say, no scum of the earth is going to steal my hard-earned possessions. So, if you do get lucky and manage to see him before he sees you, what are you going to do? Shoot him? You'd better have the best lawyer in the business because the above situation is not justification for using deadly force. Now you're off to the pokey for 20

This homeowner is on a kamikaze run. Force your enemy to come to you whenever possible. Perfoming a single-operator house clearing is, plain and simply, rolling the dice.

years for losing your temper. No, it's not fair, but "fair" is just another dirty four-letter word.

What are you going to do if you don't shoot? Nothing that you couldn't have done better and more safely from your initial location.

What's the big deal, you say? Why is it so dangerous to negotiate an area on your own? After all, it's your house, you know the layout and where all the pitfalls exist, right? After all, all you have to do is kill the lights and you're "home Jerome." Not! (Wrong answer.)

Inevitably there's going to be ambient light—enough to get you hurt. Shadows, reflections off concave TV screens, mirrors, coffee pots, etc., can all lead to an early demise. Bear in mind that the intruder doesn't need target identification. If he can locate your immediate area he can crank off rounds through a wall until he gets a lucky hit.

You will give away your location by tripping over one of the kid's toys or Rover's doggie bone or by misusing the flashlight. The only way to avoid these potential problems is to go at a snail's pace—one to two hours to search an average room with relative safety—searching and scanning in 5- to 10-degree arcs and then pausing after each scan to regroup.

This brings us to the $64,000 question: if it's literally going to take hours, what's the point of doing it at all? Would you really risk life and limb for a stupid VCR?

If you don't suspect an immediate and potential deadly-force threat to yourself or a family member, don't go looking for trouble—you'll probably find it.

It is far better to plan. Keep a spare front- and backdoor key securely attached to a Cyalume stick. This can be pitched out of your bedroom window when the boys in blue arrive. Turn on the light before you heave it out the window, because Murphy's Law dictates that your aim will be off. The stick—and keys—will land in the darkest area of your garden where nobody will be able to find it.

Dial 911 as soon as you suspect a problem. Notify the powers that be of your location and what you are wearing. Let them know that you are armed and then leave the phone off the receiver and don't change your location. Don't complicate the police officer's job any more than it already is. Then sit back, defend only a threat coming in through your bedroom doorway, and let law enforcement handle everything else. The 911 recording will help later in your defense.

There is nothing more dangerous

This homeowner has intelligently "played the angles" to spot the mirrored reflection of an intruder.

This is an excellent vantage point. The homeowner is proned out at the top of a stairwell, not visible to the intruder, and relatively safe from indiscriminate fire.

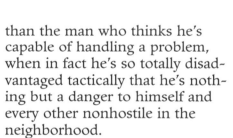

than the man who thinks he's capable of handling a problem, when in fact he's so totally disadvantaged tactically that he's nothing but a danger to himself and every other nonhostile in the neighborhood.

If you don't have backup, and if you don't have an immediate deadly-force threat emanating, for example, from your child's bedroom where you are obligated to approach the problem area, let him come to you. Discretion is the better part of valor.

Don't let your ego—and body—get in the way of a bullet . . . not for a lousy VCR. Let it go.

This is another good observation point, but a head shot here could traverse at an upward angle, raising potential backstop considerations before firing.

Positioning Yourself to Win a Gunfight

*E*ssential to small-arms weaponcraft is the ability to instantaneously adapt shooting positions relevant to a tactical scenario. While this statement may not exactly rank with the splitting of the atom, the objective of this text is to analyze the pros, cons, and finer nuances of shooting positions.

There are textbook shooting positions taught on shooting ranges, and there are field-expedient positions. Unfortunately, once the dogs of war start barking, most of the textbook positions—as usual—get the old heave-ho out the window.

Field-expedient positions are adopted for a variety of reasons, but any or all have one end objective: personal survival or the survival of a third party or parties. For every position there is one basic tenet: There is always a trade-off. This trade-off often entails a sacrifice. Sometimes it's comfort; sometimes it's a small amount of stability. However, this sacrifice is never an excuse or reason to accept a reduced level of accuracy. If you don't hit your mark, you don't win.

Basic positions are primarily composed of standing, kneeling, squatting, sitting, prone, and their variations. Where the above-mentioned trade-off comes into effect is during a gunfight—not on a flat, smooth shooting range. In the latter case you invariably have a known target and scenario, and you have been informed of your specific end objective by a range master or instructor.

In the street or on the battlefield the only rules are to win as quickly as possible and to inflict as much damage as possible, using the dirtiest tactics and techniques available to you at the time. Under these circumstances you also have the added problem of avoiding incoming projectiles—always an incentive to win!

There are essentially three facets of achieving success in this type of situation:

A field-expedient "bastard" shooting position gives this shooter as much cover and concealment as he can possibly get from the available surroundings.

- Use of cover and concealment
- Marksmanship and weapon manipulation ability
- The intelligent use of field-expedient shooting positions relevant to the situation at hand

STANDING

Standing is the least stable of all the positions, but it is used more often than any other. It should be used only if you cannot access the target—either optically or geometrically—from a more stable, secure shooting platform or if you don't have the time to use a better and safer location/position. Obviously, you are easier to hit standing out in the open than if you use cover, concealment, or a lower body position to make a smaller target area of yourself.

The biggie under these circumstances is, "Do I drop to kneeling to make a smaller target of myself and wind up with a ricochet round in the head, which would have hit me 'only' in the leg if I'd remained standing?" This type of tactical decision will have to be an instantaneous coin toss, based on the specific action prevailing at the time.

For example, you wouldn't have won the Nobel Prize for Physics for "standing up like a man" during Custer's Last Stand. On the other hand, using a Camp Perry-type prone position during a carjacking isn't the action of a mental giant either.

Remember: Trade-off, trade-off, trade-off.

KNEELING

There are two types of kneeling positions: braced/supported kneeling and quick, unsupported tactical kneeling.

Supported kneeling allows a right-handed shooter to dead-rest the left upper arm on the left knee, giving most shooters a stable base. It does not, however, allow for much elevation adjustment and negates tracking of a laterally moving target.

A variation of this for the handgun is the Phillips position, which, in addition, allows the shooter to fire strongside around a barricade without targeting himself.

Quick-kneel positions, such as the single-knee FBI position or the double-knee "California" position, are much quicker to get into (and withdraw from) but lack the stability of the braced positions. They do, however, allow for instantaneous change in elevation and windage holds and are invaluable for firing around barricades, performing one-handed malfunction clearances, etc.

Two important survival aspects of kneeling:

- At contact distances it is extremely easy to be punched or kicked on to your back.
- Kneeling doesn't make you as small a target as many people think. You will still be about two-thirds as "tall" as you are when standing.

SQUATTING

The military squat gives much the same pros and cons as kneeling, but in addition it provides support for both elbows on top of both knees. It also further lowers your target profile. Unfortunately, many people, because of their physique, cannot assume this position.

SITTING

Like the various prone positions, sitting provides an extremely stable base,

with resulting potential pinpoint accuracy. Most applicable to sniper-type scenarios where you have time to dig in, it is relatively slow to assume. Only the open-legged sitting position allows for elevation change. In a quick, unforeseen firefight, sitting is rarely used and invites serious bodily injury from incoming fire.

PRONE

Prone positions are the most stable of them all and make the shooter extremely difficult to hit with direct fire. They do, however, result in peculiar problems.

One problem is that of ground ricochets. Another is that, to shoot precisely from prone, one needs to lie at an angle that will result in a natural point of aim. This can often lead to unintentionally extending body extremities (such as feet or legs) past the leading edge of cover and/or concealment.

• • •

The bottom line with shooting positions, as with most everything else, is that of obvious necessity: they must be field-expedient, quick to get into, and quick from which to retreat. Terrain and time are the two main factors that invariably negate the use of Camp Perry-type shooting positions in a firefight.

Dirty tactics, quick reflexes, familiarity with one's weaponry, and use of natural or manmade outcroppings (e.g., river banks, trees, mailboxes) combined with tactical practical shooting positions will win the day in a real fight every time.

Don't Volunteer
to Be a Victim

There are no victims, only volunteers.

—Seen among some rest room graffiti

The above prose may not be the absolute in veracity, but there is a large element of truth to the statement. But it is also nothing new. From Sun Tzu to Pancho Villa; from Zulu impis to Rommel—only the site of the battlefield and the specific societies have changed.

With the United States in a societal state of degradation currently mirroring that of the fall of the Roman Empire, it's no wonder that the content of bathroom graffiti is changing from lurid poetry to that expressed above. It's a reflection of the attitude of someone who is willing to fight and win.

People are sick and tired of hollow political rhetoric, a judicial system that favors the criminal, and a law enforcement system that most of the time is hampered by logistics and finances until the thin blue line is stretched to the breaking point.

While it's obvious that defense will almost certainly have to be of the "God helps those who help themselves" variety, can the average Joe Citizen truly tactically avoid becoming a victim? Mechanically, to a large extent, you can. By means of firearms, blades, or Fred Kavey's combat assault bricks—and diligent practice in the use thereof—you will probably hold your own in a deadly force encounter.

The trick, however, is (1) to preferably avoid the situation or (2), if that's not possible, to make the battlefield one of your choosing. If you lose, it doesn't necessarily mean you "volunteered" to be a victim. What you can do—and the subject under discussion here is Joe Average—is reduce the odds against you, even minimally.

Tactics are always a Pandora's box. If you win, fine. If you lose, the whole world dances on your grave and calls you an idiot for using "the wrong tactics."

If, however, as an individual involved in a defensive urban situation, you believe you can reduce the odds from 100 to 1 down to 10 to 1, you're probably in for a rude awakening. What you can do is reduce the odds to where you have a fighting chance *most* of the time.

So how can you reduce these odds and turn the tactical tide in your favor? The obvious answer is to be tactically aware of your surroundings at all times, as best you can. The problem is that you can't always choose your surroundings, and you won't always be able to see the trouble before it hits you.

One can choose a safer and potentially more efficient battle plan, i.e., a defensive housebreaking scenario as opposed to reacting to a deadly-force threat from several armed individuals who storm a crowded restaurant. In the former instance you usually have more time to formulate a game plan: you are familiar with your surroundings, and you have some control over your environment and terrain.

In the restaurant you don't always have your choice of the ideal seating position, the "targets" (if it comes down to shooting) are usually a difficult challenge—and you are risking other people's lives if you miss or if your bullets don't immediately stop the threat.

On the other hand, you can avoid much of the "volunteer" aspect initially quoted in this article by using constant observation as part of your daily routine. It doesn't mean you have to become a student of paranoia; all it entails is practicing a couple of simple observation techniques until they become second nature—a subconscious procedure.

If, for example, on a hot summer day you notice a man entering "your" bank dressed in a heavy overcoat, it doesn't mean he's concealing a Thompson or a shotgun. There are myriad reasons why he is unusually clothed for the season, and all of them could be innocent. The point is, however, that you did notice something out of the ordinary.

Similarly, if you notice that specific rooms in your home that you left illuminated when you went out are darkened on your return (or vice versa), this may or may not mean that there has been an intruder during your absence. Again, the crux of the matter is that you have noticed something out of place.

You don't switch traffic lanes without glancing at your car's rear-view mirrors. It's not a big deal, merely a second-nature facet of your daily driving technique. Similarly, simple observation of a downtown street situation can forewarn you of potential violence, allowing you to either avoid a confrontation or at least have several seconds to think about a game plan.

Unfortunately, in a crowded urban environment, such as at an Academy Awards ceremony, you can't see everything. This may sound negative, but it is a cautionary statement—if someone wants to nail your hide to the wall, sooner or later he'll do it. Pessimistic, maybe, but it's the brutal truth.

The only answer to the overall problem is to be observant and to train diligently with the equipment of your choice. Remember that if it comes down to it, instant reflexive reaction is the clue to your survival. Don't play fair!

If you're involved in a deadly-force riot situation, a 350 V-8 beats a .45 ACP every time; regardless of whether you choose fight or flight. Your truck can, however, be stoned, overturned, and set on fire. "Volunteers" drive into a riot situation without thinking of the consequences. To avoid becoming a victim, as long as you've seen and read the situation, you have the option and the opportunity to make a U-turn or formulate a battle plan at your discretion. Forewarned is forearmed.

Performing While Not in Top Physical Form

Having endured the pleasures of encephalitis for five months as of the time of this writing, I had the opportunity to relearn a valuable axiom over and over again. It is commonly accepted in the firearms field that "what you practice on the range you will do in the street." This is mercilessly hammered home when you lose some of your faculties. While the viral brain infection didn't reduce my normal single-digit IQ, it did have decided neurological effects and implications. Intermittent dizziness, lethargy, and numbness in various body parts aren't exactly conducive to qualifying you as the last of the red-hot gunfighters.

Fortunately (?!), I'd had meningitis a dozen years ago and had learned from that experience. The meningitis struck at the zenith of my competition shooting "career," so one of my first priorities was to regain the ability I'd had prior to the meningitis. After hospitalization, the path I chose to achieve this—plan A—was to head for the range with as much ammunition as I could carry. That was my first mistake.

After approximately a week, several thousand rounds of ammo, and many misses and screwed-up drawstrokes, I realized it was time for plan B, which entailed driving a circuitous, time-consuming, nondirect route to the firing range and packing only 25 practice rounds. In other words, I forced myself to go to a lot of trouble to fire 25 lousy rounds. The net result was going back to the basics, enforcing quality and not just quantity. Once I achieved this, I gradually increased the ammunition capacity until I'd regained both quality and quantity.

The encephalitis was a different kettle of fish—almost total frustration. Now I know how Muhammad Ali must feel watching a young boxer fighting for a title belt.

I am independent and self-sufficient by nature, so it wasn't a thrilling proposition to literally have to be physically helped into and out of bed, a vehicle, or a shower cubicle. To cut a long story short, the dizziness was the major problem, but I didn't consider ditching my firearms because of a safety or inability-to-operate problem, for one rea-

Left-handed clearance of a stovepipe malfunction, if the right arm is injured and out of commission.

son only. Although I was physically weak at times and often not fully aware of my surroundings, there were some pertinent facts that penetrated the fog of my tiny little brain. My handgun draw-stroke, press-checking of the chamber, and general manipulation of the weapon never altered from the norm. I can attribute this to only one major reason: years of manipulating and handling the weapon in precisely the same manner time after time after time.

My marksmanship suffered to a certain extent, but probably not enough to lose a fight. Although the loss was enough not to risk a for-real, absolute pinpoint shot (such as the classic hostage-taker head-shot scenario), it was directly attributable to "the shakes" and served to increase shot group and placement size by only about 10 to 15 percent. As long as the front and rear

sights were moved/shaken together, and not relative to each other, the problem was not insurmountable.

Another facet that was a pleasant surprise was the safety aspect (primarily safe muzzle direction and a straight trigger finger when not on target), which had somehow ingrained itself into my synapses. The former I owe undoubtedly to my late father, the latter to Col. Jeff Cooper. To both, my belated thanks and appreciation. Again, both are the result of continuous and repeated actions conducted over a long period.

Obviously, some of my shooting positions were atrocious, but "necessity is the mother of invention." They took care of themselves the same as happens in a fight when range shooting positions have to be modified for field expediency.

To sum up: this article was not written to elicit sympathy (we all know where to find that in the dictionary), but to point out that, at a time when I was incapable of driving without endangering myself or others, years of ingrained training allowed me to both carry and, if necessary, defend myself with a firearm with virtually the same ability that I normally possess—and without being a danger or safety hazard to myself or others.

My affliction happened to be neurological, but the same rules apply if you are taken by surprise, if you are wounded in the process of a fight, if you run out of ammo or encounter a weapon malfunction.

Consistent habits and reflexes will get you through unless you run out of luck. If you choose to carry half a dozen types of handguns in different holsters and holster positions, that is, of course, your prerogative. But there's nothing like a bout of encephalitis to prove that it's not going to work. Whatever the Murphy's Law of the Day, there is no substitute for conscientious, repetitive training.

For Those Who Want to Do More Than Quote Sun Tzu

*T*he basic tactical tenets are, and always will be, governed by five major aspects, as laid out by the all-time guru on the art of war, Sun Tzu:

1. *Those who know when to fight and when not to fight are victorious.*

   Often in modern society, we (especially males) are reticent to retreat when withdrawal would have been a viable and intelligent solution to a specific problem at hand. For the most part thin-skinned and egotistic, too often we let our machismo get in the way of our common sense. This invariably leads to a bloody nose at best. As times change and guns are used at the slightest pretext, however, these days a more common result is a bullet wound or death.

   If there is a need for deadly force, use it with discretion backed up by sound tactics. If it is not necessary, walk away from it. Don't let such comments as "yellow" or "coward" push you into a deadly-force encounter when turning the other cheek will solve the problem—especially over something as stupid as somebody whistling at your girlfriend's butt in a bar. Better yet, stay out of bars.

2. *Those who discern when to use many or few troops are victorious.*

   In certain tactical situations, manpower is essential. Negotiating a flight of stairs, for example, cannot be executed safely by a lone operator. One person cannot look in two directions at once. If you don't wait for assistance in the form of extra personnel, you will find out for sure if there's life after death. On the other hand, trying to cram a half-dozen Conans into a tiny bathroom or closet is going to result in either "friendly" crossfire or several participants taking hits from an enraged subject engaged in a turkey shoot. Under varying scenarios, more isn't always better, but is sometimes requisite under other circumstances.

3. *Those whose upper and lower ranks have the same desire are victorious.*

   If a situation requires a team to achieve the desired result, absolute unanimity on goals and decisions must be reached before execution.

If, for example, "Hubby" decides that he should gallop off downstairs in search of a housebreaker, and "Wifey" thinks the idea sucks, it's time to reconsider and discuss a plan B. By the same token, in a law enforcement or military situation goals and requirements must be discussed and a majority decision reached before going into action. From there on out, each man must stick to his job as best he can (taking into account, of course, the parameters of the inevitable Murphy's Law situation that is going to arise). Cowboys belong in a rodeo, not on a battlefield.

4. *Those who face the unprepared with preparation are victorious.*

Preparation in this context can mean one of two things (or both): prior training, which will allow you to deal reflexively with an instantaneous problem (such as a carjacking) or a time-consuming tactical plan. Needlessly rushing into a bloodbath when you have the luxury of time to formulate a game plan isn't going to reward you with a Nobel Prize for Ingenuity. Too often, "fools rush in where wise men fear to tread."

Again, the old machismo rears its ugly head. Read it any way you wish, but if you want to be Gen. Suicide Custer and get yourself killed, that's your problem. Just don't get the rest of the company butchered because you are impatient and put glory before sanity.

If you have knowledge of the terrain and have the time to repeatedly go over available tactics until such time as you and yours have reached what seems to be the most viable alternative, chill out. Rush in with no plan when speed is not a criterion and you'll smash your forehead on your own tombstone. Never underestimate your enemy.

5. *Those whose generals are not controlled by their government are victorious.*

It doesn't take a genius to figure out that Desert Storm was a bigger success than Vietnam. The quality of the troops was the same. Terrain, technology, and objectives did differ, but the main difference was that in Desert Storm President George Bush—a fighting man himself—left the decisions and fighting to the generals. He didn't try to control a war from an oak desk thousands of miles away from the front lines—a tactical error committed so many times to this day that it's almost predictable, even in law enforcement.

There's a wall poster that has been in print for years, basically comparing the army that exists to the real army I should have at my disposal to get the job done. Would that we were always furnished with the "real" army . . .

Although Sun Tzu's fifth axiom applies (as do most of his other writings) to a military situation, any deadly-force encounter is a war. His tactics are as valid and pertinent now as the day they were written. There's no substitute for experience. Experience comes with age and history. Two-day sergeants are a sure-fire recipe for a graveyard.

Maybe it's time we finally started listening to and learning from the "Old Ones."

Placing Your Shots Where They'll Do the Most Good

Whether you're using a flyswatter or a shotgun, if you don't hit the target you won't get the job done.

"Well, golly," you say, "I could never have worked that out myself. Thanks for the brilliant advice." No, the objective of this article is not to insult the readers' intelligence, nor is it to impress the world with my omniscience. The intent is, however, to discuss the potential difficulty and complexities of hitting a human enemy where it will do the most good—in other words, where shot placement has the most likelihood of immediately ending a lethal confrontation. And *likelihood* is the operative word; there are no guarantees, even with perfect shot placement.

So rule number one—and in fact the only rule—is follow through. Once gunplay commences, be ready to follow through both tactically and mechanically. Always be ready to fire ensuing rounds immediately if the initial gunfire hasn't neutralized the threat. Once body alarm reaction sets in and the rounds don't take effect, you will have a Freddy Krueger clone to deal with.

CENTER-OF-MASS SHOT

The most commonly taught/used/practiced hit zone is "center of mass." This is normally assumed to be sight alignment superimposed on the target's upper torso. It is very easy to center-punch under controlled range conditions, as it is a large, uniform target. Contrary to this idea, however, it needs to be remembered that the human torso is not one-dimensional; it is convex. In a fight, the torso of a clothed, moving assailant is often not easy to discern.

In addition, if your assailant twists his/her body, the huge torso area instantaneously "shrinks" by anything from 10 to 50 percent, resulting in many missed shots or ineffectual glancing blows. Center of mass could—or should—be defined as the center of mass of the specific target area you have selected to impact.

Another thought to consider seriously is that a perfect center hit may not necessarily neutralize your assailant immediately, even though it is a mortal wound. While a nonrepresentative range target may appear to always offer the upper torso as the easiest available hit area, this is often not the case for real, depending on such factors as target movement, light conditions, or clothing.

HEAD SHOT

An alternative is the head shot, which needs to be delivered between the eyebrow and mouth line from the front or an equivalent if the head is angled. The head is a smaller target than the torso, and invariably there is more target movement involved. The plus side of the situation, however, is that while the movement and angle can be a big problem, the target doesn't change as markedly in size as does a twisting, turning torso. In fact, occasionally the head offers a bigger target area side-on than does a side-on upper body.

But precise shot placement for a head shot is an absolute necessity. Any inaccuracy usually results in an ineffective glancing blow—and you probably won't have the luxury of a second shot.

PELVIC SHOT

A third—and often overlooked—prospect is the pelvic area. It is invariably easier to hit than either the head or torso, regardless of body position or movement. The biggest bone in the body (with the least amount of movement), the pelvis can be struck repeatedly within minimal time frames, the objective being to halt your enemy's forward progress—or potential thereof—by smashing his gearbox.

Essentially, the lower the area you select from pelvis to head, the easier it is to hit, but the downside is that the hits are usually ballistically less efficient than either a heart, lung, or head shot.

So it comes down to the same old game—tactics. How much force can I deliver? How much is warranted? And, if the threat is of dire proportions (dependent on your assailant's weaponry, distance, etc.), you may very well have to shoot for a "second choice" target area and then move on to plan B, which may entail repeated firing.

If, for example, you are awakened by a knife-wielding lunatic lunging across your bedroom, you may have to aim at the center of mass of his entire body, because you don't have the time to go for the "perfect hit." This is not a situation where you have the luxury of two or three seconds to coolly and calmly wait for the opportunity to implant a couple of textbook slugs in his chest. This is a situation—as it so often is—where you have to go for broke, probably breaking him down with repeated fire, because the ideal target isn't offered to you. And if it were, you'd probably have no legal entitlement to shoot.

While much poor shooting in real-life situations can be attributed to fear, lack of trigger control, and sight picture, etc., many seasoned fighters have to deliver rounds to their enemy's stomach, legs, or various other "undesirable" areas because the target offers nothing else.

If this weren't the case, textbook firing-range center-torso and head hits would be a lot more prevalent in the morgue than they in fact are. The truth be known, these perfect hits are rare—and for more possible reasons than the Monday morning quarterback would have you believe.

Reloading Made Easy

*T*he ability to reload a firearm quickly, smoothly, and with economy of motion is an essential component of combat weaponcraft.

For several reasons, as we approach the 21st century, more and more rounds are being expended per enemy stop. It doesn't take a brain surgeon to balance the Ledger of Poor Marksmanship—the more often you miss your appointed target, the sooner you will exhaust your ammo reserve. While the art of street and battle accuracy has retrogressed in direct proportion to the advance of the 21st century, it is also not as easy as some pundits espouse.

Added to this are the continuing change in enemy mind-set—currently bordering on an air of invincibility—and the increased use of body and vehicle armor protection. In short, even accomplished fighters are expending more rounds to neutralize opponents than they did 10 years ago, often for reasons other than mere inaccuracy.

This in turn emphasizes the need to possess the dexterity necessary to quickly and reflexively replenish a dwindling or exhausted ammunition supply.

The reloading process comprises two facets: the tactical reload and the speed load. Each is used under different circumstances in the field.

In theory, the tactical reload should be used far more often than the speed load—the assumption being that the operation will run smoothly and the enemy will be quickly neutralized with a minimum of ammunition expenditure. The good guy is then free to use the lull in action to recharge his weapon.

This assumption is based on a utopian premise that Murphy's Law won't raise its ugly head. Unfortunately, the exact opposite is usually the case. The situation often goes to pooh-pooh, more rounds than expected have to be sent downrange, and your brain train becomes a loose caboose. This is often closely followed by a resounding *click* emanating from the weapon instead of a *bang*—time for a speed load.

Another occurrence that can necessitate a speed load is a malfunc-

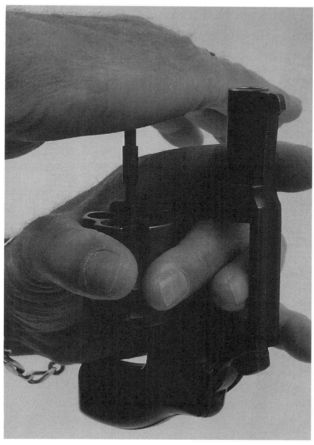

With the revolver muzzle vertical, the ejector rod is "pumped" to eject fired brass.

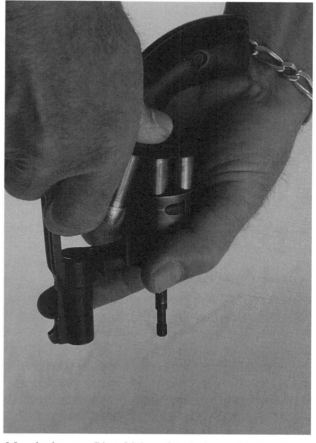

Muzzle down, a Bianchi Speed Strip is used to load two .44s at a time.

tion. Whatever the cause, if a speed load is required, you are in deep, deep trouble. The load has to be accomplished with maximum alacrity and dexterity, because you will almost certainly have to shoot again after recharging the weapon, unlike the scenario that prompts a tactical reload.

Unquestionably the fastest "reload" consists of switching to a secondary weapon, but this is not always tactically viable or feasible, especially in a military situation. Hand in hand with this is the less than comforting thought that the secondary weapon is usually less ballis-

tically efficient than the primary weapon—but *anything* is better than an inoperative primary.

Most box-magazine-fed full-auto and semiauto weapons can be speed-loaded by the same sequential process. The first step is to ensure with the non-firing hand that there is a replacement magazine within your reach. Along with this goes the obvious fact that the spare ammunition should be carried where it can be grasped regardless of body position or tactical gear worn at the time.

Having ascertained that the fresh supply does indeed exist, remove and jettison the original magazine from the weapon. Some rifles and submachine guns, because of inefficient placement and operation of release mechanisms, may require the shooter to use the non-firing hand to remove the magazine. In this case you'd better pray that your reserve supply is where it's *supposed* to be.

If you're one of the breed who chooses to clip or tape together your primary and reserve magazines, then obviously you won't jettison the equipment, but merely extract the empty and reposition and insert the adjacent back-up magazine into the magazine well.

Once a weapon or cerebral malfunction has been cleared and a fresh magazine has been inserted, pull down on the magazine to ensure that it is seated. Following this, cycle the bolt. This latter step will ensure that a round has been chambered. However, it is totally dependent on the fact that you have already pulled down on the magazine. Otherwise you may extract and eject a live round and replace it with a black hole. (The weapon may not have been "dry" or malfunctioned. Not releasing the trigger during the firing of multiple rounds often leads people to believe that their weapon has malfunctioned or run out of ammo.)

If the weapon is of the open-bolt operation variety, it is still vital to cycle the bolt to recock the trigger mechanism.

Obviously in the case of a pistol, magazines should be seated by pushing upward, as opposed to the "pull down" techniques mentioned above.

A tactical reload is less of a brain drain than the speed load because you are in control of the situation and are merely replenishing an already existent—albeit reduced—cartridge capacity.

In this situation you bring the

replacement magazine to the weapon before releasing the primary magazine. Utilizing one of a variety of systems (and everybody and his brother has a version of the "only" way to hold the spare) acquire a firm grasp on both magazines with the nonfiring hand before completely removing the primary magazine from the magazine well. Remove the primary, insert the replacement, and make sure the latter is securely seated. The partially depleted magazine is then deposited somewhere where it cannot be later mistaken for a full magazine if circumstances dictate another reload.

It is probably not a good practice to remove the first magazine and then reach for the backup, as some advocate. This downloads the weapon to only one round for an unnecessarily long time frame—or worse, in the case of an open-bolt mechanism, to zero rounds in the gun. Limit weapon downtime to the shortest possible time, even though the confrontation is supposedly over.

It's the same mind-set as the one platoon that consists of personnel who all simultaneously break down their weapons for cleaning, versus the second platoon whose members clean their weapons in relays.

It is in the field of reloading where revolvers fall behind the power curve, primarily because of the problems encountered with ammunition management. If a speed loader is employed during the reload, any remaining live rounds from the initial cylinder load end up kissing Mother Earth. A tactical reload can be performed by individually removing fired brass and replacing it (or them) with live rounds, but the process requires more manipulation and a cooler brain than that needed for a magazine switch. Probably the best overall system to use for wheelguns is the strip loader. This enables the operator to accomplish both tactical and speed loads with relative speed, utilizing only one equipment system and technique.

Another alternative is to modify the revolver to accept half-, third-, or full-moon clips.

The important fact to bear in mind is that a revolver cylinder, irrespective of whether it is of 5-, 6-, 7-, or 9-shot capacity, will always have two adjacent chambers in a straight line. A straight-line strip loader can therefore be manipulated to load two rounds simultaneously, with a minimum of fuss and bother. Similarly, when loading by means of a cylindrical speed loader, allow two adjacent bullets to make contact with two adjacent chambers, then "rotate" the remaining cartridges into their respective chambers. This virtually eliminates the frustrating task of attempting to simultaneously line up six male cartridges with six female chambers.

If tube-fed shotguns are your weapon of choice, the loading/reloading process is normally achieved by the individual insertion of cartridges. This system does, however, allow the operator to select different types of ammunition at his discretion, at a moment's notice, which cannot be done with box and drum-fed shotguns, though the latter is generally quicker to speed load from empty to full. The Striker and its clones are a notable exception to this rule. Trick speed loaders for the shotgun are usually a disaster for serious gunfighting and seem to be more trouble than they're worth.

Whatever your weapons system, you would be well advised to expect the worst case scenario; be prepared to expend at least twice the amount of ammo that the mission should require. While you may, on occasion, be able to keep track of rounds fired in a short, idealistic fight, most gunfights usually end up in an unexpected tactical and marksmanship logistics zoo.

A positive, smooth, reflexive reload is your insurance policy against an ammunition recession.

Ready or Not

Be one with your gun.

—Lori Jordan

Much as the baseball pitcher's windup is a prerequisite for accurate delivery of the ball from mound to plate, a good "ready" position is essential for safe, quick, precise projectile delivery for the defensive shooter.

Assuming one has prior warning of a potential deadly-force encounter, which obviously escalates the state of preparedness from a holstered or slung firearm to that of hands-on readiness, the weapon must be in a geometric position that is relative to the threat to allow fast operation if required.

You must become a unit with the weapon, much as a tank turret is part of the entire vehicle. Your body and audio, video, and olfactory senses are the tank—the shotgun, submachine gun, handgun, or whatever firearm you deploy is the cannon.

In essence a ready position is just that—no more, no less. If used intelligently, it allows the shooter to deal with an assailant quickly, with accurate fire, and it won't block the field of view in a tactical situation. The ready position doesn't "telegraph" the defender's position or location and it keeps the gun at a distance or angle, safe from being "snatched."

There are three primary ready positions for a shoulder weapon: the high ready, low ready, and indoor ready. The first is the high ready, initially popularized by John Satterwhite for use with the shotgun. Although extremely fast, it is debatable whether it is a tactically sound position for most situations. The butt of the weapon is placed on the belt line, and the front sight or muzzle is positioned to intersect the desired impact area and the shooter's eye. This obviously places the impact area, the front sight, and the eye in one plane. All that remains to mount the weapon and fire is to rotate the butt of the weapon into the shoulder "pocket." As soon as a cheek-weld is obtained you're in business. (The front sight/muzzle has remained on target all the way

High ready position. The shooter's eyes, front sight, and target are in one horizontal plane, prior to mounting the gun and firing.

Low ready position. Operator's vision is umimpeded and makes for difficult gun take-aways.

Indoor ready position. This position is used in tight quarters on a stealth search, the objective being not to "telegraph" one's position by overextending the gun muzzle.

through the mounting process and is therefore automatically on "target.")

There are, however, three downsides to this technique. One is that you tend to blot out visual control of the threat (i.e., the subject's hands and feet) and may end up with an unjustified shooting. It largely depends on whether the "target" is also the desired impact area. Secondly, one tends to project, or "telegraph," one's location when moving because the barrel is extended way ahead of the shooter's body. This leads to the third problem, which is potentially allowing your enemy, seen or unseen, to get underneath the barrel, giving him all of the leverage advantage.

The second basic ready position for a shoulder weapon is the low ready. Here the butt remains in the shoulder, and the muzzle is depressed below any potential threat, be it physical or optical. Full view of the terrain and enemy is available at all times, and leverage advantage is retained. This is probably the one position that is more tactically viable than others for most situations, whether a handgun or shoulder weapon is being used.

The low ready has the big advantage of leaving the good guy in total control of the scenario before and after the shooting—or even if there is no shooting, which is by far the more prevalent case. The sole downside of the long gun low ready is the "telegraphing" of the muzzle during a slow search, but this can be overcome by the third position, which is termed the indoor ready.

The indoor ready totally eliminates muzzle projection by sucking back the muzzle closer to the body. This is accomplished by sliding the support-arm elbow back past the "weak-side"

kidney, which automatically reduces barrel projection to a more vertical line. The muzzle is held off either to the "weak" side of the body or between the feet. This will be determined by body armor, stomach girth, and tactical terrain—the last determines whether a left- or right-handed turn needs to be executed.

Obviously, it's not a brilliant idea to pass the gun muzzle directly over your own feet when stepping, and extra care must be taken with short-barreled weapons when utilizing this technique. The indoor ready is useful in close-quarter terrain during a stealth search. The low ready is more appropriate in a dynamic, on-the-move scenario, where the shooter is less concerned about muzzle projection since he will round a blind angle at virtually the same time as the gun barrel, giving away nothing tactically. It should be remembered that the word *indoor* is somewhat of a misnomer, since it can be used outdoors, in thick vegetation, for example.

There are many other "ready" positions such as port arms, Rhodesian ready, and on and on ad nauseam, most of which people have plagiarized and named after themselves. They are all, to some extent, variations of the big three, though there are some that are more relevant to an out-and-out military situation and are, for that reason, older by decades than the "urban" positions described above. The big three are essentially relevant to urban law enforcement or civilian home-defense situations. The safest, and possibly best, ready position for the handgun under most situations is the low ready.

Also to be mentioned are extremely close-quarter confrontations, where the shoulder-weapon stock can be slipped underneath and to the rear of the armpit in the classic underarm assault, or where the handgun is brought back one-handed alongside the pectoral muscle. These, however, fall more into the weapon retention category than ready positions. And that's another story. *Be one with your gun.*

The Mark of a Smart Shooter

*M*ost people in the defensive firearms field seem to agree that marksmanship alone is not enough to win a fight. The general consensus is that marksmanship needs to be combined with tactics, reflexive gun-handling capabilities, and a large slice of Lady Luck. These days, marksmanship seems to be regarded as preeminent, almost to the exclusion of tactics, during training.

Marksmanship is obviously vital, but it is a useless attribute if you don't get the chance to use it. The greatest sharpshooter in history is of no use to anyone if he's dead. Being firearms oriented, we tend to forget that the gun is but a medium to deliver power. A 99-percent shooter with a 1-percent brain will almost invariably be beaten in a gunfight by the 1-percent shooter who has a 99-percent brain. Since the dawn of mankind, humans have had to rely on their thinking prowess to survive. The firearm is merely the means to attain the end.

Unless on a predetermined law enforcement or military operation (and often in these cases as well), most force-threat situations are defensive in nature. In other words, these situations are in reaction to an action. The classic scenario is that of the homeowner who believes that there is an intruder in his house.

Grabbing a g-u-n—his security blanket—he gallops off through the building in search of the Cookie Monster. His reasoning (or lack thereof) goes, "I've got a magic wand; I can handle the situation." The fact that it is successfully accomplished many times doesn't change the fact that he's on a potential suicide mission.

Even though it's your house, you are entering a battlefield where all the odds are in favor of your enemy. If you decide to approach him instead of forcing him to come to you, you're starting off at a disadvantage.

First, a motive has to be decided on, and then tactics relative to the motive must be applied. If, for example, your child is screaming for help, you have no choice but to get to his bedroom as fast as possible, and a firearm would be useful as a potential problem solver.

Yes, he has your wife's handbag, but he's fleeing and is no physical threat. While some other countries' laws differ, in most states in the United States you are not justified in using deadly force under these circurmstances.

On the other hand, if you hear an unfamiliar sound emanating from the bowels of your domicile and there is no known immediate threat to life and limb, why would you haul your biscuits down there at 400 miles per hour? Under the latter circumstances you would be negating every intelligent tactical advantage because you've allowed everything to be governed by a red mist of anger and stupidity. Ask General Custer.

We're all sick and tired of the wackos, weirdos, legal injustices, and gun laws that are so prevalent in today's society, but I'm not going to jail for 30 years for unintentionally shooting a social degenerate who was stealing a $60 pair of boots—and I'm definitely not dying in a gunfight over those boots either. The moral of the story is: If it's not worth dying for, don't do it.

The usual answer from the average homeowner is that he knows the precise layout of the house and, for the most part, has control over the lights. In other words, if he can control the illumination, knows the floor plan, and has a g-u-n, he is in command. Unfortunately, here's where Murphy's Law and stupidity step in.

Since you went to sleep, Rover has deposited a muffin on the carpet outside your bedroom door, and your teenage son has sneaked into the living room with his girlfriend, hell-bent on extending the family bloodline.

Being a master tactician, you elect to use no artificial illumination because you "know the layout of the house." Step one is into the Rover mine, and you slip and slide halfway down the passage with a resounding crash. Your judgment overridden by anger, instead of consolidating your position, you decide that valor is the better part of discretion and hit Mach 1 down the passage, figuring you've lost the surprise advantage.

Low-flying into the living room, you encounter two shadowy human outlines. You're going too fast, you're too close, there's no target identification, and Mr. G-u-n is already at work. Yes, you got your bloodline—except it is all a steady red trickle seeping into the carpet.

Thanks, Dad. I hope you can sleep at night for the next 30 years that God curses you to live.

Is it caused by the g-u-n? No, it's caused by y-o-u. Is the preceding text unrealistic? No, it's happened over and over, in one form or another, since time immemorial, with guns, knives, meat cleavers, clubs, and fists. The problem with tactics is if you win, it was the right tactic to have used. If you lose, everybody Monday-morning quarterback is on your grave. Tactics have to be constantly practiced, reviewed, and amended, no matter who is involved or the nature of the operation.

Anytime you're feeling lucky, get a friend to lie in wait for you in your own house and you'll discover how easy you are to take out.

Whenever possible, you have to choose the battleground and the weapons and then apply the tactics that are relevant to that specific scenario if you are to have any hope of success.

"Here lies John Doe, ~~Humanitarian~~, ~~Philanthropist~~, ~~Expert Marksman~~, ~~Tactician~~, Fool."

Cover and Concealment

*T*he purpose of using cover and concealment is to come out of a confrontation with the same amount of body orifices the Good Lord initially supplied you with at birth.

Cover is a material object that will stop most small-arms projectile penetration. Concealment will not stop projectiles, but an unseen enemy is difficult to engage. Concealment can, therefore, be as protective as cover under certain conditions.

The British attack at Magersfontein in 1899 didn't exactly resound with brilliant military tactics. Attired partially in red uniforms with shiny brass buttons, the British marched headlong into the rising sun—and a hail of bullets from Boer marksmen hidden in trenches. Dropping like flies, the British troops never broke ranks and paid the inevitable price.

Obeying military commands is one thing, but saluting Lord knows what while the *Titanic* is sinking doesn't top the survival list. I'll bet the ship's officers started swimming like crazy when the water reached nostril level, irrespective of captain's orders. Too little too late. As Kenny Rogers sang, "You've got to know when to hold 'em, know when to fold 'em . . ."

While this "for king and country" conduct is truly admirable, it is also often foolhardy. Nobody is suggesting that you disobey your leader's commands, but nobody can suggest that Magersfontein, Little Big Horn, or Gettysburg was conducive to a senior citizen's program either. The old adage of "stand up and fight like a man" is applicable in a boxing ring, not when three loonies have invaded your home and are hell-bent on unraveling your mortal coil.

Cover and concealment are as essential to one's tactical operation as are any of the other facets, maybe even more so. Let's face it: if you take a hit in act one, the rest of the concert becomes that much more difficult to conclude.

Unfortunately, the necessity for concealment or cover often doesn't manifest itself until the fight has already commenced, so if possible plan

While this hedge may well conceal you visually from an enemy, it won't stop incoming rounds and should not be misinterpreted as cover.

On the other hand, proning out behind a wheel well affords protection from incoming rounds and can be used for cover.

their potential availability should the operation collapse in midfight (which it invariably does). In other words: be aware of your surroundings at all times so you have an "escape hatch" if the need arises. And this brings up what is probably the most common urbanite's failing—not seeing what we observe optically.

Most people who are raised in the woods, or, for that matter, the Bushmen in South Africa and Namibia, invariably bag more "game" than the average Joe Citizen because they haven't lost the art of identifying what they see immediately and subconsciously. Pit an average urbanite against one of the aforementioned after sundown, and he probably couldn't find the woodsman or Bushman without hundreds of dollars worth of night-vision equipment.

If you're "hunting" for the bad guys you are still, in effect, in a defensive mode from a tactical standpoint, because if you're within the enemy's optical or physical range you've lost the advantage. To survive the Bushman/woodsman's attack, you have to identify your surroundings—be it hard cover, concealment, or light conditions—and see the situation from your enemy's perspective. That's how the expert sniper gets in, does the job, and gets out. The same game applies whether you're defending your home, participating on a law enforcement operation, or dodging bullets in a supermarket robbery.

If you're on terrain or in a building that you know like the back of your hand, make sure you've identified the difference between cover and concealment. Cranking a couple of rounds through your kid's bedroom wall makes your IQ appear to be that of a mud

flap. If it's not a thick brick wall, the bullets are going through. The corollary, of course, is that if Mr. Baddie knows your location, he can do you through the wall. Just because he can't see you doesn't mean he can't hit you through concealment.

Darkness can be a good concealment ally if needed, so use existing light conditions—be they ambient or induced—to your advantage. Never silhouette yourself against back lighting.

If you have the luxury of hard cover, bear in mind that projectiles ricochet off a hard surface within a 12-degree angle after impacting that surface. Ergo, you can be hit by a primary, secondary, or tertiary ricochet simply because you are within a 12-degree arc of the last hard object impacted by the bullet in question. This will include you in the "killed by skip fire" tombstone department—which has the same end result as the "killed by any other way" category. You're still dead.

Cover need not necessarily obliterate your entire body from enemy view and fire—though it's obviously preferable. If you're two feet wide and a telephone pole is all you have, use it. Hopefully, it will stop incoming rounds from penetrating, but the big trick is that most people will try to shoot "around" the pole, missing you by more than they normally would have.

A classic example of this was a man accosted on a New York suburban train by a gun-wielding robber. The more the good guy waved his hands around, the more the robber mirrored his movements, trying to line up the pistol around the side of his hands. It never occurred to Mr. Nasty to merely shoot through the accostee's hands.

Back to the "aware of your surroundings" subject. If you're approaching an area and something does break loose, it's always nice to have a plan B—in this case, a place of relative safety to which you can advance or withdraw. Why would you need it in midfight? Because something always goes bad. If you don't take a hit, your one and only pistol will malfunction. And, if you think you can clear a malfunction quickly on a shooting range, try it in the middle of a gunfight sometime.

Yes, carry two guns, and, yes, utilize cover and concealment whenever and wherever possible. Don't stand out in the open, "like a man," if you don't have to.

To answer the mocking question, "Are you a man or a mouse?" Me, I'd rather nibble on cheese than feed the worms.

I Can See Clearly Now

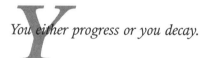
You either progress or you decay.

—Clint Eastwood

At age 46, I like to think that my mind and attendant tactics progress. But the Good Lord has seen fit to allow a certain amount of physical decay with the advancing years—primarily eyesight.

Shooters usually end up with one of two problems—myopia or hypermetropia—and this, in turn, leads to either a lack of front-sight focus or distance-vision problems (such as target identification). Either condition can often be cured by corrective glasses, contact lenses, or surgery, but the person involved sometimes doesn't respond to any of these solutions or can't use, for example, a pair of trifocal eyeglasses in the middle of a gunfight in a trash-strewn dark alley.

While many greats, like Bill Jordan and Thell Reed, could perform hip-shooting magic on a range, they didn't resort to this technique when shooting for blood, because it doesn't work on a moving human antagonist unless in extremely close quarters. And at the eleventh hour, they didn't have optical problems. Under these circumstances, Col. Jeff Cooper's "Flash Sight Picture," incorporated into his Modern Pistol Technique, is perfect—but again, is reliant on a focused front sight.

Jim Cirillo's answer to the problem is to focus on the entire hand-gun for sight reference. In other words, his technique relies on cylinder or slide alignment. If the revolver cylinder is "out of round" or the semi-auto pistol slide isn't square on the target, you know you're off center on your sight picture. While this works well at close distances, where most pistol fights occur, the assumption is to switch focus to the sights at longer distances if your optics are mechanically sound. So we're back to little old me and my inability to clearly focus on a handgun sight (my "china blues" are still okay at arm's length for shoulder weapons and excellent at distance). Having exhausted all of the normal channels of contact lenses and eyeglasses—which didn't work for me—I wended my way down the well-worn path to Steve Wickert's door. Steve built the first all-steel ghost ring for shoulder weapons after succumbing to my sniffling and weeping five years ago (see "Product Evaluation," *S.W.A.T.* Magazine, February 1990) and has since sold a huge amount of these sights to law enforcement, military, and civilian buyers. (For more information contact Wickert Precision Machining, 4980 N. Badger, Prescott Valley, AZ 86314.)

Gunsmiths such as Robar and Gunsite Training Center order them on a regular basis. In this author's opinion, there are few other reliable, sturdy ghost rings available for shoulder weapons except for Steve's and Scattergun Technologies' Trak-Lock ghost rings.

After discussing the problem with Steve and gun builder par excellence Fred Wells, I got Wickert to accept the challenge of building a sturdy pistol ghost-ring sight. While the concept of an aperture rear sight isn't new (few things are), the end objective was to retain fast, accurate fire at any distance without having the optical problems that are normally associated with conventional Patridge-type rear sights—and without adding bells, whistles, lasers, etc., to a fighting carry pistol.

There were several problems to overcome. A good sight picture is reliant on a blurred rear sight, focused front sight, and blurred target. My main problem was that I knew going in that I wasn't going to have perfect front sight focus, but optical problems were causing a slow pickup of sight alignment with conventional pistol sights. An aperture sight not only continued to result in slow sight alignment, it also blotted out some of the target because of the

Shooter's perspective through a well-constructed ghost ring.

thickness of the sight rim. This resulted not only in zero gain over a conventional rear sight but an actual loss in terms of real combat effectiveness.

After hours of experimentation and prototypes, Steve finally came up with the finished product: a ghost-ring pistol sight that has put my shooting back on track.

Why and how does it work? The "how" is easy. It's the same principle as a shoulder weapon ghost ring, except the focal distance is a lot farther from the eye than a rifle or shotgun. The "why" is less obvious, but easily explained. With the ring "ghosted," the eyes automatically "hunt" for the front sight, and peripheral vision automatically self-centers the front post, giving lightning-fast alignment. Even with a blurred front sight, my accuracy and speed have returned to days of yore; I am now shooting a pistol with both eyes fully open for the first time in 15 years. No more of the frustration of trying to align three blurred sight blades of a conventional front and rear setup before acquiring the sight picture.

As an added bonus, there was enough "meat" on the sight for Innovative Weaponry Inc. to install two vertical tritium bars on the ghost ring (one on either side) making the system, if anything, faster in dim light and canceling out all of my optical problems. Two dots would work for those who like a three-dot system but would have put me back to square one in dim light. (Normally, I've used Innovative Weaponry's horizontal "Bar-Dot" system on standard pistol sights for this

reason.) It also fits the original pistol slide dovetail, but Steve does require your front sight height when ordering the ghost ring.

Designated the YFA/P model, the sight sells for about $19.50 plus postage without tritium inserts. It is part of Steve Wickert's lineup of all-steel ghost rings and a brilliantly designed, fully portable tripod for shoulder weapons.

Although this article has deviated from the normal "Training and Tactics" forum, it is not a product evaluation. It was felt, however, that the sight is of huge tactical benefit and simplicity, especially for us dim-eyed old fogies.

"In the land of the blind, the one-eyed man is king."

Tactical Responses to an Attack

A frontal attack, while unenviable, leaves you with one small edge—at least you can instantly identify the problem. Being blind-sided or assaulted from the rear, however, is usually—but not always—a more difficult situation to resolve, because it invariably entails weapon and body manipulation over and above that required to deal with a belt buckle-to-belt buckle confrontation.

For the purposes of this article, it is assumed that the threat is so violent and close that gunplay is required to neutralize it. In essence a rear attack is, surprisingly, normally easier to handle than one from left or right, assuming that neither you nor your firearm has been physically constrained. Any time that you have already been restrained—be it from north, south, east, or west—a combination of punching, kicking, and gouging is probably going to be the primary order of the day before you can do any real damage.

If, on the other hand, you have even the remotest warning, you're in with a chance. In the lightning-strike scenario under discussion, several aspects are absolute necessities: a fast, reflexive drawstroke gun mount, close-quarters gun-fighting ability, and the capability of maintaining balance while delivering fast, accurate (probably multiple) rounds to the felon or felons involved.

Much depends on the scenario and the weaponry that you are carrying and where the weapon is positioned at the moment of attack. If, for example, you are a right-handed private citizen carrying a pistol in a strong-side belt holster and you are blindsided from the left, it is a relatively easy situation to handle. The left hand can be used for a block, diversion, or strike while you simultaneously draw the pistol and fire it from a weapon-retention position. This usually entails locking the firing wrist tightly alongside your right pectoral muscle and, in this specific scenario, will also probably require twisting your body toward your attacker. Foot movement won't be necessary, but it would be a good idea to keep your left arm and hand out of the line of fire!

Startled homeowner tries to draw pistol under impossible circumstances—a day late and a dollar short.

While you should incorporate force continuum, gaining distance, and the like into your range training, this text will cover only the primary-reaction stage of various scenarios.

LESSON NUMBER ONE

If you carry only one pistol on your "strong" side, carry your groceries or any other packages with your "weak" hand. Also, whenever possible, keep any potential danger away from your gun. If you suspect a possible threat in the above specific scenario, walk around the problem and keep it on your left side, even if you have to enter your car through the passenger door.

Should the preceding scenario remain the same but you are jumped from your right side, all of the above should be applied except that at least one footstep will be necessary to both keep the holstered pistol from being entrapped and allow you access to the gun.

This leaves you with a dilemma: either you will have to sweep your right foot back and away from the attacker, or you will have to step in to him with your left foot. Both techniques will gain you enough body twist for gun retention and access, but neither is at the top of the Christmas wish list. They are absolute last-ditch evasive maneuvers that will hopefully gain you enough of an edge to continue fighting. Under no circumstances should you ram the muzzle of a semiauto or full-auto pistol into your attacker's body in an attempt to contact-wound. The slide can be pushed out of battery, and the weapon could fail to fire.

113

A lone homeowner or law enforcement officer armed with a shoulder weapon is in dire straits if blindsided, especially from his strong side. A weak-side attack can be dealt with by lowering the stock beneath and to the rear of the strong-side armpit and clamping hard onto the stock with the inner part of the upper arm (the classic underarm assault position). The bottom line with a shoulder weapon in close quarters is to move into a ready position that uses a lowered muzzle. This not only allows you visibility, but it also enables you to get to work ballistically on your attacker's lower appendages after an upper body twist.

Do not engage in a stealth search with the muzzle up—you lose visibility, leverage, and the ability to shoot. Similarly, one currently taught technique if caught in the above nightmare is to "merely drop to a kneeling position and shoot him in the chest." God help you if he gets his hands below the muzzle because he'll level you onto your back like a three-day-old kitten.

If you are jumped from the right, you can apply the footwork used with the handgun; again, start "working" on your attacker's lower body. You have all of the leverage advantage, but bear in mind that in these extremely close-quarters scenarios you won't have the ability to acquire the underarm assault position if you are hit from your strong side.

A rear attack has both good and bad news. It is usually easier to detect than a side assault but often results in your losing your balance or being trapped into fighting a retrograde battle. Most criminals won't come in from the front unless their prey looks totally helpless

or they have a big advantage in numbers of personnel.

If you're rushed from behind—whether standing or in a carjack situation—apart from the surprise element, the enemy has the ability to push you forward off balance (you have nothing to bolster your stance) or entrap you in your car or truck. The carjack problem is unique and requires instantly accessible weaponry, but you can deal with it if you have a contingency plan.

Being shoved forward, however, is your worst nightmare. The good news is that, although you should be able to optically pick up a side attack more easily than one from the rear, normally you have more visual and audio "warning aids" for the latter. A sidewinder usually operates surreptitiously, such as leaping out from behind a blind corner, a parked truck, etc. Cover and/or concealment is usually predictable in advance if you maintain a level of awareness.

A backstabber, however, normally relies on surprise and must move quickly. Thankfully, this often causes an audible warning. Also, in most street scenes or carjack situations, there are optical aids everywhere, such as mirrors, store window reflections, etc. As stated above, a carjack has a unique solution. If an attempt is made from the rear, a simple 180-degree pivot toward your "weak" side will both move the weapon out of the assailant's reach and provide access for the muggee.

The only remaining problem would be maintaining balance, and under the circumstances, this should be attainable by a single sidestep. It is critical to remember that mirror images are literally reversed, so optical identification of the target is essential prior to the initial pivot.

While it is easy to write down solutions to hypotheses, it bears mentioning that the above scenarios are representative of about the deepest doo-doo you can ever get into. They are extremely dangerous situations, and, as a result, you must conduct range training in techniques to counteract them with extreme caution.

As always, there is no perfect tactical solution. The above text covers some viable techniques, but this article was written only to promote tactical thinking.

"Skill, Cunning, and the Powers of Observation":
The Klingon Formula for Victory

*T*actics and techniques are as old as the hills, and through the pages of time various masters such as Sun Tzu, Musashi, and, in the 20th century, men of the caliber of Col. Jeff Cooper, have taken the time and effort to analyze the finer points in print. Additionally, while foolhardy tactics and weapon manipulation are the order of the day in movies and television "blood'n'guts" shows, every now and then a brilliant diamond emerges from the fecal pile. Two such examples follow.

Script or screenwriters for presentations such as *Highlander* obviously—at least to this author—have an insight into fighting that is a cut above the rest (no pun intended).

Another winner is *Star Trek: The Next Generation,* Attempting to drug myself to sleep with a dose of TV recently, I was awakened from a half-stupor by pearls of wisdom emanating from a Klingon warrior. While his statement was nothing new, it was so succinct and all-inclusive in its simplicity, it encompassed every attribute necessary for a successful warrior in one sentence: "Skill, cunning, and the powers of observation."

Everybody and his second cousin have written reams of paper, produced videos, and run training camps to achieve this end in the trainees' minds and bodies, and here the whole nine yards is summed up in seven little words: "skill, cunning, and the powers of observation." Like everything else that works, simplicity once again rules the day.

Does this mean that one can become a samurai or the "gunfighter from hell" merely by reading one sentence? Obviously not. And equally as obvious is the fact that training is a lifelong process of study and labor, an ever-learning cycle that can never reach perfection

What the Klingon statement does cover, however, are the three elements of a fighting triad concept. Once one understands the concept of what is required for success, the goal is half achieved. The rest is years of practice, dedication, and experience. The Klingon concept is comprises three elements, much like Musashi's *Five Rings* or the Marine Corps/Jeff Cooper color code stages of mental awareness.

SKILL

The skill requirements should be self-explanatory. This is the one aspect of fighting that is usually understood because it is obvious. If you don't have marksmanship, swordsmanship, or whatever the case may be in your field of weaponry, you don't have a prayer. Naturally, this extends all the way through to unarmed combat—the game is the same. Skill, also, by nature, must incorporate such facets as footwork, maneuvering, and tactics, but this is where many combatants close out the overall concept.

CUNNING

There is an oft-seen T-shirt that is emblazoned with these words: "Old age and treachery will overcome youth and skill." Amusing and for the most part true on the battlefield. The problem is if you don't learn treachery (cunning) early in the game, you won't make it to old age. One of the least utilized aspects of battle, especially by Westerners, is that of cunning.

Because most Westerners were brought up to believe in fair play, cunning is often missing from the soldier's makeup when he hits the war zone. This is displayed in such suicidal situations as a reluctance to shoot a female enemy or an unwillingness to gouge out a rapist's eyes because it "goes against the grain." While this essentially falls under the heading of ruthlessness, people are still being killed in bathrooms and rest rooms because the enemy has retained the centuries-old ninja "trick" of waiting for hours—or even days—in a latrine cesspool.

Same song, different singer. We play fair, and the bad guys don't, so we lose again. Following the Marquis of Queensbury boxing rules isn't going to win a down-and-dirty street fight. Finding a technique mind-set to turn your assailant around so you can hit him from behind will bring a more successful resolution to the fray.

Cunning? Yes. Unfair? Yes. Treacherous? Yes. Does it get the job done? YES!

POWERS OF OBSERVATION

You have to understand your enemy to beat him, be it in a military, law enforcement, or civilian context. If you don't understand how a rapist thinks or moves, you will he raped.

You have to take a page from Sherlock Holmes and put yourself in your enemy's shoes and then employ your powers of observation to gain the edge. My single-digit IQ tells me that somebody holding a knife in his left hand is probably going to cut me left-handed—so maybe sometime before I start bleeding I might want to consider a southpaw counter.

Or maybe it's a nonhostile situation. Perhaps you've noticed someone wearing a wristwatch on his right wrist. While you can't assume he's left-handed, it's still worth salting away in the back of your mind. On the other hand, you may want to be cunning and wear your watch on your right wrist to make someone think you're left-handed when you aren't.

If the same car follows you through 30 left and right turns in the city, there's a slight chance the driver may be following you. Use these observations to assume the worst and drive to an area that will give you the advantage if it does turn to war. See what you're looking at.

Paranoid? No. If somebody is out to nail you, he'll get you sooner or later. But why hand it to him on a plate?

Skill, cunning, and the powers of observation.

Oh, and one last suggestion—don't ever mess with a Klingon unless you've been to Klingon school.

The Pros and Cons of Various Body Positions

Cover, concealment, and fighting body positions are essential on a battlefield—but the disadvantages of the latter are often not taken into consideration. So while the positive aspects of body positions will be discussed in this article, the disadvantages need to be scrutinized, and a balance between the pros and cons must be established to avoid your becoming the recipient of incoming rounds.

STANDING

To this author's mind, there are only two intelligent reasons for firing from a standing position: either you don't have the time to acquire a more stable, low-profile position, or you cannot access the desired target area because of terrain or bullet trajectory (such as standing waist-deep in a river or needing to angle the bullet path upward because bystanders are in a horizontal plane with the shooter).

There's no point in standing out in the open like a fool if you can make a more accurate shot in the same time frame from a safer, more stable position. If standing is your sole viable tactical option to deliver a round, it should preferably be combined with the judicious use of cover and/or concealment or dead-rest support, such as that offered by a fence post, tree trunk, etc.

This is, of course, based on the assumption that you are not involved in a "must shoot immediately" close-quarters confrontation.

KNEELING

There is a plethora of kneeling formats over and above the classic military braced kneel, but kneeling has become both the boon and the curse of modern gunfighting.

The boon is that because of the many variations, much can be gathered tactically by employing a kneeling position. The downside is that many people look no further than the advantages and consequently don't realize how much trouble this position can potentially cause for the user in a fight.

The positive and negative aspects of kneeling can be briefly summed up by tabulating the different variations:

1. *Braced kneeling.* You can supply a dead rest for your support arm by bracing it atop the "weak" side/elevated knee. This also provides a lowered self-targeting silhouette. While the weapon platform is solid, elevation cannot be altered, and tracking a laterally moving target is virtually impossible.

2. *Speed kneeling.* Developed by the FBI many moons ago, speed kneeling does not yield the solid platform afforded by the braced kneel, because both elbows are free-floating. It does, however, lower your body line and allows instant elevation and windage adjustments. In addition, by switching knees on the ground, combined with a simultaneous 180-degree pivot, you achieve instantaneous 360-degree area coverage—a valuable addendum discovered by Massad Ayoob several years ago.

3. *Double kneeling.* As the name implies, both knees are on the ground, allowing left and right roll-outs around a barricade. It lowers the body line, allows elevation and windage trajectory to be instantly changed, and is also an excellent position for one-handed weapon operation and manipulation, such as malfunction clearances when wounded.

4. *Phillips kneeling.* A little-known pistol technique brought to this author's

attention a decade ago by Ron Phillips, this position requires a relatively slim body, as both wrists are locked around the "weak" knee and the head must be lowered to knee level. The pistol and head are both horizontal during firing. Difficult to describe in print, the Phillips kneel gives all the pros and cons of the braced kneel and, in addition, is extremely useful tactically for firing strong side around cover if you can acquire the position.

There's one constant with all the kneeling positions—a lowered body line. That's the good news. The bad news is that most people don't realize how little they're actually lowering their

Speed/unbraced kneeling position.

120

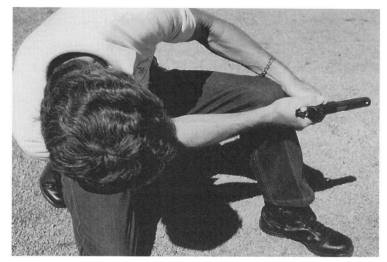

Phillips kneeling position.

Braced kneeling for shoulder weapon application.

Military prone position.

profile. Most women will lose at best about half of their body outline when adopting a kneeling position. The average male will lose only about one-third of his profile—much less than many people realize. The percentage gain by women is because their legs are invariably longer than those of a male of equal overall height, and the legs are obviously the means by which you "lose" height when kneeling. The torso remains a constant size.

Skip-fire becomes more of a hazard because vital hit areas are lowered into the bullet's path (rather be gut-shot than hit in the heart or lungs) and, at close quarters, an opponent can use kneeling against you to shove you onto your back, as there is no body balance to counteract this.

This is the same old game. Apply everything in a specific scenario to your advantage, but always be aware of the potential disadvantages.

MILITARY SQUAT OR "RICE PADDY PRONE"

Reputedly taught to U.S. armed forces in Vietnam—though there is no evidence to back this up—the squatting position gives a solid weapon platform because both elbows are braced atop the knees with both feet flat on Mother Earth. Though elevation cannot be altered, fast windage changes can be made by means of a "bunny hop" until you are naturally aligned with the target. There appears to be about 50 percent of the population who can acquire this position, and for those who can, it works well. The same "rules" apply as with kneeling vis-à-vis skip-fire and close-quarters balancing.

SITTING

Extremely stable for "sniping" at the enemy, it provides only two positives: excellent accuracy potential on a non-moving target and low body line, dependent on which variation you use. Relatively slow to get into and out of, and a nightmare for the trauma staff if you take a hit, sitting should probably be reserved for targets who don't return fire. By nature of the bunched-up, hunched-over requirements of the position, you will probably sustain multiple injuries from one projectile. Furthermore, it is not a position you can sustain for long periods of time without numbness, cramps, etc.

PRONE

The closer you are to the ground, the more stable your position, and for pinpoint low-profile shooting, prone is the epitome of the axiom. The one big downside to prone in a street fight is that you require, as in all shooting, a natural point of aim if you are to apply the basic rules of marksmanship.

If, for example, you drop into prone and aren't "naturally" aligned with the target, you will have to angle your entire body differently until the weapon comes to a point of aim on the target without using muscle tension. Prone relies solely on relaxed bone support of the weapon.

For example, if you're using a car's wheel well for cover and can't get a natural point of aim, you may end up offering your lower extremities as a target from an oblique angle if you try for a textbook position. It is better under these circumstances to use one of the "bastard" prone positions as opposed to the classic military prone. Another comforting thought is that if you're fighting "Mr. Claymore" (front toward the enemy!), don't worry about taking a hit. It'll be in your head and your problem becomes nonexistent anyway.

What's the bottom line? Use everything to your advantage, be aware of all the disadvantages, cheat like hell, and make sure you can acquire the various body positions of your choice in full battle gear before hitting the battlefield. There's nothing so disconcerting as becoming proficient on a training range dressed in jeans and a T-shirt and then finding out on the battlefield that you can't get into a desired shooting position because of body armor and a gas mask.

The Legend—and Lessons—of Wyatt Earp

The most important lesson learned from those proficient gunfighters was the winner of a gunplay was usually the man who took his time. The second was that if I hoped to live long on the frontier, I would shun flashy trick shooting—grandstand play—as I would poison.

—Wyatt Earp

And live long he did—long after the OK Corral debacle had ceased to be front-page news. Even though Mr. Earp's morals and ethics may have been in question during his earlier days, he was one of the few who survived to old age, based on his above-quoted logic. And both lessons can be invaluable tools in the fighting toolbox.

LESSON ONE: "THE WINNER OF A GUNPLAY USUALLY WAS THE MAN WHO TOOK HIS TIME."

Obviously, this doesn't literally mean taking your time, as was borne out by several other quotes by Earp during his lifetime. What it does mean is that the man who keeps his cool should win. This is epitomized in Kipling's poem "If" and in another thousand written works besides his.

The Earp trick was to plant the first bullet, even if it meant holding his fire for fractions of a second. While this may have been pushing the envelope, he did attain longevity—and he did qualify his statement with the word *usually*.

A century later and nothing's changed, save weaponry and technology. The same rules apply, and the same lessons have to be learned—usually the hard way.

If you lose your cool, you lose the fight. And if you resort to haphazard slinging of rounds downrange, you will probably lose a lot more. Indiscriminate launching of projectiles can have one of two dire consequences: (1) you pay in blood, or (2) you pay in court for the stray rounds that hit innocent bystanders.

Logically, you have to hit the target to stop the threat. Equally as logical is the fact that you don't have all day to accomplish this feat. So a compromise must be reached to accommodate both situations. While most training conducted these days concentrates on staid, static range drills (like two rounds to the upper torso in X time from X distance), this is nothing but marksmanship and weapon manipulation exercises—no more, no less.

First, the target invariably doesn't offer this neat, clinical availability on the street. (If an assailant is facing straight on and not moving, usually you have no business shooting.) Second, if these range drills are so wonderful, how come bodies in the morgue don't have the classic perfect shot placement results? Last, but not least, perfect body shots may not necessarily stop the threat, irrespective of how good the shot placement.

What this all boils down to is that shot placement is more critical than any other aspect of gunfighting—and it may necessitate immediate follow-up rounds to de-escalate the problem. The one factor that seems to be least understood is that the torso is the one body area that can shrink to less than half its width in a fraction of a second (with antagonistic body movement such as an assailant reaching for a sidearm).

This usually means that you may have to find a different target area—such as the pelvis, head, or whatever—but you have to hit! And if it means taking an extra eighth of a second to make sure of target acquisition, sight picture, backstop, and foreground, then so be it.

LESSON TWO: "FLASHY TRICK SHOOTING AND GRANDSTAND PLAY"

Annie Oakley was one of the premier trick shooters of all time, but she never went to war. Bill Jordan hip-shot aspirin at 10 feet—and he went to war more times than can be counted. The subtle difference between the two is that on occasion Mr. Jordan had to shoot for blood, and on those occasions he relegated his aspirin- and balloon-shooting tricks to the bottom of his hit list (no pun intended). This author grew up with a pro boxer who, like Mike Tyson, specialized in early-round knockouts. When asked why he didn't "make the fights last longer" to give the public their money's worth, his stock answer was "there's no overtime in the boxing ring." He was right.

Anytime you make a grandstand play in a gunfight, you'd better be able to back it up—ask General Custer. The only consolation prize in a gunfight is a tombstone. And Tombstone is where this article started and where Mr. Earp's logic first bore fruit.

Building a Better Bullet

*T*here are times when I feel like a dyslexic theologian in search of the true meaning of Dog. Hand in hand with the "my bullet is better than yours" arguments goes the endless discussions on projectile overpenetration. There is no question that improvements in ballistics technology are beneficial. There is no question that bullet overpenetration can be a tactical nightmare. And there is no question that apparently either I'm the village idiot or I can't see the forest for the trees.

After all, what else could explain my relative lack of concern for either bullet design/configuration or overpenetration through walls or so forth? Not having Nostradamus' ability to predict the future, I've had to base my admittedly pathetic lack of knowledge on what has happened in the past.

Yes, better bullets give better results, and, yes, accountability for the terminal resting place of each and every projectile sits squarely on the shoulders of the shooter—save in some military situations. I'm not suggesting carrying a .17-caliber BB gun for self-defense, nor am I advocating turning your local supermarket into Alamo II merely because you've had your purse snatched.

If we cut out all the hysteria, egos, and ranting and raving and humbly admit that most of us know a helluva lot less than we proclaim, all that remains is to examine the facts. And, as it so often happens, the facts belie the printed word.

Somehow I can't see two cavemen arguing about the respective merits of their clubs and rocks while Tyrone Rex was about to stomp them into the ground, or Central American Indians discussing the relative velocity imparted by their atlatl while their neighbors were in full charge.

The point, of course, is that shot placement is vastly more important than caliber, velocity, or anything else. If you miss, you lose—period. It's the same old story, ad nauseam. Throughout history, from the cavemen to the 1990s homeowner, the solution has always been the same—only

Although Dad is probably justified in shooting with an escalating threat this close, note Miss Ruby in the room behind, directly in the line of fire from a 12-gauge—and invisible to her old man through the swinging bar doors. Be sure of your backstop!

hits count. The weaponry was always adequate—it's marksmanship and tactics that decide the outcome.

There have been marked improvements in bullet design and performance in recent decades, but so inconsequential against the late-19th-century weapons like the .30-caliber Broomhandle Mauser as to make no difference in a fight.

Perhaps it makes more sense to look at the bullet design/overpenetration subject from a layman's point of view than from a ballistician's hypotheses. If, as is currently theorized, about a foot of projectile penetration is preferred for reliable bullet performance, how does this apply to different angles of entry on differing parts of human anatomy—and with different weaponry?

Obviously, based on this theory, a straight-on upper torso hit with adequate penetration should do the job. But a blown-up heart or lungs can still leave the victim's motor skills operational for close to 20 seconds—an eternity in a gunfight. The scenario will differ if bone is struck first or if the bullet has ricocheted off a weapon before entry or if the round had been delivered side-on to the torso, or if . . . you get the message. There are too many ifs, ands, or buts to make any kind of coherent prediction on which bullet will do what, whenever. All that we can do is say what the bullet should do; no more, no less.

Also, it is apparent that a side-on head shot fired by a .308 rifle will invariably result in overpenetration, while specialty ammo, such as frangible rounds, can only result in a bastardized version of the ballistician's wish list most of the time. Much is based on the gunfighter's hope of what the tactical scenario will be, as opposed to what usually actually transpires.

For example, many people carry birdshot as a first-choice shotgun round for home defense, essentially for two reasons: (1) the round should have enough power to stop a threat, and (2) "if I miss, the pellets won't penetrate the Sheetrock bedroom wall and hit my kids."

Problem one: if your enemy is farther away than five or six yards, birdshot probably won't stop him. Problem two: if he's at contact distance, a couple of feet from the bedroom wall, and you miss, guess what? The round is going right through the wall like a slug anyway.

While everybody seems concerned about indoor overpenetration through trailer home and apartment walls, ceilings, and floors—and understandably so—it doesn't seem to overly bother anybody to empty the guts of a 16-round 9mm weapon in a crowded parking lot, often with 14 misses. And these rounds will carry on trucking downtown for well over a mile.

When you have a large police department averaging 19 percent hits, the answer is not to change the ammo and weaponry. With 81 percent of your rounds missing the adversary, the problem of overpenetration is a lot less of a priority than training to increase your hit potential. This will automatically reduce overpenetration problems.

The good news is that there is a solution.

Stay with the weapon and ammo best suited to your envisaged potential tactical situation, use cover and concealment, be aware of your backstop, and use the 36 fighting strategies laid out in the Japanese "art of war." In this author's humble opinion, the above is far more important than worrying about minuscule inconsequentials about whose bullet can better murder a wet telephone directory or block of gelatin.

Me, I'm off to enjoy a ride in my turnip truck, accompanied by my 80-year-old pistol.

What to Do in a No-Shoot Situation

There's an old joke about taking a knife to a gunfight. At face value this doesn't exactly appear to be a display of ingenuity. The flip side of the coin, however, is that most potential gunfights—both law enforcement and civilian home defense—de-escalate to a nonshooting situation.

The purpose of this article is not to suggest that you should revert to Jack the Ripper status at this stage, but rather to examine the complexities of controlling a scenario that has—as so often happens—reverted from a shoot to a no-shoot situation.

Law enforcement personnel usually have two slight advantages over a lone civilian: (1) more manpower, which either awes perpetrators into submission without deadly force having to be used, or alternatively gives a force-of-numbers advantage, and (2) police officers often know prior to a specific problem what they're walking into. This obviously allows a formulation of some kind of plan of engagement.

The home defense scenario, however, often degrades into a semblance of the following: Homeowner hears noise, grabs gun. Homeowner gets lucky and finds intruder before intruder nails homeowner. Homeowner proudly announces, "I have a gun." Intruder replies, "Big deal." Homeowner proudly announces, "I have a gun." Intruder replies, "Big deal."

After 20 minutes of this ludicrous debacle, Mr. Homeowner becomes frustrated and shoots Mr. Intruder—and goes to jail for 20 years. Or the intruder, realizing that the homeowner is bluffing or out of ideas, wrestles the gun from Mr. Homeowner and shoves it where the monkey put his peanuts.

Moral of the story? If shooting is warranted, you'd better do it and continue shooting until the threat stops. If shooting is not required, you'd better have a game plan to deal with the sudden de-escalation and resultant lack of necessity for the use of deadly force.

Many training centers cover hostile and nonhostile target scenarios but offer no solution as to what the trainee is supposed to do in a no-

He may be cocky, he may be an intruder in your house, but U.S. law doesn't regard this man as a deadly-force threat unless further escalation transpires.

shoot situation. All this does for the trainee is to teach him target recognition and marksmanship. No more, no less.

Do you have to be a combination of Bruce Lee, Kathy Long, and the Highlander to survive a nondeadly-force confrontation? No, but it would help if we didn't automatically assume that gunfire is going to erupt just because a firearm is available as an option.

There are two essentials to the successful conclusion of a confrontation: a brain and a plan. Law enforcement officers understand comparative use of force relative to the threat because they have administrative rules of engagement by which they have to abide—but they, as well as civilians attempting to defend life or property, must have the aforementioned brain-plan combination to draw upon, or all is lost.

Discretion is the better part of valor—use cover and concealment instead of trying to look like Clint Eastwood. Better yet, stay in your bedroom and let the loony downstairs steal your damned furniture. If it's not worth dying for, it's not worth doing. If you absolutely have to do your thing, consider your "what if" variables before you enter the fray.

So we're back to the "I have a gun/big deal" scenario, Well, you could withdraw, if that's not too much of an insult to your misguided machismo. Or you could quickly file off the front sight so it doesn't hurt so much when the intruder inserts your gun barrel where the sun don't shine.

Or as an absolute last resort you could inject into your range training program weapon retention techniques and tactics, as well as some to help you develop the ability to control a scenario that doesn't require shooting but also doesn't allow you to blithely bypass a Pepper Popper merely because it's painted a "nonhostile" color. This last option just won't cut it for real.

Another aspect that bears scrutiny is equipment, especially flashlights. If, for example, you have a shotgun fitted only with a pressure switch on the fore-end, how do you maintain illumination and simultaneously open a latched door? Or, worse, how do you dial 911 and keep the light trained on a trapped suspect? Have a pressure switch that can

be operated by the firing hand or mount an on/off switch.

Similarly, if armed with a handgun and a remote flashlight, can you control a nonshooting situation? Can you reholster quickly? What if it's 3 A.M. in your house—you'll probably be in your birthday suit, which means no holster?

Nonshooting situations usually pose a more difficult problem than an out-and-out gunfight and need to be addressed during training. Trying to work out a game plan while Mr. Sump Plug is giving you the "big deal" speech is not the answer. In fact, telling an intruder with 20/20 vision that you are armed probably doesn't rank with Einstein either.

Taking a knife to a gunfight isn't bright, but bluffing with a firearm in a no-shoot situation is just plain stupid. Welcome to the Real World.

Playing by Today's Rules

Ruthlessness is a necessary evil. It's evil because nobody in his right mind wants to splatter somebody's brains and snot all over the bedroom wall. It's necessary because if ruthlessness is what it's going to take to stop a lethal-force confrontation then it's essential if you don't want second place in a two-man gunfight.

The problem with instilling ruthlessness in a training environment is the obvious fact that the targets are not human. Depending on the quality of the instructor and the scenario, adrenaline can be induced to the maximum, but the salient point is that the trainee is not taking human life if shooting is required in a specific range training situation. He is merely delivering rounds to an inanimate material.

While the scenario can be totally realistic and street/battlefield representative, there is no substitute for seeing and experiencing the destruction of human tissue along with the attendant emergence of blood and gore to hammer home the message. No amount of *Rambo* movies can instill the realism and violence of a for-real confrontation. On the other hand, I cannot for the life of me understand an adult juror running out of a courtroom barfing at the sight of an autopsy photo. One wonders whether that same person could retaliate with enough ruthlessness and necessary force if, for example, his or her children's lives were being laid on the line by a machete-wielding fruitcake?

I personally don't get my jollies from seeing fresh entrails hanging over the railings, but I do feel that much of the post action horror and sleepless nights we're supposed to experience is a direct result of modern society's telling us in advance what we should feel, so some people do indeed have those emotions if the situation arises. It's the old Pavlov's pooch syndrome.

I've been accused of being callous and indifferent, but I've reached the stage with the extremes of political correctness and psychology where the entire planet can perform an anatomical juxtaposition with its orbicularis oris muscles in a state of contraction with my aurelear orifice. If you're old enough to point a gun at somebody with malicious intent and with full knowledge of the destructive potential, you're old enough to eat a couple of bullets. It's called *responsibility for your actions*. I really don't care if your daddy sucked on too many Jack Daniels or if your mommy temporarily loaned out some of her body parts for pecuniary gain. If you don't like warm rooms, stay out of the kitchen.

What's brought on this tirade? The almost daily routine of abuse being lumped on police officers for shooting "children." Let's try some veracity just for a change. The "children" shot by law enforcement are invariably over 6 feet tall and weigh in at 200 pounds. And, oops, almost forgot, they're cranking off rounds at the cops and anyone else in the vicinity for that matter.

Or we get the young lost waif in Arizona on his third auto-theft joyride in four months shooting at the pursuing officers engaged in a high-speed pursuit. That poor child is 11 years old. Or the 13-year-old in L.A. with seven counts of murder one—gainfully employed as a "mechanic." And the list goes on. And the do-gooders sit in their ivory towers and bring lawsuits. And it's not going to stop.

I hate to mention this, but the only "thousand points of light" I've seen in evidence lately were incoming tracers. This is a wake-up call. The entire country was horrified by the Oklahoma City bombing. Albeit horrific, it was still *one* bombing. The same thing has been going on worldwide for a full generation and has been labeled as "freedom fighting" by the United States. Now, all of a sudden it's "terrorism."

It's a rose by any other name. That's why we keep losing. When Vice

President Dan Quayle mentioned "family values" everybody collapsed with mirth and regarded him as a buffoon. Well, who's the fool now? We've reached the dizzy heights of trying to play the therapy game with gun-toting (and shooting) 10-year-olds. Face facts: either raise your kids to behave or, if they're going to play with the "big boys," expect them to have to endure a man's punishment.

What all of this mess boils down to is that the normal so-called urban "civilized" Western fighting mind-set will have to change. It will have to be replaced by the fighting man's requisite ruthlessness at least until the kinder, gentler world I've been hearing about finally shows its face, if it ever does. It means that you may very well have to rip the mortal coil off a 10-year-old kid or light up a woman. And if this thought disgusts you, maybe you should pay for your tombstone now—because you're going to freeze if it comes down to it. Too little, too late.

Or pretty soon, if things continue the way they are, you may have the dubious pleasure of dealing with a female terrorist. Middle Easterners and Teutons have utilized them for a long time for two reasons: they are more vicious than their male counterparts, and they know they have the reaction-time edge because Western "nice guys" tend to freeze momentarily at the thought of lighting up a woman—a result of their "civilized" upbringing and social graces. Of course, if you concentrate on the threat and not on the child's size or the woman's cleavage the problem is no big deal—but tactically for most people that is easier said than done.

And before anyone out there thinks this article is the ravings of a paranoid

133

madman, it may behoove you to realize that while North America is one of the few continents where this is a new phenomenon, it's old hat most everywhere else. The "age of chivalry" is fast replaced by the "law of the jungle" when you're hungry.

So until the "Well, it's the 90s now" expression stops being the stock excuse for every degenerate . . . until a *mild* derriere-warming isn't called child abuse . . . until mealy-mouthed cowards who lack the intestinal fortitude stand up and fight for what's right instead of expecting outcast "dogs of war" to help them when the self-induced crap finally lands on their ivory walls long after it's hit everyone else—the situation can only worsen. To quote George Santayana, "Those who cannot remember the past are condemned to repeat it."

And this *is* merely history repeating itself.

Over the last quarter-century my sword and armor have rusted, and my white steed was carted off to the glue factory. I no longer have philanthropic dreams of riding off into the sunset to help people who won't help themselves. If I have to resort to ruthlessness, violence, and callousness to survive a deadly force confrontation, so be it—irrespective of who or what the opponent is. At least I'm honest, and slowly but surely society is degrading to the stage where this is the only recourse left for self-defense when attacked.

This is not a pleasant subject, and I would dearly like to see the age of chivalry return. But if it doesn't there are not going to be any politically correct Marquis of Queensberry rules from this quarter. If the goose don't have to, the gander don't have to. And frankly my dear . . .

How Far Is It Anyway?

The one tactical facet of fighting that cannot be mastered by most people is that of range estimation. But while this is indeed a frustrating problem, it is a double-edged sword. Even if you can estimate range to the nth degree, it doesn't help if you can't shoot up to your firearm's trajectory potential. If, for example, you are blessed with a rifle that can shoot a three-inch group at 600 yards, but you have the ability to shoot only a 12-inch group, there is absolutely no sense whatsoever in bothering to learn range estimation.

Obviously, there is no point in using the requisite hold-over at this distance (dependent on the weapon's zero) because you don't have a clue (in the aforementioned example) as to where the bullet will impact within a 12-inch strike zone. So why hold over a couple of inches under these circumstances when your basic marksmanship ability just doesn't cut it, irrespective of your range estimation expertise?

This having been said, there is plenty of "hot dog" equipment that bolsters the human inability to estimate range, in the form of binoculars, monoculars, telescopic sights with duplex reticles, built-in range finders, bullet-drop compensators, etc.

But what of the man who doesn't have all this fancy, toasty-canine equipment? After all, probably the only two people who really need long-distance range estimation equipment are the sniper and the humane—but unendangered—small-game hunter. For the most part, anybody else has a buffalo, elephant, or human adversary to contend with, and close-range self-preservation at that stage is usually a bigger problem than range estimation.

So how do you take the "guess" out of guesstimation, armed only with a couple of brain cells and simple, mundane equipment?

The first and most common technique is to envision the length of a football field and then deduce the distance to your enemy by multiplying, adding, or subtracting increments of this base measurement. This works fine unless you're a baseball player; the terrain is not flat and uninterrupted by foliage, buildings, etc.; or if you just plain can't envision the length of a football field, as is the case with most people. Usually this technique leaves students of the art as frustrated as they were before they learned the technique—and often more so.

Technique number two involves using a common, known, man-made object, such as a telephone pole. Knowing the height of such an item can be invaluable, as structures like these are invariably staggered at regular distances, allowing easy distance evaluation. Know how long the painted intermittent highway lane markers are? (They're longer than most think.) This last example is a piece of cake for appraising distance. Unfortunately, as in the first technique, technique number two has a huge downside. If the gunfight doesn't erupt on Route 66 or somewhere near where Mrs. Bell has strung her communications lines, you're back to square one.

An excellent technique originally attributed to the FBI is that of using one's thumb extended at arm's length in the pilot's classic thumbs-up position. "Posting" your enemy on top of your thumbnail can roughly establish the distance to your target if he's walking side-on to you. One pace "across" your thumbnail equals approximately 50 yards; three paces equals about 150 yards. Because of the variables of the technique, however, it's an iffy last-ditch technique, usually good out to only a couple of hundred yards and usually reserved for snipers—who should have better equipment than a thumbnail to rely on. The last sour note to this technique, of course, is that somehow you have to convince your

An auto ignition key can be used for range estimation.

enemy to stroll straight across your field of fire. If he alters compass direction, it doesn't work.

So far all the techniques that have been discussed relate to the long-distance rifleman. What is needed is a simple, basic technique that will work, for example, for the handgunner who is forced to take a shot at 146 yards, the shotgunner who needs to deliver a slug at 192 yards, etc. In other words, a system that will work each and every time to estimate distance from shooter to target, irrespective of weaponry, weapon trajectory, or terrain. And here's the scoop.

Most firearms, other than scoped rifles or belly guns, have some form of front sight. Learn how much this sight will laterally obliterate a human torso at specific distances. Humans, whether they be a Twiggy or a Schwarzenegger, have essentially the same torso width for the purposes of range estimation.

Experiment also with your front sight on objects of known unvarying size, such as gallon gas cans, various modes of transportation—be it a 1946 Buick or an enemy tank—mailboxes, etc., all at varying distances. This will allow you, if the enemy is adjacent to one of these objects, to accurately estimate target distance.

Obviously, you need to know incremental amounts so that your sight will laterally cover these objects as well. For example, "If my front sight laterally covers one-third of a human torso, the target is at X distance," etc. Or, conversely, if the target is four-fifths the width of the sight, the distance is . . .

Being off by 60 yards in an estimation on a 200-yard handgun or shotgun attempt will be disastrous to your point-of-bullet impact. If you use several weapons and find yourself reduced to a

myriad of bewildering formulas because of differing front sight widths, you can use something at arm's length you always carry, such as your favorite knife or an ignition key (which, incidentally, allows you several "distance markers" because of the varying sized cut-outs necessary to trip lock tumblers). That one's been around since Moses was a corporal and works better than any football field trick. (Note to law enforcement personnel: use your cuff key—it has enough different sizes and configurations to work.)

One final plea to the military rifleman: battle zero your rifle at 25 and 100 yards and hold point of aim/point of impact out to 250 meters. Don't mess with the sight adjustment afterward and don't "hold over" out to 270 yards in a fight. After 47 years I'm tired of seeing rows of white crosses in cemeteries.

No Brain, No Gain

God doesn't build junk. Man, however, in his infinite stupidity, has an amazing penchant for taking the ultimate God-given machine—the brain—and relegating it to the battlefield scrapyard.

This article is both an admitted plagiarism of quotes from some the greats, past and present, and a dedication to a couple of acquaintances of the last few decades. To the John H's and the David S-D's, my eternal respect for having mastered the ultimate computer—the tactical brain. To my late father, who spent five years on battlefields after a six-week boot camp—I'm still not fit to stand in your shadow. And, finally, to the garbage who should print their 10-page résumés in Braille and send them to Venus de Milo for proofreading:

> *The men that can do things are going to be sought out just as*
> *surely as the sun rises in the morning. Fake reputations, habits of glib*
> *and clever speech, and glittering surface performance are going to be*
> *discovered.*
>
> —Dwight D. Eisenhower

And now on to the tactics of fighting: There is one golden rule to fighting: "He who has the gold makes the rules." No more, no less. Since time immemorial tactics have been more important than weaponry; that is why the pen is mightier than the sword (unless, of course, somebody destroys your printing press with a baseball bat or you take a typewriter to a gunfight).

The trick is to know and fully understand that tactics have to progress and change as the fight progresses, irrespective of whether you have a prebattle plan or not, because you can bet your bottom dollar that something will go awry before the fight is over.

No plan of operations extends with any certainty beyond the first contact with the main hostile force. Only the layman thinks that he can see in the course of the campaign the consequent execution of an original idea with all details thought out in advance and adhered to until the very end.
                                        —Field Marshal von
                                                Moltke

In fact, Napoleon said, "I have never had a plan of operations," and he did just fine until he met his Walerloo—and sooner or later we all do (death, taxes, and the bullet with your name on it). On the other hand, it's nice to stave off the inevitable for as long as possible. As Sir Winston Churchill so aptly put it, "Nothing is more exhilarating than to be shot at with no result."

On the other hand I can personally do without Frederick the Great's "Rascals, would you live forever?"

What part of yes did he not understand?

Let's be honest. The ultimate objective is survival, and survival means winning both the battle *and* the war. It means having the ingrained ability to be absolutely ruthless when required, tempered with the ability to walk away if intelligence dictates that the latter is a more viable alternative to solving the immediate problem. The war is more important than individual battles, but losing the battles will cost the war.

And then there's the age-old wisdom of the sages, all saying in essence the same thing: Brain power is more important than firepower. All who earned success in this field for several thousand years have stayed with this basic concept. Those who didn't have lost.

The seven military classics of ancient China (including the much-vaunted Sun Tzu's *Art of War*), the Japanese art of war, Moltke's art of war, Machiavelli's art of war, and on and on ad nauseam. And still we don't learn. It doesn't matter how many guns you own or how well you shoot—if you have snot for brains, the only way you'll win is by luck.

There is no question that there have been many occasions when people have won on luck alone, and that lends the lie to the truth. For those who have had the misfortune to have been involved in multiple incidents, or those who have been forced (either voluntarily or involuntarily) into repeated situations by the nature of their profession or circumstances, this has become painfully apparent. You can practice and train 365 days a year, every year, and all you gain is an edge. But if you don't have the edge you run on luck alone, and there are very few bankrupt casinos or unoccupied cemeteries.

In the past decade, many institutions have sprung up, especially firearms related, that proclaim that you can become a "gunfighter from hell" with several days' or a week's training. No you can't. You can learn marksmanship extremely quickly, and you can pick up one or two basic life-saving tactics. Fighting, on the other hand, is a life-long study, and the longer you live the less you know. Fighting isn't learned by merely pounding 500 rounds of ammo into a stupid piece of paper or steel.

In war we must always leave room for strokes of fortune and accidents that cannot be foreseen.
                                        —Polybius

In 1944 Captain Sir Basil Liddel Hart stated that the only thing harder than getting a new idea into the mind was to get an old one out. He was both right and wrong. The "old" ideas we need to get out are the relatively recent ones. The "new" ideas are new in name only—their tactical roots go back to the dawn of man. Survival fighting is based on thousand-year-old ideas—only the weaponry changes.

The sword is more important than the shield, and skill is more important than either. The final weapon is the brain. All else is supplemental.
—John Steinbeck

It's time to sweep the crap out of the chicken house, have a surgeon operate on our opto-rectumitis, and get back to the fighting man's creed: No brain, no gain.

Paring Down to the Training Basics

After nearly a half-century I think I've finally figured it out. Apparently there are two different types of gunfights. A basic fight requires virtually no preparatory training—merely a regimen of the elements of sight alignment, sight picture, trigger control, and tactics.

An advanced gunfight, on the other hand, is a whole different kettle of fish. This latter situation requires that all participants rush around like a herd of turtles, employing extremely advanced techniques such as sight alignment, sight picture, trigger control, and tactics.

Or maybe if it's an Armageddon of an advanced fight then you need to be accomplished in awesome high-speed/low-drag capabilities—like sight alignment, sight picture, trigger control, and tactics.

No, this article isn't meant to be farcical, but apparently along with the rest of the degradation of the fighting man's ability is our ever-increasing late-20th-century optical problem—that of failing to see the forest for the trees. You can jump out of helicopters and rope down buildings like a ninja from hell, but if you don't stay with the basics when it comes down to trigger time, all else is for naught.

Yes, basics are boring to practice ad nauseam, but we may as well face facts. When all is said and done, basics are what win the day every time. Unfortunately, it goes against the human grain to stay with crawling once you can walk, even if a "crawl" is required to solve a specific scenario—besides, you don't look like a big deal if you don't run when you should walk. Well the good news is you don't exactly look like Mr. Hollywood in a body bag either.

Put it this way: A Porsche is a magnificent piece of machinery. It runs like a bat out of hell, handles and brakes beautifully, and has air conditioning and leather seats. But the sorry truth is that it's essentially an overgrown Volkswagen, and most people buy it to impress the neighbors more than to appreciate the machinery.

If you apply these principles to a gunfight, with a bit of luck the only person killed will be yourself. Usually this attitude ends up with the

"Porsche owner" getting other people hurt unnecessarily, and that just isn't going to cut it. If it is beneath you to "drive a Volkswagen" because of what the neighbors might think, get off the pot before you cause somebody else's demise. Better yet, if you absolutely have to be a cowboy, drive a horse.

Gunfighting basics are composed of several aspects, but the emphasis should always be placed more on fighting than on the gun itself. The gun is a medium, a tool—no more, no less. All is supplemental to (and dependent on) the mind and its attendant tactical ability.

Following are some suggestions as to paring down training to plain, simple basics that provide a foundation for the building. Crack the foundation and the entire building will topple.

Naturally, it goes without saying that these are suggestions only; because they are merely personal opinions they can be nothing else.

1. *Ballistics:* "My bullet's better because it's bigger/smaller/faster/slower/expands/doesn't expand . . . Who cares? Hit the damn target, and if it doesn't do the job, hit it again until the threat stops—but hit the target and stop worrying about ballistic hypotheses. If you don't have 100-percent accuracy on the training range, you're starting off with a handicap in the street. Ninety percent is not good enough on the practice range.

2. *Equipment:* "L.A. SWAT is using X equipment so it must be the best for my application." Wrong answer. The L.A. SWAT team is very, very good at what it does, and its equipment is geared toward its specific mission requirements, but it has worked this out the hard way over a quarter of a century. This does not mean its equipment is necessarily applicable to your situation. Stay with what works for you, tried and tested.

3. *Training targets:* If you figure on being attacked by humongous pieces of paper and steel, practice on humongous pieces of paper and steel. Otherwise . . .

4. *Accurizing weapons:* If you're not a sniper, forget it. A pistol that shoots into two inches at 50 yards is pointless, especially if it malfunctions more than once in 1,000 rounds. And if you can't shoot a half-inch group with a rifle at 100 yards in a fight, you don't need a sub-MOA rifle because you can't shoot up to your rifle's capability. Buy a Volkswagen.

5. *Tactics.*

6. *Tactics.*

7. *Tactics.*

There are more concepts and misconceptions, but these are the most commonly found on the "list."

Come to think of it, I need about another 200 to 300 years to get my feces coagulated, but one thing's a given—if you want to be like Bruce Willis in *Die Hard*, there's some bad news: (a) life isn't a Hollywood movie, and (b) you WILL "die hard."

Equipping Your Mental Toolbox with the Proper Tools for Training

*T*wo heads are better than one—as long as each head contains an operational brain.

You are always better off in a conflict with more manpower, but the absolute criterion is that each individual sticks to his job. If this is not done, all you have is a herd of extra bodies running around like freshly decapitated chickens.

The objective of having backup is to operate as a team. If you're on your own you're in deep trouble—but at least you know this going in and don't rely on inefficient backup, which may drop you into deeper doo-doo than you would have encountered running "man alone."

The downside to being on your own is obvious. You cannot look in more than one direction at any given time and consequently cannot optically cover any potential threat area greater than about a 100-degree arc. Naturally, the "about" 100 degrees shrinks in direct proportion to the size of your anal orifice—a phenomenon called tunnel vision. This can be compounded by terrain. In other words, if you are virtually anywhere other than the Sahara Desert, you can be hit from above or below, as well as from the sides or rear. This leaves you with an unprotected 200-degree+ lateral and vertical problem, as can occur with stairwells, attics, tree limbs, etc. And if you are attacked by more than one assailant simultaneously, you cannot protect yourself from all quarters. That is why law enforcement uses backup whenever possible, and why military units have used flanking techniques since the dawn of time.

But if you are in the fortunate position of having the availability of backup, each member must be cognizant at all times of what the rest of the "team" is doing—primarily their physical location. Outflanking the enemy is great, but crossfire is not.

If there is such a thing as "tactical rules," there are two that have to rank near the top of the list. One is *no crossfire under any circumstances*, and the other is *communication with other team members*. Lack of communication is what usually leads to the crossfire problem and many others in addition.

Here the instructor observes as two officers tag-team on a moving-target hostage problem.

Communications is the first thing that breaks down in a fighting environment. The object of having more manpower is to gain a tactical advantage in the field of optics, auditory senses, and force of numbers. Unfortunately, if it isn't done right, all you're doing is setting up more potential targets or hostages for the bad guys than you would if you were on your own.

If you're alone and you screw up, you will probably get hurt. If you're part of a team and you screw up, you're probably hanging somebody else's rear end out to dry. Try sleeping with that on your conscience.

A "team" doesn't necessarily comprise only law enforcement or military personnel. It could be a husband-and-wife duo at home, it could be a gaggle of family members at a Thanksgiving dinner from hell at a restaurant, it could be a couple of buddies being preyed upon by a gang at a gas station. The bottom line is not to run around like a herd of turtles screaming, "Why me, Lord?" God just doesn't like you, that's why. A more productive plan is to do something in a combined effort.

Bottom line? Have a game plan for emergency (or, for that matter, planned) situations. While it may be easier said than done, the only alternative is to stand by for a load of lead in your Thoracic Park. In days of yore, the game was to nail the radio man, then the man adjacent to him. After that, you watched the rest of the headless chickens scurrying around sans communication, leader, and game plan.

The antithesis to the nonintelligent use of available manpower is the sometimes-heard military or police comment of, "No problem. I'll always have backup."

Don't bet your life on it. Troops have become separated from their units in the past, and two-man law enforcement patrols have had an officer go down during a building search or vehicle suspect stop in the past. When this happens you have to immediately revert to *one-man* tactics and *one-man* thought processes—no easy matter when under pressure.

There are some absolutes in tactics.

1. You cannot safely negotiate a building on your own, especially stairwells. So don't do it if you don't have to.
2. Murphy's Law operates 365 days a year, 24 hours a clay. Don't tempt Fate.
3. Whether you're a battle-hardened six-star general or the diminutive elderly dowager from Pasadena, the scenario is the same: a deadly-force confrontation or the potential thereof.

You have to have both one-man and backup/team tactics in your mental toolbox. If you don't, you can bet your bottom dollar that the one wrench you need on D-Day won't be around when you need it.

It's Better to Give Than to Receive

Some say that if you're not operating on the edge, you're taking up too much space. The corollary is that there are old pilots and bold pilots, but there are no old, bold pilots. And while discretion is often the better part of valor, fools persistently rush in where wise men fear to tread.

These days it seems that many people are so concerned about looking like Wyatt Earp in front of their peers that they throw caution to the wind and end up eating a bullet instead. But with the passing of time you run across enough backstabbers, sidewinders, and self-important people that you realize you really don't care a rocking-horse dropping about anybody's opinion, save for that of family and friends, if you're lucky enough to have either. Survival takes precedence.

And there's one absolute: when it comes to trading projectiles, it's far better to give than to receive. Tactics and brainpower will stand you in good stead in a fight, whereas ego or stupidity won't stop a bullet.

If somebody wants your epidermis, he will undoubtedly get possession of it sooner or later, but that doesn't mean you have to hand it to him on a platter. On the other hand, wandering around expecting Jack the Ripper to be lurking behind every corner with your demise as his sole life's ambition won't do much for your sanity. Somewhere there's a happy medium.

Self-defense training is like every other facet of your life. The only difference is that if you goof in a deadly-force confrontation, somebody is going to get hurt, possibly terminally. You don't stick your tongue in a light socket to see if the current is on. Why do it in a gunfight?

For the most part, there are three primary causes of good guy injury or death on today's urban battlefield:

1. Lack of training
2. Overconfidence/cowboying
3. Complacency

Lack of training, sooner or later, will lead to the inevitable demise of you or a third party. Unless you are very, very lucky you probably won't even make it past round one, and, as such, this specific aspect isn't even worth discussion. Training is mandatory—period.

Overconfidence, cowboying, cockiness—call it what you will—is an open invitation to a "fools rush in" funeral. It is most prevalent in the young, usually short on field experience, who display bravado in a desperate attempt to gain "recognition" from their peers. The fallacy of this pathetic situation—and it is embarrassingly pathetic—is twofold: (1) nobody cares what a "big deal" you are, and (2) you will probably cause the death or injury of a partner. Most "cowboys" don't get hurt—they cause other people to get hurt.

Much of the above situation stems from an ego that overrides common sense. It is extremely difficult for some to admit that they are not omniscient, and they try to cover up this fact with "bull in a china shop" actions in battle. As stated before, the best in the business will readily admit that they are always hungry for knowledge. The sole exception who comes to mind is the 17th-century samurai, Miyamoto Musashi—but he could back up his mouth and never, *ever* lost a fight.

The cavalier "I don't need to use cover and/or concealment" attitude is fine if you're on your own. Go ahead and get your rear end blown out of the water. Believe it or not, nobody gives a damn. But if you're operating with a team, extend the common courtesy to your partners of not hanging their rear ends out to dry.

I was condescendingly informed by a SWAT team member about a year ago that "we always do it this way because we trust each other." Silly me. In my infinite stupidity, I'd presumed to suggest that there might be an alternative to pointing a submachine gun muzzle at a fellow team member's back while "stacked" for a live-fire building entry exercise.

Go ahead, Mr. 22-Year-Old-Hotshot. Double your powder and shorten your fuse.

As Colonel Cooper was wont to quote from his commanding officer in the Marine Corps: "If you want to be stupid, do it in your quarters; don't do it out here."

Complacency is a killer. The only sad (but also good) news about complacency is that it usually causes harm only to the complacent person in question. The "it hasn't happened for 17 years so it won't happen" syndrome is a death-trap. Too many long-time officers are getting hurt or killed because of lackadaisical approaches during a vehicle stop or the old standby: "It's too hot to wear my vest."

I readily admit that I have a brain the size of a pea, but for once I'm going to presume to make a statement, which I humbly but firmly believe to be a non-negotiable fact: Any police officer in America today who doesn't wear a vest is either crazy or a fool—or both.

Yes, it can happen to you. It's happening every day to other officers on a regular basis. If you want to gamble, play the crap tables in Vegas. If you want to keep the edge, leave your money in your wallet. Keep operating on the edge and sooner or later you'll fall off. Become paranoid and you'll drive yourself nuts. The happy medium to the problem is to split the difference, and you'll be all right unless

Lady Luck frowns on you—and there's nothing you can do about that.

I'll let Jon Bon Jovi sum up the situation: "There's no more Joneses to keep up with anymore." But it's also as well to remember that only the mediocre are always at their best.

The Great Shotgun vs. Carbine Debate

There they were—the ultimate pearls of wisdom screaming from the magazine cover: "Single Action vs. Double-Action: A New Look."

Dear Lord, how many times can the same rhetorical subjects be swallowed, regurgitated, and expectorated ad nauseam? "The 9mm vs. 45 auto"; "The Auto vs. Revolver"; "The Ankle Holster vs. Uncle Harly's Undercover Backpack Concealment Rig." All of these earth-shattering subjects have been covered over and over again since the Dead Sea was only ill.

And it's always "a new look." Change the date on the magazine cover and the author's byline, and for the most part we're merely rereading a 30-year-old plagiarized article.

Just for once I'd like to see the Indians beat the cowboys, or see an interstate road sign that reads "Slippery When Dry," "Stale Oil on Shoulder," or "Tight Gravel"—or maybe a new store advertising a "Pathetic Opening" sale.

The latest on-again/off-again debate—second only to the "Point Shooting vs. Sighted Fire" debacle—is the "Shotgun vs. Carbine" argument. This inevitably stems from the age-old question of which specific firearm you would choose if you were relegated to the situation of selecting only one do-it-all, jack-of-all-trades firearm. The blunt answer is either (a) go with whatever tactical situation you are envisioning or (b) there ain't no such thing.

There are pros and cons to all weaponry and tactics. Apart from a pistol, which for the most part can be carried easily and unobtrusively, most other firearms are (to a greater or lesser extent) mission specific. For example, I wouldn't hunt a rogue elephant with an MP5. Then again, being admittedly cerebrumically challenged, I'd never considered using an electric hair dryer in the shower until I read a warning label on said instrument stating that above-stated action "could be dangerous."

It seems like about every five years somebody decides that the shotgun is a dinosaur and "needs to be replaced" with a rifle or carbine.

"You know, all those buckshot pellets flying around, and God help us if somebody misses their intended target with one of the .70-caliber, 500-grain slugs: half the city could be flattened. Besides, the guns kick like a mule, weigh a ton, and are difficult to handle in training," goes the logic.

So the shotgun is ditched and replaced by a carbine because "anyone can hit with one of them puppies." Five years later, after countless bullets have pockmarked city walls half a mile from their intended target, some Einstein clone decides, "Maybe we should have a look at one of them smoothbore suckers; you know, that thing in the trunk with the big hole in front." So the call rings out for the "gauge" again.

Sooner or later someone is going to cotton on to the revolutionary concept that if you don't practice until you need to neutralize your intended target, it doesn't matter what you use. And even if you achieve this rare level of ability and maintain it, doing entry on a dope house with a bolt-action rifle, for example, probably isn't going to bolster your Social Security investment ideals.

Fighting and tactics are mental concepts—the gun is but a medium or tool. Yes, you need the right tool for the right job, but you can't arrive at a solution if you don't understand the problem. And while you can gain information from books and videos, the only true learning academy is the School of Hard Knocks:

man gets old, man bleeds, man learns. Judge Roy Bean was fond of saying that men respect books—"especially when walloped over the head with them." There's nothing like having your nose broken to fully understand the joys of a sinus problem.

And speaking of a problem, the current "fashion" of knife fighting, a centuries-old martial art, is a snowball fast heading for hell if it isn't put into perspective. There's something perverse about waiting for aeons for Sam Colt to design an Equalizer only to revert back to a blade out of choice. The old saying, "A little knowledge is a dangerous thing," has never been more in evidence than with the present rash of rhinestone Clipit Killers wandering around displaying the two or three basic flashy moves that are the mark of an amateur ripe for the picking.

That's tantamount to waving a pistol at someone who wolf-whistles at your date. It's all been done before, and the end result has always been the same. If you don't use your brain, if you don't use the right tool for the right job, and if you don't rigorously train in the judicious combination of both, sooner or later you will lose.

If you absolutely have to yank on the elephant's tail, make sure that you are fully equipped—both mentally and mechanically—to handle the repercussions that will emanate from the other end of Jumbo. He has a long memory and no sense of humor.

The Two Absolutes in Life:

Death and Reaction Time

*I*t's a matter of simple math. There are 5,280 feet per mile. Therefore at 60 miles per hour you will cover 5,280 feet in one minute and 88 feet in one second.

With this as a mathematical absolute, it is merely a matter of division to work out that at eight miles per hour—the pace of a fast-moving adult—one covers approximately 12 feet in one second. This computes to about six feet in half a second.

Having duly impressed the reader of this column with my Einstein-like brilliance, let me get to the point. While many people have heard of the much-bandied-about "21-foot rule," which is hammered home in training circles from a (usually) knife-wielding frontal-attacker perspective, the underlying problem of reacting to a threat seems to be ignored under most other training scenarios.

And here's the kicker: it's not so much that your opponent's speed is so devastating as the fact that, over and above all else, the one thing you cannot control or improve is your reaction time.

For example, you can fool yourself that you can, under stress, perform a one-second reload or malfunction clearance, but the man hasn't been born who can perform said feat when the situation coldcocks you—when it happens unexpectedly in the middle of a confrontation with no cover and at close quarters.

If you have average to above-average reaction time, it will take approximately half a second before it sinks into your brain that you have a mechanical malfunction or have run out of ammo. Bearing in mind that your assailant has already closed distance by six feet in this half-second—as established in the second paragraph of this article—and you still have not physically even begun to fix the mechanical problem, it is obvious that at contact distances you don't have a snowball's hope in hell of neutralizing your incoming attacker with that firearm.

Compare the above situation with the motorist's nightmare:

Driving at 60 miles per hour you travel 88 feet per second. You see a soccer ball roll out into the street 30 yards (90 feet) in front of you. Fearing that a child is in pursuit of the ball, you attempt an emergency stop. Only half a second later does your foot initially contact the brake pedal, because of reaction time. At this stage you have already traveled 44 feet. No car can stop in another 46 feet at 60 miles per hour. Here's the shocker—one second after you first see the ball, the child is a hood ornament on your truck.

Practice to perfection reloads and malfunction drills, but don't delude yourself that it can be accomplished for real without distance, cover, or concealment as an ally. At contact distances it cannot be done. Period. This is tantamount to attempting a 200-yard rifle shot at a springbok running at full tilt (and bounding six feet into the air while he's at full bore). The word *lunacy* comes to mind.

Many people are training for arm's-length encounters with the envisioned scenario being that you are accosted while your handgun is still holstered. While there are viable techniques that may or may not work (as is the case with any tactical situation), the sorry truth is that if someone unexpectedly charges or "spins" on you from three feet, you will not have the time to use said pistol unless you have the luxury to change the angle of attack or can combine the drawstroke with some

other form of physical defense. You're probably looking at a down-and-dirty fistfight instead. This is not to be confused with a situation where you smell the potential of trouble and can gear up for it, even though your reaction time is still a constant.

Erratic lateral movement of an assailant or hostage holder is another aspect where reaction time can get you into trouble. If you insist on practicing on pendulum-type targets that can be "tricked" or "led" like a clay pigeon, sooner or later you will light up the wrong person in the street.

Unless it is a sniper/predator situation where you can pick and choose the time and place for the enemy to walk into your bullet, there is only one way to deal with movement. The firearm has to be maintained on target all the way through the firing cycle up to and including the follow-through stage until target neutralization has been achieved. This is a basic tenet of marksmanship, be it bull's-eye shooting or a defensive gunfight. If you try to "beat" the target movement and "snap" the shot, you will hit where the target "was" before reaction time weaves its deadly web.

I've been told of a "charging" target system whereby the operator yanks the target straight into the shooter from close quarters at about 20 miles per hour until the target frame base cracks the shooter on the shins—the operator all the while telling the "trainee" to verbally challenge the target continuously and perform an obligatory automatic failure drill (two body shots followed by one to the head) on a piece of cardboard.

I have two humble suggestions. (1) To the shooter: if this happens for real, go for the biggest piece of meat and bone you can hit and get the hell out of the way. You don't have the reaction time to get fancy. (2) To the "instructor": don't play pachyderm games with people's lives until you've seen the elephant somewhere other than the San Diego Zoo.

There are only two *real* absolutes in life—death and reaction time. You can face your personal reaction time as an absolute that must be worked around, or you can delude yourself into a false sense of security and hope that the Grim Reaper appears disguised as a stationary Pepper Popper.

Eight Reasons to Avoid One-Man Searches

Let's try it again—hopefully, for the last time: you cannot safely negotiate or search a building on your own. While fortune favors the brave, and the good Lord apparently suffers fools gladly, it's not worth betting your life that you'll be one of the Chosen Few.

Training in the science of one-man tactics can net you only two advantages: it will school you in the rudiments of tactical movement—such as not crowding blind corners and not skylining yourself against backlit areas—and it will give you a last-ditch tactical edge if you lose or become separated from backup personnel. For both these reasons it is essential to your training curriculum, but to be misled into thinking that you hold one whit of a snowball's hope in hell when walking alone onto someone else's battlefield is absurd.

If you can't maintain control of your surroundings, you're running primarily on luck—and sooner or later every gambler runs out of that commodity.

The two most utilized senses in a building search are sight and hearing, with vision undoubtedly the more important of the two. While olfactory and tactile stimuli can help one to maneuver and locate a possible suspect, for the most part in civilian or law enforcement applications, you can't deliver force or contain a situation unless you can see what's transpiring. If you can't identify the enemy, you can't toss in the ol' grenade and just hope for the best, unless it's an out-and-out military conflict where both the enemy and allied locations are absolutely, positively known. Too many well-intentioned good guys have nailed family members or other "allies" because of lack of target identification.

The biggest problems with one-man tactics are not so much the actual physical encounter with the bad guy(s); that part of the scenario will have an absolute black or white result one way or the other if there is force applied from both sides. Either you win or lose, and that's all she wrote. On the contrary, the problems are (a) to locate the transgressors while all they have to do is lie in wait and (b) to contain the situa-

154

tion on your own until help arrives. And this latter is a big problem if deadly force has not been applied.

Any time you want to see how stupid you look or verify how easy you are to take out while you're engaged in a lone "Kevorkian Kommando" house search, invite an acquaintance or friend to act out the part of the bad guy and see how long you last. Then reverse roles and watch the curtain go up on Act Two of "How to Commit Suicide 101."

As mentioned above, you may very well have to do the honorable thing and beetle off into the setting sun on your white steed to rescue a family member, or if you lose your support personnel, but all you can do with single-person tactics is cut down the odds against you by a couple of percent. No more, no less.

Why is it so difficult or ludicrous to go it alone, as opposed to having more manpower? Assuming that the scenario dictates moving with stealth—and I can't imagine any homeowner situation that is worth your life to require this (unless it entails withdrawing from a potential danger area, and that's a whole different ball game), there are various aspects over which you have no control. Let's face it—if your daughter is screaming bloody blue murder from her bedroom, you're obligated to advance quickly, such as on-the-move, where you can maintain control but still cover ground within a minimum time frame. Navigating through your house at a snail's pace under these circumstances is obviously ridiculous—but here you have to go.

However, having decided that you are obliged to so-called stealthily investigate the inevitable scenario—"The

Noise in the Night Downstairs in My House for Which I'm Prepared to Commit Suicide"—we come down to the salient points of why you will immediately become sucker bait. And these boil down to the aforementioned aspects over which you have no control.

Number one: "You possess one tiny pair of eyes and one gargantuan rear end."
You cannot cover 360 degrees at any given moment. Ergo, wherever your eyes are looking is diametrically opposed to where your rear end is a potential bull's-eye. It is all very well to say, "I have to check everything before I advance further." Unfortunately, while you're checking the clothes closet, you're nuked in the back from under the bed or from the bathroom or from behind an interleading door. So either strap a pair of rear-view mirrors to your shoulders or cancel number one.

Number two: "All I have to do is stay clear of blind corners and steer wide of them as I slowly 'slice the pie' and negotiate my way around them."
So who's watching your back while you're executing these maneuvers as you wind your way through your 10-room, two-story house? Bearing in mind that blind corners are not necessarily only walls but include furniture, doors, refrigerators, etc., we can cheerfully cancel number two.

Number three: "It's my house; I know the floor plan and I can control the lighting."
In a swine's optical organ you can control the lighting. Maybe you can some of the time, but most of the time during daylight hours you can't. And if it's after sunset, that cozy fire burning in the living room hearth is going to

155

play hell with your game plan. If you turn on the lights to override the fireplace illumination, the intruder knows where you are. If you leave the lights off, the flickering shadows from the embers will look like a thousand specters before you finally lose your mind with the adrenaline pump and start emptying your 12-gauge at the ghosts of your imagination.

Light and shadow are close to being the two most dangerous problems to overcome when you're alone on a hunt, and throwing a shadow or causing a dark area to lighten are each as dangerous as the other. If either natural or man-made lighting will cause your shadow to be projected either forward of your avenue of entry, laterally onto a wall or furniture, or, for example, underneath a door, you're sunk. If the intervening structure between you and your enemy isn't hard cover, he knows where you are without having to physically see you and will drill you through a wall or door. He's not concerned with the niceties of target identification—if he's hostile, you're done, and you'll never see it coming.

Ever tried moving across a furnished room while an accomplice spots reflections for you? Reflections on concave TV screens, reflections on glass-fronted stereo consoles, reflections on overhead brass chandeliers and ceiling fans, reflections on lamp stands, reflections on kitchen cooking ware, reflections on microwave oven glass fronts, reflections on soda cans, reflections on door knobs and mirrors, and on and on ad nauseam. That's a helluva lot of reflecting.

As for the "I know the floor plan and he doesn't" idea, how do you think he came into your house in the first place? He knows at least half of your house layout as well as you do.

Cancel number three.

Number four: "My reaction time is not a problem."

Having finally tracked down Mr. Badbuttocks, all that remains is to pop open the closet door, identify him, analyze whether he's armed or a threat, and then make a decision whether to shoot or not.

All of this in under half a second from a brain exploding with adrenaline and a sphincter the size of a pinhead. With nobody to open the closet door for you, you are forced to compress your thought processes into analyzing a situation in a fraction of a second from a distance of two feet. There's a loud yell; all hell breaks loose; you focus on a Halloween mask and shoot.

Nice going, Sherlock. Your sister's going to be ecstatic when she finds out you've just wasted her practical-joking drunk husband. Chalk up another family tragedy—and about 25 years in the Big House.

Cancel number four.

Number five: "I can keep my cool. I collared me a couple of unarmed, stoned burglars, and now I've got them right where I want them—and without shooting."

Yup. And a lot of dogs chase cars and don't know what to do with them once they catch them either. If those two brain-dead drain plugs don't immediately capitulate, hog-tie themselves to each other, and magically transport themselves by teleportation to the local hoosegow, you're in trouble.

Because now a conversation starts, escalates to an argument, and reaches the stage where even their cobwebbed IQs realize you're bluffing with the gun. So they outflank you and call your bluff. Now you have to double-bluff by shooting them.

And next week, in a lot of jurisdictions in the U.S. of A., the judge is going to ask you why you didn't attempt to retreat from your house if you suspected a threat, as the law requires in some states. And when you don't have a vestige of an answer, he'll put you behind the Wall for a long, long time.

Cancel number five.

Number six: "Too bad. He shouldn't have been in my house. I'll put one of my kitchen knives in his recently deceased hand. That'll fool the cops!"

Oh yeah. Your last business venture was probably opening a kosher deli at the Vatican. Number six goes out the door.

Number seven: "I know they're downstairs. I'll creep down the stairs and then work out a brilliant battle plan."

If ever there's time when you are mandated to look in two directions at one given time, it's while descending or ascending a stairwell, staircase, or stairway. Lie down at the farthest point from the top of the stairs, such as at the front entrance to your home, and see how much success you'd have if someone was lying there in wait for you during your descent.

So far the score is Lions 7, Christians 0.

Number eight: "The outdoor arroyo training scenario."

It's instructive, it's a learning experience, it's a test of marksmanship, one

learns rudimentary tactical movement, but it's an impossible mission.

Asking a lone hunter to blithely murder half a dozen steel targets in 15 minutes in a huge expanse of terrain just isn't going to happen for real. He's a sitting duck, and that's all there is to it. End of story.

The reason this outdoor training scenario has been lumped in with the first seven examples is that there are several common denominators: you may be pushed into a situation beyond your control, where you are forced to use tactics that wouldn't, under normal circumstances, be anywhere near your first choice. A lone military sniper, for example, often has to traverse large areas of terrain to reach his objective; he is often successful if he can control his mind and body to move at a pace so slow and tortuous as to be beyond the realm of the common man.

A military man unintentionally separated from his allies may be in a similar situation, but he may or may not have to move faster in retreat, as might the sniper on withdrawal from his completed mission. Unlike a special unit dropped in behind enemy lines, the lone military man cannot afford a firefight with enemy troops.

Lone law enforcement officers, for a variety of reasons, are often forced into employing plan B from the get-go— usually because of lack of manpower on duty. Nobody forces an officer to choose law enforcement as a vocation, but once he takes on the job his life is on the line day in and day out for precious little money, no thanks, and a toss-of-the-coin future.

This is what makes the homeowner's house search so stupid. Unless it's a situation akin to the "screaming daughter" scenario, he has the *choice* of not looking for trouble. He has two tactical variables that he can employ:

1. If he is forced to do the hero act because violence is imminent, he has to throw caution to the wind and act and move quickly, but under control.
2. If there is no immediate threat, there is absolutely no intelligent reason to "find that SOB downstairs and teach him a lesson."

If there is, indeed, the potential of physical violence, let him/them come to you, at your convenience, on a battlefield of your choosing, where you hold all the aces. Law enforcement is restricted on manpower. Response time varies, and you may have to deal with the problem yourself before help arrives. That doesn't mean you have to provide the "fools rush in" routine.

To safely clear one room in an average house will take a lone hunter more than an hour—and once you exit the room you don't own it anymore; if you return you have to retake the area all over again because you have no tailgunner. Ergo, if you want to "clear" your home while maintaining maximum safety unto your epidermis, it will, at best, take six or seven hours, and you're still not sure the "ghost intruder" hasn't circled around onto your back trail. If ever there is an exercise in futility and stupidity, this is it.

People get away with it every day, and more power to them. However, a quotation comes to mind: "Genius has limits; stupidity doesn't."

The Object Is to Win—
Not to Fight Fair

*I*t all began about a thousand years ago when I started boxing. After going through the requisite battering before some small modicum of sense was beaten into my thick skull, I finally managed to dump an opponent onto the canvas. It took a long time after that initial victory to discover the whys and wherefores of my success on that occasion when I'd been beaten to a proverbial pulp in prior fights.

I knew I was quick, I knew I had fast reflexes, and I knew I had a good right hand—but I'd still lost those early bouts. Then I finally found the common denominator: although all the prior opponents had obviously been under the same weight limit constraints and of the same approximate age, the above-mentioned pugilist who assumed the horizontal position was the first I'd come up against in the ring who was of equal height and reach as I.

After all the punishment sustained, Mr. Smallbrain came to the brilliant conclusion that a boxer with a 60-inch reach can't fight an opponent with a 66-inch reach from 66 inches. Pure genius. What I'd been doing was punching the 66-inchers on their fists, cunningly using my 60-inch face as an impact weapon. It had taken a lot of blood, sweat, and tears to realize that I had to move inside the taller adversary's reach, cause damage, and get out fast.

Unfortunately, boxing was, and is, governed by rules of conduct prescribed by some idiot Marquis of Queensberry who decided that it was better to be a gentleman who resembled raw hamburger meat than to be a dirty, unfair (and unmarked) fight winner.

Then came high school and the adolescent fights behind the gym hall with the damsel in distress as the trophy. I won that one too—I hit him from behind before he'd realized the fight had started. Naturally, the lady in question wanted no part of either of us, so I had no Dulcinea. But I also had no Marquis of Q.—and my nose was intact, complete with its full capacity of blood. I duly gained the disrespect and disgust of the school populace. I lost at least two minutes' sleep fretting

159

over that one—but I never had to fight at school again. Nobody wants anything to do with a lunatic.

Years later in the military and during ensuing decades of weapons and tactics training and instruction, I came to realize that the only battles I'd ever won had been won, wittingly or unwittingly, fair or foul, predominantly by *tactics*.

If you have only a 60-inch reach and Mr. Drainplug has 66, you'd better have a game plan. It's all very well having a quick, fluid drawstroke with your pistol. But while it's essential, the Samurai could do that with his sword 300 years ago. If you carry only one pistol, you'd better have a lightning weak-hand drawstroke perfected. That's one of the reasons why the ninja carried more than one weapon. It's the singer, not the song.

Obviously, equipment can make a big difference to the outcome of a fight, but without tactics you're starting off five seconds down on a standing eight-count. If a knife is all you possess to take to a gunfight, you'd better get in real close or, failing that, utilize cover and/or concealment to remove thineself from the battlefield—since tomorrow's another day.

If you decide to use a knife against a gun when you have the choice of tactically withdrawing, do your dependents the courtesy of leaving enough money to pay for your funeral. Don't saddle them with the financial burden resulting from your stupidity and misguided bravado. If your name isn't James Coburn and the words "Magnificent Seven" don't ring a bell, don't try to beat a gunman with a knife when he's calling the shots (no pun intended).

On the other hand, if you are armed with a pistol and he's wielding a knife,

you'll still lose if you screw up tactically. In a contact-distance situation the weaponry becomes almost irrelevant— "No brain, no gain." The last of the 36 military strategies of ancient China, colloquially translated, suggests that you "haul mule" from the scene to fight another day. You can always exact vengeance later.

So much emphasis is placed on the weapon and accessories during weapons training these days that tactics have become almost nonexistent. Probably the most predominant weapon in this field is the handgun, with particular attention paid to the drawstroke, target acquisition, and the resultant discharge of said firearm, all conducted from a Weaver or isosceles shooting platform.

The problem is that, for the most part, the assumption is made that the opposition is at standing elevation facing straight on to the good guy. Virtually no attention is paid to the fact that either the target(s) or the shooter— or both—could be moving, at different elevations or angles, or situated in dim light or on rough, uneven terrain.

So you can slam two rounds from 10 yards into the chest area of each of three International Practical Shooting Confederation (IPSC)-style paper targets in microseconds. So you have marksmanship. So whoop-de-do. The 64-caliber question is—can you fight?

News flash: if three people are standing facing straight on to you 10 yards away, you probably have no business lighting them up in the first place. And even if you do have some justification, and if you somehow plant the two "miracle" hits in the terrible trio's chest cavities (which, incidentally, almost never seems to materialize in documentation and mortuaries), the chances of all three immediately desisting from their foul intentions are extremely remote.

Just because you luck out and vaporize somebody's heart and lungs doesn't necessarily mean he'll be stopped in his tracks. He may even die in a short space of time, but the object is to immediately shut down the threat, not to kill—at least in a "conventional" defensive situation anyway.

So it's back to the ring and one Charlie Weir, a middleweight boxing acquaintance. He was, like Mike Tyson, a one- or two-round knockout specialist. He had a punch like a mule and eventually fought Davey Moore for the world title. Moore won in a long, drawn-out brawl. When I asked Charlie what had happened, he told me he'd set up his opponent like all the others before him, landed his Sunday punch—and nothing happened. He had no backup plan, and when Moore smiled at him he knew he was going to lose the fight.

He was never the same boxer after that.

There's a saying that if somebody outdraws you, smile and walk away—there's plenty of time to look tough when you're out of sight. And it's also said that you can't tell how good either a man or a watermelon is until you thump it.

It's 30 years later, and I'm not salivating at the mouth anymore to find out how good I am. What I'm trying to do is use whatever tactics are available—fair or foul—to avoid personal loss of blood. The modern pistol is wonderful, and so is the Weaver stance. But the Weaver stance is merely a rifle shooting position that has been used for a long time. It was also used by American Indians for centuries to shoot the long bow and by boxers.

The Indians "lost" because they played by the rules and signed treaties with people who had no intention of honoring the script. The majority of boxers lose because they fight under regulated Marquis of Queensberry rules. Neither lost because they used the excellent Weaver stance. The former lost because they displayed trust instead of fighting dirty; the latter lose because they are not allowed to fight dirty.

If you want to win, you use intelligent, dirty tactics—or don't fight. Take your choice: you can be a world champ or a thumped watermelon; there's no in between.

Setting Your Sights on the Right Tactical Accessories

*T*he plethora of tactical accessories available in recent years to aid dim-light and night-shooting capability is a definite plus, but a caveat must be put on the intelligent use of this equipment.

While flashlights affixed to firearms are nothing new (the Owl—a handgun system—was in use in the early 1940s, and shoulder-mounted weapon accessories were available before then), ongoing research and development has resulted in outstanding products, such as those of Laser Products, among others. This has made it much easier to achieve tactical control of a situation via enhanced target acquisition, identification, and neutralization capabilities.

The one downside to the whole shebang is that it still requires an operator who is blessed with an IQ of at least double—and preferably triple—digits. It's not only the car's horsepower, it's the nut behind the wheel that decides the outcome of the race. The real marketing genius wasn't the inventor of the Pet Rock; it was the Johnny-Come-Lately who sold $5,000 diamond-studded leashes for those who wanted to take their Pet Rock for a walk around the block.

The current corollary of that leash is the laser-dot sight. While there is a definite application for a laser-dot system under specific tactical circumstances, seeing an advertisement depicting a laser system mounted to a snub-nosed revolver accompanied by the words "Accurate to 300 yards" leaves one gasping in awe at the prowess of the test-firer. Most people today can't shoot a six-inch group with a sniper rifle under perfect range conditions in broad daylight, let alone with a snubbie. And speaking of broad daylight, that little red dot just isn't going to be visible at any "reasonable" distance.

That doesn't mean everybody shouldn't rush out and buy one for only half a million dollars per unit—especially when you get a free blender and a bottle of car polish if you order it before midnight at the 800-number listed on the bottom of your TV screen. It also doesn't mean that you shouldn't derive hours of pleasure taunting your cat by flashing

Laser Products integral flashlight fore-end mounted on a Remington 11-87.

the dot on and off and watching him go nuts trying to catch the red or green dot—or possibly shining it into your buddies' eyes so they can sustain permanent retina damage and sue your buns.

What the laser dot is good for is specific situations such as punching through smoke where a flashlight beam would merely bounce back, akin to headlights in fog, or—for example—where a conventional sighting system couldn't be used because you have a set of black sights overprinting on dark clothes in a dim environment, or where a "normal" shooting position would force you to give up too much cover.

Laser-dot systems have to be zeroed to the weapon's point of impact. They will not help identify a target, and they will not compensate for poor trigger control or follow-through. They are also hell to keep locked on a moving human adversary, they can visually pinpoint the shooter's position, and—the last piece of good news—if more than one person

has his laser trained on the same opponent, how do you know whose weapon is aimed where? The popular laser is, therefore, in this author's brain-dead opinion, primarily good only for out-of-the-ordinary assignments such as those conducted by special response teams— or for annoying your cat.

The flashlight, on the other hand, makes the one-eyed man king in the land of the blind. Second only to the firearm itself, it is probably one of the most important accoutrements necessary for those who frequently carry, use, or expect to possibly have to use a gun in a defensive role. You cannot hit what you cannot identify—legally, morally, and, for the most part, tactically. While it is a tremendous asset to your fighting equipment, it can also be your death knell if it isn't used intelligently.

There are two variations commonly taught with one-on-one flashlight gunfighting. System A entails turning off the illumination and stepping laterally after firing the weapon (the obvious objective being that if your opponent is not out of action he won't know where you are). System B suggests leaving the light on until help arrives, enabling you to "own" or control the downed adversary.

Unfortunately, as with all tactics, there are pros and cons to both techniques. If you turn off the light you'd better be absolutely sure beforehand that the terrain will indeed allow lateral movement—otherwise you'll be jammed in the initial location without eyes. Additionally, sooner or later you'll have to turn on the light a second time to see the result of the conflict—and guess who's going to win this one if the bad guy isn't out of action?

On the other hand, if you don't kill the illumination after discharging your gun, there'd better not be another enemy in the vicinity or you'll be blindsided by number two and never see it coming The above scenarios presume that gunfire did erupt; if it did not, you have a bigger tactical problem of controlling the situation, because you now have a fully operational enemy who may or may not re-escalate his initial violence. And if you have to resort to nonlethal force to resolve the problem, it becomes difficult with a pistol in one hand and a flashlight in the other—and almost impossible with a shoulder weapon. Try accomplishing this trick with a pump shotgun and a remote flashlight.

Hitting the target can be done relatively easily. Controlling any tactical situation is an entirely different matter.

There is only one guaranteed solution to the above: a permanently attached flashlight is mandatory for serious work with a shoulder-fired weapon. A combination of pressure momentary and "click" on/off switches wouldn't hurt your chances either. That way you have all your bases covered.

Tritium sight inserts are another invaluable innovation. Relatively modern, they will allow you to shoot with surgical precision as long as you have enough ambient light to identify the target(s). Their sole detraction seems to be that they are visible from above and behind the shooter from a distance. On the other hand, if your adversary is above or behind you, you're probably a "gone dog" anyway.

Available in different "bar" and "dot" configurations, tritium sights vary greatly in quality from manufacturer to manufacturer. As with most things, you generally "gets what you pays for."

Dim-light and night tactics are a critical part of one's training curriculum. There is, for the most part, an innate human fear of the dark. It's one time in a fight where high-quality, sturdy weapon accessories can help turn the tables.

Use only quality equipment pertinent to your envisaged potential battlefield—and leave the damned puddy-tat alone!

Who Needs All Those Gizmos?

*T*here's an old legend of the bird born with one black wing and one white. Not being overenamored of his physical appearance—and wanting to appear cosmetically perfect—he proceeded to chew off one of his wings. The good news is that he attained his monochromatic ideals. The bad news is, of course, that he lost a bird's greatest asset, the ability to fly.

On the training range over the last decade there have appeared so many gadgets and gimmicks affixed to firearms that oft-times it's almost impossible to actually identify a gun buried among all the junk bolted, screwed, and glued to the basic weapon. The "Beware the One-Gun Man" adage has held true for over a century, and in a real fight it will continue to do so for at least as long as most of us retain our mortal coils.

We're our own worst enemies and never more so than in the recent misguided practice of trying to replace brain power with technology. What's scary is that it's no longer the backyard mechanic who's the "modification maniac"—now everybody's jumping on the bandwagon.

God forbid somebody should buy a new pistol, swab out the barrel, and actually shoot it. Instead, it apparently has to go to half a dozen gunsmiths to be throated, polished, beveled, checkered, ramped, and "accurized"—all for the princely sum of your firstborn's college funds. And if you're rolling in the green stuff you can add on some "essential" gizmos like lasers and recoil reducers.

This is not a reflection on gunsmiths or manufacturers of equipment. But there seems to be a direct correlation between the ace street performers who always seem to be running well-maintained (but simple) hardware and the also-rans with rayguns from hell. This is also not to say that there have not been some advances in technology, such as the Wickert pistol ghost-ring sight and Pattern Master's brilliant shotgun choke, but most are merely regurgitated decades-old proven ideas.

If you don't like black feathers on one wing, get a can of white paint. Keep on nibbling at that black wing and you'll find aerodynamics don't

Stock H&K P7 pistol alongside Robar-modified Glock 26.

apply when you have only one remaining wing. In other words, *if it ain't broke don't fix it.*

There is a definite need in military and law enforcement special operations for specialized equipment, but that's where it ends. For the most part, the only other place where absolute precision equipment is required is on a Camp Perry-type marksmanship range. Unfortunately, precision instruments are all too often too fragile or impractical for everyday carry and use.

It started with the "accurizing" of handguns. A defensive pistol that reputedly will shoot into two inches at 50 yards is simply ridiculous, especially when it's usually accompanied by a reduction in factory reliability. First of all, nobody can shoot a two-inch group at 50 yards with a handgun in a fight—

in fact not many people can shoot a two-inch group with a rifle from 50 yards free-standing in broad daylight on a target range. And, second, most accurizing entails "tightening" the reciprocating parts of the weapon to the stage where lack of functioning reliability becomes unacceptable for serious battle.

By the time you've removed all the fancy high-dollar junk from the weapon to get it to actually function, there're usually enough parts left to build a turbocharger for a Ferrari.

Closely following the accurizing rage is the recoil and muzzle-flip reduction gadgetry. While some of this equipment may indeed reduce muzzle rise or recoil, one's time and money would probably be better spent understanding (a) the difference between muzzle rise and recoil and (b) the finer points of how the human hand operates and the benefit of an effective shooting stance and firing grip.

If a 90-pounder can control a 12-gauge and a 12-year-old can shoot a .45 auto, there's no reason why the average adult needs five pounds of trash and a barrel that looks like Swiss cheese to deliver accurate, continuous fire from a shotgun, rifle, or handgun—unless he is shooting a big-bore heavy rifle or physical stature or hand size prevents a decent firing grip or shooting stance.

Of course, because people are perverse by nature, the first thing most of them fit to a pistol is a set of oversized rubber stocks, which immediately compounds the problem for many shooters with average-sized hands. A classic example of this is the current spate of prophylactics that are appearing on the ubiquitous Glock—a pistol that is

already too big (or almost so) for many hands. Rare indeed is the man whose hands are so big—à la "Cop Stuff's" Chris Pollack—that he actually has to have a "beaver-tail" on a Glock to prevent "slide bite."

Are oversized pistol stocks necessary for some people? Yes. Do muzzle brakes sometimes serve an effective purpose? Yes. Are laser dots needed in some tactical scenarios? Yes. Is there a need for some weapons to be accurized? Yes. The operative words are *some* and *sometimes*.

For the majority, most of the time, it's usually just a fad. No computer will work if you don't know where the "on" switch is located.

It's your wing, and it's your beak. If you want to chew off the wing, that's your prerogative. It's merely a matter of a pinion.

How to Protect Yourself at Your Most Vulnerable

Fornication, defecation, and urination are probably not the most tasteful of subjects for discussion in this book. But it is a fact that, for the most part, when man lets down his foundation garments—for whatever physical reason—he invariably synonymously lets down his guard.

Encompassed in a warm cocoon of sex or personal waste product disposal, one tends to concentrate on that one specific activity to the exclusion of all others. And for centuries man's enemy has taken advantage of this behavior. A dog, for example, will circle several times and "sniff the wind" before opening the bomb bays. Humans, on the other hand, head for the first available latrine in a crowded rest room, hell-bent on instant relief to the exclusion of everything else.

Again, this subject is not the ideal dinner table discussion when you're trying to impress your newly introduced future in-laws, but if you're serious about personal defense it deserves tactical consideration sometime during your "what if" training regimen.

Any public rest room is a tactical nightmare. There's usually only one entrance/exit, so if you need to beat a hasty retreat your egress can invariably be easily blocked. The doors and separating walls on individual cubicles are a joke—not only can they be broken down by a 10-year-old, they hardly ever stretch from floor to ceiling. This obviously means that you can be smacked on the cranium by someone standing on the adjacent pot and leaning over the intervening communal wall, or your legs can be jerked out from underneath you by the simple act of someone grabbing you by the ankles through the gap underneath the door or adjacent cubicle dividers. And there are two simple rules to human geometry—(1) wherever the head goes on a vertical takedown, the body will follow, and (2) if your feet are jerked out from underneath you, the body will follow. So in the above scenario, the best you are looking at is having your wallet or valuables snatched. The worst case is cracking your skull on the pot if someone violently yanks your feet toward the cubicle door.

Another potential ray of sunshine is the technique whereby the door is smashed in and you are immediately upended and given the old royal flush. Any way you look at it, once you begin egestion you lose mobility, with a correspondingly large percentage of your ability to fight.

So here's the good news: the content of public bathroom graffiti is often poetic and entertaining and helps to while away the time. The floors are often polished to enough of a degree where you can see the "lowdown" ankle assault coming by means of reflected shadows. And by reason of what they are designed for, there is usually a multitude of mirrors in front of the wash basins that will enable you to keep an eye on your current companions.

If you are male (or female and weird) and use one of a bank of several adjacent urinals, the most preferable would be an end unit alongside a brick corner wall. That will give you at least one side that is protected from attack. Logically, if you're armed and right-handed, the far right urinal is probably your best bet; a pistol can be drawn and used more easily from this location than most any other. Virtually any other attack in a public rest room when you don't have advance warning is probably going to end with whoever is the better tactical ground fighter being the victor.

Reverting back to the potty cubicle for a moment, if you are armed with a handgun, don't place it atop the cistern behind you where it can be seen by your neighboring Peeping Tom and where you don't have immediate access to the weapon. Don't lay it on the floor for the same reason, and if you're wearing a law enforcement Sam Browne-style rig, don't remove the entire rig en

masse and hang it on the back of the cubicle door. If you can't work out the last one on your own, it's probably time to change occupations.

A relatively safe pistol depository in the above situation is in the "hammock" formed when your foundation garments are lowered to ankle level. This places it in a position of quick access and keeps it reasonably hidden from sicko prying eyes.

Port-a-johns are a holdover from centuries-old cesspits and outhouses and are an absolute death trap, as can be attested to by people who've had practical jokes played on them by their buddies while using these facilities. You are open to attack from six sides, though these days the sixth side (à la the ninja technique of lying in wait for your enemy to answer nature's call and then skewering him from below) would probably be extremely rare.

The bottom line with any publicly accessible rest room/bathroom is get in, do your business, and get out as quickly as possible. It's like boxing: the longer you hang around, the better your chances of sustaining a beating.

Your own private john at home is tactically easier to control, because you will have more time and distance to read the situation—and because Mr. Baddie has to come to you on your battlefield. Forewarned is forearmed—keep a weapon where you can reach it fast from a seated or standing position.

The shower stall/bath, however, is a different kettle of fish. You are, to all intents and purposes, blind, probably half asleep or at least in a relaxed state of mind, and are often in the process of doing your best Pavarotti imitation at a million decibels.

Extremely difficult question: do you

think Mr. Rapist might possibly be able to work out where you are located from the sounds of running water and "Nessun Dorma" and then perform his own version of a Hitchcock *Psycho* thriller? You can't see because of the steam, you can't hear because of your opera antics, and you can't shoot because the pistol you so cunningly left in the shower stall for five years for just such an occasion is now rusted and the ammo is waterlogged.

Nobody from this side is suggesting you religiously wash your carcass with the latest designer gun-on-a-rope, but have a plan. If your plan is, indeed, a firearm, it needs to be in a water/steam-proofed container and immediately accessible. How you do that is your problem—but there are ways. But the same system had better work in an unfamiliar motel room as well. Having some illumination system to backlight your attacker's approach may also warrant looking into.

The last subject covered in this admittedly crude—but in this author's opinion, necessary article—is the sex act. If you have sex with someone you don't know or trust, see ya and good luck. That's about as vulnerable a position as any into which you can place yourself.

If, on the other hand, you tell your wife to shut up while she's yelling your name in ecstasy "because you have to pay attention to what's going on out-side"—bad move. You do that when she's yelling someone else's name in ecstasy. How you get around this prob-lem has to be a mutual decision and it has to be discussed and planned before the situation arises, just like any other tactical game plan.

As stated above, when man takes down his pants he often takes down his brains at the same time.

If you are killed in a toilet it has to be one of the most degrading ways to die. If you are killed during sex, at least you die happy.

But guess what? Either way you're dead.

We're All Gonna Die— Get Used to the Idea

*F*rom the day you're born, you start dying. You may get a couple of years, you may get 50 or even a century, but nobody is immortal—and you know this almost from day one.

So why are most people so afraid of death? Let's face it, in the middle of a gun battle nobody is thinking, "Oh, God, I may he wounded in an arm or foot!" You're probably thinking, "If I lose this one I can finally shrug off the IRS (or words to that effect)." You're thinking of two things: winning and dying. Throughout history, achievers and heroes have attained their success from one, two, or all of three things: ability, willpower, and ignorance. Ability is a necessary attribute that speaks for itself, but over and above that, it's a tossup as to whether you win because of willpower or ignorance. The man who keeps on trucking against all odds is probably going to get to the winner's circle sooner or later simply because he won't admit defeat.

The "ignorant" person who doesn't know when he's beaten is a totally different kettle of fish. A bumblebee, for example, cannot fly. A physicist can prove that flight is impossible for this creature. The only problem is that bumblebees don't go to school and they don't study physics—so they fly anyway.

The three most dangerous opponents you can ever face are the man who doesn't care whether he lives or dies, the man who doesn't know when he's beaten, and a madman. Nobody ever wants to mess with a lunatic—leastwise not if you have one iota of common sense in your skull.

Someone who cares not one whit about whether or not his life is about to be snuffed out is usually a religious fanatic or an extremely dedicated soldier (like a samurai warrior or kamikaze pilot). Or his life has reached such desperate straits that he literally has nothing left to lose. You can't bluff him, because he's not listening to what you're saying and even if he does listen he just plain and simply doesn't care. You may be a dog lover, but if Fido is foaming at the mouth, crazy-eyed, and about to rip out your jugular, it's not because he's swallowed a couple of Alka-Seltzers—you have to kill him if you want to survive.

Ignorance of the depth of the surrounding feces pile will always be trouble for the good guy, irrespective of whether it's you or your opponent who's displaying a lack of knowledge of how much trouble is brewing. Obviously, if you become complacent, overconfident, or simply unaware, you're probably going to lose the fight. The same would equally as obviously apply to an opponent who's exhibiting the same traits, but in an enemy in the context of this article we're not discussing the same traits—we're talking about somebody who doesn't know when he's whipped. Cut off one of his arms, he punches you with the other. Chop off his remaining arm and he kicks you. He doesn't know when to quit because he doesn't understand that he's supposedly already beaten. So he becomes a flying bumblebee, and you're the puzzled physicist—and in a lot of trouble.

How do you get through to this person that he's beaten? You don't. You destroy him because you have no other choice; he doesn't speak the same language of reason you're trying to use. Not because he doesn't want to, but simply because he's ignorant of your method of reasoning and the only way you'll get through to him is by tissue or neurological destruction.

The last and—in this author's opinion—most dangerous enemy you will ever run into is the madman, the lunatic, the crazy man. Not only is he a combination of the first two because he doesn't care if he wins or loses, nor does he understand when he's beaten. In addition, he's like a mad dog and will take you down with everything at his disposal until he runs out of breath or blood or both. Added to this is the fact that, despite the connotation of words like *madman* and *lunatic*, this one is no fool.

Socrates said that there's a fine line between genius and madness, and it works both ways. The madman may be regarded as a fruit loop by society, but he can revert to genius in an instant. The 250-IQ physicist, on the other hand, still can't work out bumblebee propulsion, even though he can launch rockets into space.

The main thing the so-called madman has going for him is that society at large often doesn't comprehend him or his mental processes—and is always scared of him. And once you feel fear you're starting from the back of the pack. Adrenaline often kicks in under stress and could provide the last kicker needed to win a fight. The problem with dealing with a crazy man is that much of his mental imbalance, killer instinct, and cunning can stem from an adrenal problem, so he's ahead of your game anyway, wittingly, or unwittingly.

The average person will use verbiage like "Leave me alone or I'll kill you," but he doesn't *literally* mean it. The loony will say it and mean it. There are some people you just don't mess with.

So we're back to the initial problem of fear of death and/or pain as evidenced by most people when trouble is imminent. If you don't have bile, anger, or a killer instinct to override your Shakespearean "distill'd almost to jelly with the act of fear" temperament, you have only two choices: you can either

WE'RE ALL GONNA DIE—GET USED TO THE IDEA

transform yourself mentally into a simulation of one of the three bad ones until the fight's over, or you can face the sorry fact that if you ever run into one of them you're probably going to lose. And you can't fake it. If you're rich, have kids, and a lot of fancy toys, there's no way you can *pretend* you have nothing to lose.

You're going to die sooner or later anyway. If it bothers you that much and you're hoping for longevity, stay away from the battlefield. Don't try to snow the snowman.

Keep It Simple, Stupid

About 20 years ago, several of my brilliant tactician cronies and I were approached by a young lady who was, by today's definition, being stalked.

She was a night-shift nurse and lived alone in an apartment. The situation had degenerated to the stage of the pervert in question following her home from work, attempting to peer through her frosted-glass bathroom window, and making telephonic threats about what he envisioned doing to her "one day."

Law enforcement was, naturally, powerless to do anything until after the fact, and after several fruitless and disappointing discussions with police officers, the lady in question contacted us omniscient geniuses to help her entrap the drain plug who was making her life a misery.

Our skull sessions ran the gamut from lying in wait for him (with the end objective being a crippling beating) to discussing the rigging of "jackal guns" to her apartment door and windows. (A jackal gun is usually a shotgun rigged with a trip-wire to the trigger, often used by sheep farmers in Africa to knock off sheep-butchering jackals.) It eventually permeated even our thick skulls that this would be regarded as, at best, assault or, at worst, premeditated murder—no matter how noble the cause. In a flash of brilliance one of us actually had the foresight to realize that an innocent party might take a load of buckshot. I'm surprised none of us thought of using claymores.

To cut a long story short, before we'd managed to contrive or carry out some idiotic version of the Charge of the Light Brigade, the nurse called to inform us that she'd come up with her own plan, it had worked, and the weirdo had been arrested in her apartment and was in jail.

What she'd come up with, looking back 20 years later, was pure genius. In an age when rotary-dial telephones were the norm, she'd connected cotton thread from both of her apartment windows and the door to a pencil. She would then, immediately after entering her apartment after work, dial all the digits to the local police precinct and jam the pencil into the phone dial, not allowing the dial to return counter-clockwise after dialing the last digit.

So when the idiot eventually invaded her apartment by way of a window, he tripped the thread, which popped the pencil, which released the spring-loaded dial ring, which allowed the phone to "self-dial" the local precinct. With the mouthpiece off the receiver the cops were there in a matter of minutes, with the pervert still running his mouth.

The moral of the story is that she solved the problem with about three brain cells and cotton thread. The Claymore Clowns had used about half a brain cell and were hell-bent on killing a mosquito with a 10-pound hammer. While I personally don't feel that there's any such thing as overkill on a battle-field, I do feel that in this case Florence Nightingale got the job done with a lot more finesse and a lot less blood and gore than her supposedly more experi-enced tactical confidantes—and with no legal or moral repercussions.

If you believe in the "forewarned is forearmed" axiom, there are various ways you can set up your house, car, or personal environment, based on the Nightingale principle. The object is, of course, to give you lead time to either prepare for or read a deadly-force situa-tion, or preferably to avoid or escape the situation altogether—unless you're psycho and enjoy the sight of blood and gore. If the latter is your choice, remem-ber that sooner or later you'll run into the man who outwits and outfights you; then you'll be admiring your own blood and guts strewn across the carpet.

Nobody's suggesting that you attach a length of cord from your house doors to your pit bull's eyelids every night upon retiring, but there are inexpensive

forewarning devices available—some built specifically for that purpose, and others that can be constructed from simple hardware and a little thought. Bear in mind that any auto or house-alarm system designed by man can be outwitted by a man. The KISS principle works every time. A simple rubber door wedge that slips between the door and floor will give a home or motel-room invader a lot more trouble than a dead bolt or safety chain. Horizontal venetian blinds that are closed with the slats fac-ing up allow you to observe outward and downward, while not allowing an outside observer to look into your domicile at normal eye level. Closing the blinds with the slats facing down, as most people are wont to do, reverses the good guy-bad guy advantage.

Many years ago I worked at a mechanical plant that required that employees keep personal valuables in a locker room. Unlike most of the other staff, I never had the misfortune of hav-ing the contents of my locker stolen. This was possibly due to the fact that I kept the hasp shut with a huge pad-lock. What nobody knew was that I never had a key for the lock but replaced the hinge pins on the opposite side of the door with drop-in hardware store nails. When it came time to open the door I merely had to slip out the nails, open the door, and leave it sus-pended by the hasp.

If you can't dazzle them with bril-liance, baffle them with you-know-what—learned that one from "the pur-loined letter."

Because sound is probably the num-ber one giveaway of an intruder's pres-ence, something that will alert the homeowner's auditory senses to a break-in can be a valuable addition to your box of tricks. While there are exotic alarm systems available, they can be taken out of commission as easily as telephone lines and, for that matter, the entire house's electrical circuitry. A simple battery-operated gizmo, such as a Halloween electronic-eye-operated toy, is totally portable and won't be detected until it's done its job. It can be positioned anywhere, but the batteries must be regularly changed, and obviously it must be placed where the family pet isn't going to trip the light sensor five times a night. Another simple trick is to place a musical birthday or Christmas card where it will spring open when tension is released from the front cover, such as in a doorjamb or in the nook of a sliding window. Simple, but effective.

Of course, you can always use a booby trap wired to a neutron bomb, but in an urban domicile or hotel room these violent pieces of equipment often end up hurting the wrong booby (usually an innocent third party), and they are, for the most part, illegal anyway. Don't act stupid and don't fight stupid.

Tactics always have pros and cons, and whenever possible both sides of the tactical coin should be studied before you decide on your game plan. If, for example, you feel that it's a good idea to turn on the courtesy lights in your car by remote control so you can ensure that nobody's hiding in the car awaiting your return in a dark parking lot, at least consider the fact that you could be a proverbial clay pigeon for any drive-by skeet banger once you enter the car.

Similarly, taping out the door-operated pressure switches won't leave you hanging out to dry every time you enter the car. If you have to scan the car from outside, carry a flashlight—it should be a permanent piece of your daily carried tactical equipment anyway. If you need light once you're inside the car and in a safe location, that's what map and manually operated dome lights are for.

Simplicity is the key to survival. A fancy gadget that doesn't work is a non sequitur. Low-key and plain equipment will work every time if coupled to an operational brain.

Forewarned is forearmed; and forearmed is forewarned.

"You Gotta Have Heart"

Not often at a loss for words, former Israeli Prime Minister Benjamin Netanyahu was floored by a question from his young son: "Which is more important, the heart or the brain?"

Piqued by curiosity, the battle-hardened father asked his son to answer his own question. The youth replied that the heart was more important "because the heart will always work."

Out of the mouths of babes . . .

While tacticians, strategists, and soldiers have preached for eons that the mind is the most critical tactical tool—and it unquestionably is—apparently even a child can see that it doesn't take much stress for one's brain to turn brown, sprout wings, and fly off into a black abyss of paralysis like the mythological Turd Bird.

The point is, of course, that the human brain is an absolute criterion for success on the battlefield—but it takes very little for the operational mind to come to a staggering halt at the worst possible moment.

Ostensibly, you train so that you can react reflexively to any and all circumstances in a fight. Clichés such as "Fight like you train" have stemmed from the above objective, and as long as the fight goes as planned and as long as your training has covered the parameters of what occurs on the battlefield, all is fine and dandy.

Unfortunately, there are very few battles that come to a conclusion without Murphy's Law intervening in one form or another. The great military generals have always maintained this through the ages, but it was perhaps most succinctly phrased by boxer Mike Tyson, who said, "Everybody's got a game plan until you're hit in the mouth."

We'd all like to believe that we're cool and unflappable under pressure, but unfortunately this just isn't true all the time, every time. There's always someone out there waiting in the wings who's better than you are, and if he has the psychological ability to bruise the Achilles' heel in your mind, he will beat you. You can maintain a level of training and preparedness that will enable you to be the eternal Mr.

Expert Hell on Wheels, but you cannot outfight an enemy and yourself. It's like shadowboxing—you're in a lose-lose fight. A sparring partner is one thing, but trying to outbox your own shadow is a joke.

Once your brain is supplanted by the Turdie Birdie, you have only two things left—intestinal fortitude and luck. And don't crack a rib holding your breath thinking that luck will run on your side. That leaves intestinal fortitude, bravery, or—in little Netanyahu's terms—heart. The will to win.

Again, clichés come to mind: "No guts, no glory," "Fortune favors the brave," and several more. The bottom line, however, is that, while ideally one should have both heart and an agile mind, it is easy to beat a chicken heart. It is not easy to beat the man who won't quit.

All of the aforementioned inevitably lead to the, "Well I've been down the road, and nothing fazes me, and I can keep my feces coagulated" self-proclaimed legend in his own mind. This one's going to end up a ferryboat operator on the River Styx. If you've never been "paralyzed" with fear sometime in your life—however momentary—you're not human. Somewhere, sometime, someplace it's going to happen—assuming that thus far it hasn't occurred.

The bad news is that you have to continue operating until your thinking brain kicks back in. Once you over-rev an engine that's fitted with a governor, you have to back off on the throttle until the revs drop down to the usable power band where the motor will kick in again. But this does not mean that you stomp on the brakes or take your hands off the steering wheel—you'll

lose the race. It's easy to just say that you shouldn't over-rev the motor in your brain, but how much incoming fire are you taking? How many times have you been cut in the last three seconds? Talk is cheap. If battles were fought with lips, we'd all be omnipotent warriors.

In this author's opinion, firearms training should be run ideally on a three-stage basis.

Stage one would encompass safe, basic weapon handling, manipulation, and marksmanship and constantly revert back to basics. Forget the fancy high-speed, low-drag tricks—basics are what it always reverts to and what will get you through when your brain freezes.

Stage two would cover tactics and techniques and fighting from "unconventional" range situations and would include drills and circumstances that would force the trainee to handle scenarios with an instructor-induced destroyed brain, so the trainee would understand that operations like split-second reloads and malfunction clearances, when unexpected, are pure myth.

Stage three would then rebuild the trainee to where he would have a running chance in the street or on the battlefield, by fair means or foul (preferably foul) with or without a firearm. Then all he would need to win a for-real fight is about 90-percent luck.

Yes, the mind is all-important for fighting, but if it's out to lunch when you're attacked by the Breakfast Bandit, you'd better have some other organ operating to carry you through until your mental revs get back onto the power band. And that organ may very well be the heart.

Jonathan Netanyahu's legacy lives on in his nephew.*

* Editor's note: Jonathan Netanyahu, the brother of Benjamin Netanyahu, was killed in the raid at Entebbe, Uganda, in 1976, in which Israeli troops freed 103 hostages being held by German and Arab terrorists aboard an El-Al flight.

Seeing the Forest *and* the Trees

Sometimes we can't see the forest for the trees. And whatever may seem obvious at first glance might not make too much sense after further deliberation. Much has been made in past articles of the mythical mid-fight, half-second malfunction clearances, reloads, and, in general, simplistic answers to tactical problems. While these comments were, and are, obviously merely the personal opinion of this author, even I am not dumb enough to state something as absolute fact unless it is, indeed, indisputable fact that can be proven beyond a shadow of doubt.

Unquestionably, subsecond reloads and malfunction clearances can be accomplished when they are set up on a preconceived basis, such as on a stipulated range training drill or even at a predetermined stage of a real fight. Unfortunately, they cannot be done within the same time frame when one is forced to perform one of these tasks unexpectedly—for one plain and simple reason. Reaction time is reaction time is reaction time.

You can froth at the mouth, you can refuse to admit it, or you can practice until you can navigate through Hades on ice skates, but you cannot improve your neurological brain-to-hand reaction time. Which means that if you run out of ammo and you need a speed load in a fight, you can automatically tack anywhere from two-fifths to three-fifths of a second on to your lightning training range times because you didn't know it was coming in advance.

So your half-second speed load has now taken a full second from shot to shot, as opposed to half a second. And if you think half a second is no big deal, try your luck with somebody like Phil Messina in an average-sized room. An originator in the study of reaction time at room distances, Messina, or any of his instructors, will clean your clock from 20 feet if you give them an extra half-second slack.

Guess what? The extra time is a given—you have no control over it, you cannot decrease it, and no amount of training will improve it. You have to accept it and train on the basis that "if I run out of ammo at close quarters I am going to do X, Y, or Z." Do not kid yourself that you can accomplish an unexpected speed load in under a second.

This is not the personal opinion of a loud-mouthed Monday morning quarterback running his mouth. This is fact. Period.

Of course, to circumvent this problem you can go on the basis of continually shooting until the weapon is empty and then automatically speed loading. Supposedly this will cut out the "brain freeze" of an unexpectedly nonfunctioning weapon. Here come the forest and the trees again . . .

One military unit that trained on this principle is now operating one man short. In fact, he's so short, he's dead. He shot his weapon to slide-lock and then executed a perfect speed load. The only problem was that his 16-shot pistol had disgorged only 12 rounds before a double feed occurred. Understandably, in the heat of battle, the shooter obviously figured he had run dry, attempted to reload a malfunctioned pistol—and died.

As far as malfunctions are concerned, your mind-lock reaction time is exactly the same. The good news is that some of the time the actual malfunction clearing time might be faster than a speed load, so sometimes the overall shot-to-shot time might be quicker. The bad news is, of course, that sometimes it might not.

It might be as well to remember that a perfectly legal, unloaded roulette wheel in a Monte Carlo casino once turned the same color 27 times in succession. Don't gamble with your life unless you're honestly ready to die or you'll end up in a crapshoot (no pun intended).

Another bone of contention is the whys and wherefores of the tactical use of equipment in dim-light shooting situations. Here it is, plain and simple:

1. Tritium sights don't help you one whit to identify a target. They enable you to shoot with precision once you've identified the target.

2. If the tritium dot is inserted halfway down your front sight and you place the top of the metal front sight on your desired point of impact in normal light conditions when shooting, you need rear-sight tritium inserts that will give you the same point of impact in dim light when front and rear tritiums are aligned, or you will shoot high in poor ambient light.

3. A shoulder weapon that has an attached flashlight should have either a firing-hand-operable pressure switch or an on/off click switch available for the support hand. You can hit a target with a support-hand-operated pressure switch. You can even hit a target with a hand-held flashlight operated by the support hand. But you cannot tactically control a situation with a shoulder weapon, without backup personnel, using either of the latter two techniques.

4. Last, but not least, the ubiquitous laser dot. While lasers and ray guns from hell will obviously be the norm in the 21st century, with the advance of technology, at the date of this writing the "magic" dot is currently in limbo. In this writer's opinion, there has been only one rational, intelligent tactical study conducted on the use of laser-dot equipment attached to hand-held firearms. It was done by Anthony Rosselli and several other officers of the Anaheim, California, Police Department, and it paints a dismal pic-

ture when the pros and cons are weighed against each other.

Books, let alone one article, can be written on a plethora of subjects based on the "forest vs. the trees" subject, such as the "this bullet beats that bullet," "this gun beats that gun," "these tactics are the only way to go," and on and on and on. The bottom line is that nobody cares, and it doesn't matter.

What does matter is that you, the individual, scramble all the informa-tion, and then you make a decision on what you feel will work for you when the pooh-pooh splashes on the wall. We're often too quick to accept others' opinions on blind faith because we don't want to face the thought of enter-ing the woods.

You may see a forest, you may see trees. Either way there's a pile of branches, leaves, bark, and twigs in front of you—and we're rapidly running out of chain saws.

What to Do if You're Attacked on Your Motorcycle

One of the few true pleasures in life is piloting a high-powered motorcycle on a warm summer day. One of the many miseries in life is being shot off a high-powered motorcycle on a warm summer day.

While four-wheel defensive driving/shooting courses are a dime a dozen, defensive driving/gunfighting techniques for motorcyclists are few and far between in training circles. This is possibly because there are many more car and truck drivers than two-wheelers, but it is just as likely a function of the fact that few people understand how complicated it can be to fight from a motorcycle.

As with so many other things in life, Hollywood has influenced people's thinking to the stage where common sense has run the gamut from the sublime to the ridiculous. How many times can you watch the classic wolf pack scenario of rampaging motorcyclists swinging chains at the victim's car windshield before you realize that a two-ton car can force an 800-pound cycle off the road at the auto driver's slightest whim?

On the other hand, how many motorcyclists have thought through the tactics and ramifications of a rolling gunfight before it occurs? Although a "static" fight (with both shooting parties stationary) is neither amusing nor common, trading projectiles while your vehicle is moving is a nightmare. Obviously, the logical (and commonly taught) technique is to ground the motorcycle and use it or something else for cover. This works like a charm on range-orchestrated practice drills, but hog heaven becomes piggy purgatory if you try this when under attack at speed on a freeway. If road rash doesn't get you, an 18-wheeler will.

There are huge differences between shooting from a moving car and shooting from a moving motorcycle—pro and con. The one common denominator is that it is impossible to keep track of both target and backstop if you're attacked from the side—it's called the theory of relativity (otherwise known as "hit the wrong target if you're in heavy traffic").

The other downsides to shooting from a moving car or truck are a limited arc of fire because of the confines of the vehicle and the possi-

Returning right-side fire from a moving motorcycle is a tactical nightmare unless mechanical modifications are made to the cycle.

bility of being hit with stray shards of metal or glass from either your own gunfire or that of the enemy. Your hearing ability will also suffer some form of permanent damage if you trigger rounds from inside an enclosed vehicle.

The primary advantages motorcycles have over other road users are maneuverability, outstanding brakes, and a much more efficient power-to-weight ratio—this last delivering instantaneous acceleration. Unfortunately, all three of these positives can just as easily become negatives. Two-wheelers, because of gravity, won't stay vertical for long without drive to the rear wheel. Cut loose of the handlebars and the machine falls over once rolling speed has been sufficiently reduced, or if the tires slip on gravel, sand, road marker paint, oil, water, etc., so you can cancel on the "look ma, no hands" gunfighting technique. Even if you merely pivot your

upper body, gravity will dump the machine if you are running without at least one hand on the bars.

Here comes more bad news: all the horsepower and almost three-quarters of a motorcycle's braking power are controlled by the rider's right hand, which, for most people, is also the gun hand. Ergo, if you pull a pistol right-handed at average road speed, you are left with about 25 percent of your braking power (foot-pedal-operated to the rear wheel) and a quickly-decelerating cycle because you no longer have the ability to throttle up.

Of course, you could launch into your poorman's imitation of a *True Grit* John Wayne by holding the handlebars in your teeth, operating the throttle and brakes with your left hand, and firing your pistol right-handed. While you're at it, you could also jam on the cruise control, do a headstand on the gas tank, and kiss you rear end farewell—because that's what this whole shebang is coming down to, unless you prepare ahead. And, as always, there are ways of cutting down the odds . . .

A long time ago in a far-off land, an acquaintance found himself lined up in a lone highwayman's rifle sights. Having rigorously trained in the art of firing a pistol from a moving vehicle, he drew his Hi-Power, spent almost too much time trying to go through the rigmarole of sight alignment and sight picture on a bumpy country road, and was suddenly struck by an earth-shattering idea. He canceled on the Browning plan, tramped on the gas pedal, and was rewarded several seconds later with a new hood ornament for his Land Rover.

So much for the fancy stuff—it doesn't work in a for-real fight. And so much for thinking you can gunfight right-handed from a rolling motorcycle, unless you make a teensy-weensy $10 mechanical alteration to the motorcycle. All-terrain vehicles have a lever-powered throttle mounted on the handlebars. This simple device can be mounted to the left side of a motorcycle's bars, and the cable can then be spliced via a junction box to the cycle's factory-installed cable, somewhere ahead of the carburetor(s). With this modification you have the availability of either left- or right-handed throttle operation, while the return spring on the main cable will still be strong enough to snap shut either unit to avoid over-revving or to allow hands-free deceleration.

You still don't have your braking advantage, but you've now retained two of the three motorcycle advantages with the addition of a simple mechanical device. And two out of three are better odds than zero for three.

If you're normally left-handed, you're obviously streets ahead of the game—your pistol is ready to hand, and you should be conditioned to one-handed shooting. If you're right-handed, you're back to the, in this author's opinion, tactical absolute: carry two guns. And you'd better practice the Hades out of left-handed shooting—even more than if you didn't ride two-wheelers.

Should the above text strike you as the equivalent of Monty Python's Flying Circus, here's a poser: If you're so concerned and serious about defensive firearms training, home defense, vehicle (car) defense, and all de udder fences, why shouldn't you be as concerned just because you're on the Harley and not in the Chevy? Defending yourself while on a rolling motorcycle is probably one of the most dangerous games in town—if not the most dangerous. Like the man said, "If you fail to plan, you plan to fail."

One caveat about using a downed motorcycle for cover: I've owned and ridden motorcycles for 37 years—including a couple years of racing when I was younger and even stupider than I am now. *Not once*, after dropping a machine, did I fail to see gas leaking out of either the carburetor overflow pipes or the gas tank cap breather vent. If there's any other hard cover you can get to fast, use it.

Like everyone else, I'm concerned about how many miles per gallon I can get with my motorcycle, but I'm a lot more concerned about how many gallons of burning fuel I consume per incoming ricochet.

Buyer Beware:

Selecting the Right Tool for the Job

A man walks up to a parrot and says, "Hey, stupid, can you talk?" Parrot says, "Yes, stupid. Can you fly?"

So what does the human genius do? He immediately goes home, loads up $20,000 worth of bass boat, and heads off to the lake to outwit a fish. No wonder sharks and cockroaches have been around for millions of years, and we're approaching the state of genocidal self-extinction.

Face facts: parrots can learn to speak because they have a brain and vocal chords. Humans will never be able to fly unless God sticks pairs of wings on our backs. There are times when you plain and simply can't get the job done without equipment.

What follows are some personal opinions—be they perceived as intelligent or dumb—on the use (and possible misunderstanding) of two items of equipment commonly used in conjunction with today's battle firearms.

PISTOL HOLSTERS

A holster system for a handgun is as vital an accouterment as a sling is for a shoulder weapon. Unless you've been forced to use extremely deep concealment or have chosen one of the "alternative" tactical systems such as Barami Grips or a string Mexican carry system, a $10 holster is a poor companion for a fighting handgun. Unfortunately, on the other hand, you don't always get what you pay for with expensive holsters either.

A couple of years ago, I had occasion to trash a big-name expensive holster after three days and somewhere between four to five hundred drawstrokes. It should have been left on the cow's rear end from whence it came. Now, every time I see that manufacturer's holsters for sale, I cringe—sooner or later somebody's going to die using one of them.

While there are good-quality, leather holster makers still out there, the shooting world lost three good ones—Sparks, Nelson, and Shoemaker—too fast, too soon. Buyer beware.

Although the recent trend has leaned towards either Kydex or ballistic nylon, the same buyer rules apply. Almost as much thought must be applied toward the acquisition of a holster as the weapon it will encase. There's a fair amount of Kydex trash on the market, the same as with leather—and I'm too cerebrally interrupted to understand how a piece of nylon becomes "ballistic" simply because it's molded into the shape of a holster. Buy what works for you, but it had better work every time, relevant to your personal tactical requirements and lifestyle. The greatest pistol in the world is useless if you can't access it.

In the same vein, while fanny packs have progressively improved in design and development, in this author's opinion ladies' concealment handbags are still way behind the power curve. This is possibly due to the fact that they are primarily designed by males—combined with the fact that concealed-carry laws and the large-scale, brutal victimization of women are relatively recent phenomenas, creating a market that didn't exist prior to societal breakdown. There are women who can draw handguns extremely quickly from a handbag, but it's a two-handed operation requiring perfection in its execution—it's an upstream swim all the way. There is a dire need for improved equipment in this field.

The bottom line with any holster is (1) if you need two hands to free a pistol from its receptacle, you could be in a lot of trouble, and (2) while most everybody should have a holster system that, for tactical reasons, will allow quick, one-handed reholstering if the need arises—for law enforcement officers the latter is an absolute.

It's the same old song. On the practice range, most every time you draw a pistol, you shoot. On the street, it's invariably the reverse, and you may need to reholster fast—especially in a law enforcement environment where the situation de-escalates more often than not, requiring less lethal physical means to solve the problem.

FLASHLIGHTS

During a recent conversation John Matthews, designer and manufacturer of the excellent Surefire series of flashlights, told me that many people don't understand what constitutes the difference between a well-designed tactical light and a $5 dime-store torch.

Like a holster, a flashlight is complementary to a weapons system and should be instantly to hand, even during daylight hours. Probably second only to body armor in the field of lifesaving tactical accouterments for serious social applications, a flashlight must have a solid bright beam with no dark patches or distortions.

The purpose of a white-beamed tactical light is threefold: to positively identify one's surroundings, to provide a "pure" background for optically perfect sight alignment and sight picture in the event that shooting is required, and, last but not least, to contain the situation whether or not gunfire occurs. Some lights, such as the Scorpion, put out a tremendous white aura for the overall flashlight size but are handicapped by spidery dark patches in the center of the beam. This can be solved by the simple expedient of slipping a five-cent fiber washer between the bezel and flashlight body, which alters the distance between bulb and reflector and results in a pure,

187

bright light. Needless to say, attempting to silhouette your gun's sights against a murky beam is not conducive to accurate shooting.

For serious gunfighting with shotguns, subguns or rifles, it is mandatory that the tactical flashlight be affixed to the weapon. While these weapons can be fired one-handed while a remote light is held in the support hand, this is a half-buttocked system at best and is no way to go to war. You can certainly hit a target using one of these bastardized systems, but you cannot fight like this unless you're either crazy or suicidal—or both. And you cannot control a situation like this, after the shooting, unless you were born with three hands. The sorry end result will probably be that you will shoot somebody who doesn't need shooting, because physically you have no other way to solve the problem. You've just run out of hands, time, lawyers—and a life outside prison walls. For some obscure reason, unnecessary indiscriminate shooting of nonlethal citizens is frowned upon in modern society.

A caveat on one of the "bastardized" systems mentioned above: the Laser Products Sure-Fire line of flashlights will provide intermittent light at the operator's discretion by squeezing the flashlight sideways against a shoulder-weapon fore-end—if the tail cap is screwed up to the stage just before the light stays on permanently. (The tail cap was initially designed to be either turned clockwise for permanent light or a rear push button depressed for an

intermittent light beam.) I'll mention here that I discovered the squeezing "trick," and I mention it not to receive the planet's accolades at my genius but as a warning. It is an absolute emergency system only. What several instructors have subsequently failed to tell people is that sooner or later, whether under weapon concussion or while operating a slide-action fore-end during multiple-round firing, the tail cap will turn slightly—either clockwise or counterclockwise. You will then be in the predicament of either having illumination when you don't want it or of not being able to attain illumination with the sideways "squeeze" when you *do* want it.

Another warning: a flashlight that does not have a cushioned bezel designed to withstand the rigors of recoil will sooner or later blow a bulb. When your world goes black, don't blame the manufacturer. You don't go four-wheeling in a Lamborghini, and you don't take a Hummer to the Daytona 500. If you have nothing else and it's a matter of do or die—if you don't use the squeeze system or something like a half-baked version of the Mike Harries handgun technique while operating a shoulder weapon, then so be it—you have nothing to lose.

But if you do have a choice, use the right tool for the right job. Maybe I'm not too bright, and maybe I can't fly like the parrot. But I'm also not locked up in a cage with useless wings, walking around on a sheet of newspaper, covered in my own feces.

Good Enough Is Simply Not Good Enough

Sir Henry Royce, cofounder of the illustrious Rolls Royce car factory, lived by the following credo: "Take the best and make it better. If it doesn't exist, create it. Accept nothing nearly right or good enough."

Most long-time firearm owners have—albeit unwittingly—abided by this principle, to the extent that many of us possess enough boxes and containers so filled to the brim with discarded aftermarket parts that we could probably put Gun Parts Corporation out of business. All in an oft-time futile attempt to chase the Rolls Royce rainbow.

Even after buying the "perfect" gun that will meet one's tactical, physical, and social needs, the "improvement serpent" inevitably rears its ugly head, and the race is on. Sometimes it entails respective modifications to factory internals or externals, such as a trigger job or different sights. More often than not, equipment is altered, such as substituting a set of personalized pistol stocks for factory originals.

The sorry truth is, apart from the obvious fact that the weapon should fit the shooter's physique, the only essential requirements on a battle firearm are reliability, a manageable trigger, and sights compatible with the shooter's optics. The point here is not so much that most of the junk added to guns doesn't improve fighting performance or potential, it is that it can sometimes be downright dangerous to the user's mortal continuum.

While it is self-evident that hand size varies widely, causing different people to feel comfortable with different pistols (except maybe John Browning's Hi-Power, which seems to fit everybody), unnecessary pistol stock modifications can be detrimental to one's tactical marksmanship—and health. A classic example is the person who has average-sized hands and who promptly slips one of the ubiquitous rubber "socks" onto the handle of the already gargantuan Glock 21. No matter that he now has a useless firing grip on the weapon and can't reach the trigger. "At least the sucker won't fly out of my hands when they're wet."

It's amazing that pistols never fell out of shooters' sweaty little paws until rubber handgun condoms were invented. If it works for you that's fine, but somehow I have visions of the dog ringing the bell and Mr. Pavlov answering the door instead of vice versa.

Several thousand rounds of expended practice ammo, plus the useless process of drifting the sights halfway off the pistol's slide in a fruitless attempt to cure a huge windage drift, finally leads to the condom joining the rest of the aftermarket parts in a huge cardboard box in the gun room.

Another common feature found on Browning-designed pistols such as the Colt and Para-Ordnance in recent years is the Detonics-style lowered thumb safety. This is to attain the opposite result of rubber overstocks—in other words, to "diminish" the size of the factory firing grip. This is sometimes fitted in conjunction with the removal of metal from the front strap or with slimmer stocks. The big joke, however, is that they are most often found on handguns that have been modified to accept a high beavertail grip safety. This safety allows a high hand position on the pistol, which is a crucial aspect of a good firing grip. Combining this with a lowered thumb safety, however, often succeeds only in promptly lowering your firing grip back to where it was if you'd stayed with a standard thumb and grip safety. There's the mutt ringing the doorbell again.

Naturally if the combination is compatible with your hand size or you need a beavertail grip safety to avoid "hammer bite," more power to you. But you'd better be absolutely sure when firing the pistol left-handed that the knuckle connecting the left-hand trigger finger to the hand doesn't push up the thumb safety enough to disallow trigger/sear operation. A mere 1/16-inch upward movement of the safety will cause this malfunction And if you think you'll never have to fire your pistol left-handed—irrespective of whether you carry two guns or not—maybe it's time to stop packing a gun altogether.

A pistol is not a security blanket—it's a defensive tool. Any tool that doesn't work when required is a useless lump of metal.

Another peculiar fad that has evolved primarily with magazine-capacity-restricting laws is the extended magazine buttplate, which allows a "firmer" grip with the little finger of the shooting hand. While these have existed for years on semiautos like Walthers, many of them were factory installed to facilitate magazine removal from pistols fitted with a European-style heel-clip release, as opposed to a springloaded, side-mounted magazine release button.

All that you will get from squeezing the little finger is screwed-up marksmanship—the strength in a semiauto firing grip comes from the middle finger. This is automatically weakened when the little finger is compressed.

Somebody please answer the door—there's an angry, impatient dog outside.

"Take the best and make it better. If it doesn't exist, create it. Accept nothing nearly right or good enough." Nearly right is not right, and good enough is simply not good enough. If it ain't broke, don't fix it.

Running Backward Will Get You Nowhere Fast

Well, I'm confused again.

If an elephant charges you, you don't back up (unless it's a mock charge) because you can't outrun him. If a lion charges you, you don't back up because you can't outrun him. If somebody tries to run you down with a truck, you don't back up because you can't outrun him.

While I'm admittedly a far cry from Sherlock Holmes, even I can work out that a human cannot move as fast backward as he can forward. If this were not the case, I'm sure Carl Lewis would be running Olympic events backward to improve his times.

So either my last remaining brain cell has followed its predecessors into a void in the Great Beyond or I'm apparently missing something else in my tactical logic synapses. It is currently commonly accepted in some close-quarters defensive training circles that you can escape the wrath of an enraged, onrushing assailant by the simple means of judicious backpedaling with your hind paws.

Here's a huge secret: you can't escape an eight-mile-per-hour charging lunatic by retreating at two miles per hour. If you hear a lion burping, it's not because he has gastro problems—he's just dined on something that tried to avoid Simba's dinner menu by running. He's bigger than you; he's faster because he's using forward motion and impetus; he has a fecal attitude and no sense of humor. All you have is a tactical brain and maybe some form of weaponry other than your hands and feet—and that's a big maybe.

If somebody jumps you from seven or eight feet you won't even have time to draw a pistol unless you have the luxury of lateral or diagonal movement. Moving straight to the rear isn't going to cut it because your reaction time is anywhere from two-fifths to three-fifths of a second behind his action. Ergo, no retention protection time for your holstered pistol unless you're angled to your assailant. People had this worked out 5,000 years ago. Why can't we understand the principle today?

There are, as always, a myriad of tactical solutions to the above problem, but one is a given—you can't retreat at 2 or 3 mph from a piece of paper on a smooth-surfaced firing range, admire your couple of good hits on the target delivered from a "ready" position, and think this will immediately incapacitate an enraged attacker in a for-real confrontation.

Of course, there are close-quarters firing and withdrawal techniques, and they, like everything else, should be rigorously practiced. But it must be understood that if we're talking about a single human under attack from another who is rapidly approaching at close quarters, these drills are Utopian in nature and will work only if you are very, very lucky.

In this author's opinion—and at best this entire article is obviously only personal opinion—the same range solution is often being utilized to handle two totally different tactical problems.

Problem one is the above mentioned, where quick backpedaling is probably tactically suicidal anywhere except on a level, designated training range. It is also not a brilliant idea to start hauling your mule in quick rearward motion when you have backup partners expecting you to be going forward. All you need is to collect a team member's bullet in the back of your head on top of your other problems.

Problem two is a situation where you have more distance, reaction time, leeway for variables of maneuverability, and cover and/or concealment. Here is where the backing-up technique is more viable because you are maintaining control or delivering projectiles—but the withdrawal can be conducted under much less duress and complexity than in problem one and is performed at a slower pace.

There are many alternatives to consider, a couple of which follow for the reader's perusal. If you believe, as this genealogically interrupted author does, that you're going to be pounded into the deck by a 250-pound, knife-wielding maniac, one alternative to consider is the "best defense is a good offense" syndrome.

In other words, go into him and do damage from close quarters—but right in his face, inside his striking distance. Before you say that nobody but an idiot heads into an enemy as opposed to withdrawing, bear in mind that we're talking about somebody who is moving a lot faster than you can retreat. You cannot defy the laws of math and physics.

It keeps coming back to the same bottom line: you can't escape a knife-wielding, doped-up windmill when he has every advantage—tactical, physical, mathematical. It's also possibly worth mentioning that your magic bullets may or may not kill him, but the criterion is that they probably won't immediately incapacitate him—this latter is what you're trying to achieve. He can't fight with a broken windpipe, but he can continue forward progress with a couple of bullets in him, dead on his feet.

Another option is to drop to the ground and either shoot or foot-fight from there. Let's face it, if you're going to kiss Mother Earth anyway—you may as well do it out of choice and own the battlefield. The ground is not the worst place from which to deliver bullets or foot and leg strikes. This goes along with the scenario where you've been punched to the ground, start shooting from a supine position at close quarters, and then immediately work your way back to a standing position.

Unless you're being sniped at from a relative distance by additional assailants, why are you standing up? You're not a boxer trying to beat a 10-count. Stay on the ground if you're winning!

An obvious caveat to shooting-upward-from-ground-level techniques is the acute angle of trajectory that the bullet path will follow. Needless to say, delivery of projectiles from and at these angles—be they straight on or laterally delivered to the assailant—can be a tremendous terminal-resting-place concern in the street if there are misses or overpenetration. And on a firing range the backstop problem is immense. The onus is obviously on the instructor or self-trainee to make absolutely sure that both the backstop and fields of fire are 101-percent safe.

Admittedly there is a quotation that immediately comes to mind when the "best defense is a good offense" adage is brought up, and that is "a good run is better than a bad stand." However, while quotes are being tossed around, another one to temper both of the above is the good old "those who can do, do; those who can't, teach."

Call your instructor while somebody's gutting you out and see if he answers his phone.

Knowing Your Limitations— and Capabilities

Fine feathers make fine birds. Unfortunately, the finer your feathers, the more your enemies want to pluck your plume. While the strutting peacock has a supposedly built-in deterrent of simulated "eyes" when his magnificent plumage is fanned, nobody is particularly interested in the peacock, save maybe a peahen selected for an amorous ritual. Any human interest in the peacock is restricted to the bird's feathers. And even cold and wet, this peafowl can probably survive bald.

The ostrich, on the other hand, is a strange anomaly, comparable to humans when it comes to a fighting mind-set. Within reason, he has the tools and wherewithal to win most of the time, but often loses because he is not aware of his inherent capabilities. Most people lose a fight not because of lack of capability but because they beat themselves. You cannot outfight yourself and your enemy—and we are our own worst enemies. Assuming that there are no rules of engagement involved, there are very few humans who cannot be outwitted, outpunched, outkicked, or outshot in mortal combat. And anybody who self-imposes rules of engagement in a deadly-force confrontation is a fool.

To steal a line from a Clint Eastwood movie, "A man must know his limitations." The corollary to this is that you also have to know your capability. If you overrun your limitations, you will lose. If you succumb to fear and uncertainty, you will lose. The tricks are to find out your maximum and minimum potential before you have to utilize them and to then stay within the parameters during a fight. That's why there are Grand Prix drivers who consistently win races, and there are other drivers who have the same inherent ability, but blow up one perfectly sound engine after another, never seeing the winner's circle.

Back to the ostrich . . .

Unlike the pretty-boy peacock, the ostrich, for the most part, is raised in captivity so that most of his body parts can be used for man's various pleasures. For over a century, his plumage has been used in the Western world for fashion adornments and feather dusters. Most of the

194

body meat is converted into steaks, sandwiches, and jerky (or *biltong*, for the South African readers). The feet become mounted table adornments, and the eggs are used for food—one full-sized egg provides enough breakfast omelets for eight to 12 people.

And the good news for ostrich farmers is that he will eat literally anything—glass, rocks, etc. So he is the perfect example of total subjugation by another animal (man)—providing food and entertainment while he's alive (eggs and surrey/piggyback races), and providing food and trinkets when he's dead (meat, feather dusters, and hat plumes).

The operative phrase in the above-mentioned is "raised in captivity." Because he's raised in captivity and subjugated from birth, the ostrich doesn't know his own fighting capability. If you think a fighting cock can do damage, you need to see the trail of blood and gore an enraged Big Bird leaves behind. He has the power, the weapons, the size, and the speed. You can't outrun him, you can't outmaneuver him, and you sure as hell can't outpunch or outkick him. One frontal kick will disembowel you from throat to crotch.

But all you have to do is drape a hood over his head, and he'll stand totally stationary, meek and mild as you please. This quality in ostriches is amusing to humans, but in the Western world, we are also "raised in captivity." Like the supposed (and incorrect) legend of the ostrich burying his head in the sand, humans do exactly the same. While the ostrich syndrome presumes that if he can't see a threat with a buried head, there is no threat, humans fresh from the womb pull the bed sheets over their heads to make the bogeyman disappear. But maroon an

adult human in a dark forest—or house, for that matter—and you can almost hear him sweat. The human feels safe in a self-made, dark cocoon, but is terrified if someone else induces darkness upon him. Like the bird, it's merely a state of mind. So much for what "civilization" has done for the Fighting Man.

A predator who wins by his prey's self-inflicted defeat is almost as wryly amusing as naming the Audubon Society after a kill-crazy man who shot more birds in his lifetime than any other man before or since.

An ostrich will stand on a railroad track, mesmerized by a locomotive's headlight until the train runs over him, leaving nothing but snot and feathers. A human will stand transfixed while a knife-wielding mugger leisurely approaches him from 15 yards away, hoping Batman will somehow appear from nowhere to save the day. And he can't understand why the blade artist has a fecal grin on his face. It's because he knows he's already won, dummy. He knows the person acquiesced the moment their eyes locked and the person showed fear. He knows that the victim instantly decided that he couldn't win. Birds of a feather . . .

Nobody on this side is presuming to suggest that everybody can be a reincarnated Bruce Lee, but one look at an irate mother finch chasing a terrified hawk six times her size might generate the idea that all is not lost because of size, lack of equal weaponry, etc. There is no way in hell that a finch can take a hawk in a fight—but the hawk doesn't know that. And Mama Finch knows that he doesn't know it.

There is more to combat mind-set than the Marine Corps/Cooper Color Code. You have to know that you can win before you can ever have any hope of beating an enemy.

Some days you get the feathers, some days you get the chicken. It's up to you whether you want to be a brainy bird or a birdbrain.

A Solution in Sight

July 4, 1997—High noon. Bright, clear summer day. Partaking in a fun shoot with Colonel Cooper and several friends and acquaintances, I stepped up to the plate (no pun intended) to shoot the Guatemalan steakhouse scenario. I cleared the table napkin, brought my pistol to bear on the first target, and was mortified to find that the front sight had "disappeared." I looked down at Old Faithful, saw the sight was still attached to the slide as securely as ever, and started a second firing string attempt.

Same thing—no front sight. The third time, I had the same problem. After a couple of pathetic firing strings during which I actually managed to hit the backstop on several occasions, we switched to shoulder-fired weapons for marksmanship and target-testing and evaluation purposes. No problem. It then became apparent that it was an ambient light/focal length optical problem, as I was—and have been—using ghost-ring rear and acute-angled front sights on both weapons systems for a long time.

After feeding our faces, the good Colonel was kind enough to drag my sorry rear end down to his armory in an effort to diagnose and solve the problem. At that stage I was using a black front sight with a deeply embedded tritium dot. The reason for the ghost ring on the pistol was to enable my virally destroyed vision to still shoot accurately with a blurred front sight. The ghost ring works on the principle that one's brain will automatically self-center the top of a front sight in a circle, and Steve Wickert's much-copied pistol sights allow the shooter to shoot quickly and accurately out to any reasonable distance (plus or minus 100 yards) even with a blurred front sight.

Some of the manufacturers who have subsequently attempted to follow in Wickert's tracks have missed the point. Thick-ringed peep sights, which may be accurate, are not a ghost ring. They blot out much of a close target and force the shooter to have to align the sights, which is in antithesis to everything for which the ghost ring was designed and intended. One can't shoot accurately using a small aperture combined with a blurred sight, and oftentimes light will bounce off the inside walls of the thick rings, feeding false information to the brain, much like the elliptical shadow effect in a misaligned rifle scope.

On the other hand, misusing the Wickert ring by attempting to align the front sight in a large, ghosted aperture isn't exactly conducive to shooting tight groups either—a vital point misunderstood by many shooters and authors.

As Lamborghini test-driver Valentino Balboni once said, "We are better calibrated than our computers." Bottom line? Don't try to out-think your own brain—it'll beat you every time.

So back to the Independence Day blues. Colonel Cooper's solution was to paint the front sight orange—a color diametrically opposed to virtually any potential target or background color. It made a huge difference in his armory and during several ensuing shooting sessions. Then, several days later, I "lost" the front sight again on the handgun. I tried the shotgun and rifle, black sights against a black background—no problem.

At this stage of frustration two things became apparent: (1) the Good Lord doesn't like me, because apparently I'm the only person on the planet who can't "pick up" orange under certain conditions, and (2) suicide was starting to look like a pretty viable option. After several days of trying blue, green, and white paint, white seemed to work the best overall under all ambient light conditions, but I was still having optical problems with a white sight against a cream-beige-colored background. White on white was great, but white on cream or beige targets and I was back to square one.

Shooter's view of Ashley Big Dot tritium sights.

Then for once in my life I lucked out. For some reason I illuminated the front sight with a flashlight and the white sight stood out like a sore thumb—this in broad daylight. All the other colors were still so-so. I tried it in different light conditions and against every imaginable target and backstop color. It worked. It had the reverse effect of what should happen ("losing" the front sight when light hits it, as often happens with silver sights, long front sight ramps when overhead sunlight bounces off, or when flashlight techniques are used incorrectly).

Realizing that walking around with a Sure-Fire flashlight permanently glued to my proboscis would not only raise some eyebrows, but probably wasn't a good idea in itself, I racked what was left of my brain for a solution. Then I lucked out again. I contacted Ashley Emerson of Ashley Sights in Fort Worth, Texas. Not only did he understand the problem once it was diagnosed, he already had a solution on the market: the Ashley Big Dot Tritium sight.

It is different from any other sight currently available. It is circular in shape (the entire front sight) and looks like a miniature golf ball. Encased in a black steel shell is a big white dot that houses a tritium dot. The trick is that the sight has specific angles and pigmentation engineered into it that makes it stand out against any colored background and in any ambient light.

Short and sweet, as this isn't a plug for, or an article on Emerson's product,

it looks like it shouldn't work, but like many other good products, it does. If there are any other "pigmentally challenged" old codgers out there, this could be the answer. Naturally, it'll also work well for somebody who doesn't have optical problems.

Suicide has been temporarily put on the back burner until the next body organ starts failing. In fact I felt almost jovial after driving past an automatic teller machine while on a recent training circuit in California—and saw instructions marked in braille.

I'm still trying to figure out that one.

# Choosing Not to Be a Victim

*T*here are four categories of victims of violence.

The first, the person caught in the wrong place at the wrong time, is probably the most unfortunate and "blameless" of all victims. He is the traveler who loses direction in a rental car and unwittingly drives into a predatory urban gang's cul-de-sac. She's the person caught in a crossfire during a terrorist attack at an international airport. He's the victim of a random act of violence, the innocent bystander taking a bullet during a drive-by shooting. She's the gang-rape victim. Out of luck, out of time, and no wherewithal to defend himself or herself, the victim loses.

The second is a designated victim—be it a targeted homeowner, a motorist stranded in the middle of nowhere, or a family member whose greedy relative has decided is better replaced by the proceeds of a life insurance policy. This type of victim is doomed. If you don't smell it coming, you can't set up a defense system. The sorry truth is that if somebody wants to nail your hide to the wall, your skin will, sooner or later, end up as graffiti.

The old saying, "Just because you're paranoid doesn't mean they're not out to get you," often rings true. While you'll probably die from an ulcer instead of a bullet if you are paranoid and figure every dung beetle is out to get you, it also doesn't mean you have to trust everybody to the hilt. The commonly used handshake, for example, originated from the ancient tradition that you trusted someone with your weapon hand. On the other side of the coin, however, I don't know that, if I were a police officer, I would entrust one of my gun hands—even to a grateful citizen—unless I had at least worked with break-away techniques first. You could easily become one of the Number Two Victim Club members in a split second.

Number three probably doesn't deserve mention. Although still a victim who doesn't instigate trouble, this is the person who won't fight back. If you are not prepared to take an eye for an eye, don't expect your enemy to show you any mercy. He will look on your inaction only as a sign of weakness. While you may think you are "turning the other cheek," your assailant will kick a different anatomical cheek than the one you thought you were turning—unless you talk his language.

If you can't or won't speak the language of the "law of the jungle," don't expect a predator to cut you slack. Don't think that the rest of the world, law enforcement officers or otherwise, is beholden to help you when you won't help yourself. It's not a matter of bravery or cowardice—it's a matter of realizing that anything worth having is worth fighting for.

Two seconds after emerging from the womb, somebody 10 times my size picked me up by the ankles, turned me upside down, and belted me across the butt. In retrospect, I think I realized then that life probably wasn't going to be a smooth or safe ride.

The number four victim often isn't a victim, for one simple reason: he chooses not to be. He reflects on tactics that could potentially apply to his lifestyle, he's neither paranoid nor complacent, and he prepares and trains to a level of his choice for an occasion that will hopefully never occur. If the worst does occur, he's prepared for it, knowing all the while that he may not win—but it won't be for lack of preparation or fighting back. This man may not win, but even in his coffin he will remain unbeaten.

There are obviously no guarantees, as tactics, luck, and God's will set up infinite variables, but you can buy a modicum of insurance by being careful without resorting to paranoia. As stated above, if somebody really wants to take you out, sooner or later he will—irrespective of how careful you are. What's

being discussed here is not a matter of trying to be Mr. Superspy, but more a system of avoiding or dealing with a potential conflict by simple, day-to-day tactical forethought and possible weapons or martial arts training.

To quote Morris Mandel, on progress: "After several thousand years we have advanced to the point where we bolt our windows and doors and turn on our burglar alarms—while the jungle natives sleep in open-doored huts."

It's hard to catch a "jungle native" off guard because he hasn't lost his animal/survival instincts. To disconnect a fancy burglar alarm installed in an urban native's domicile is two minutes' work by a trained operator. Maybe installing a high-tensile-steel Club on your vehicle's steering wheel is a good deterrent, but it takes only 15 seconds to hacksaw through the steering wheel and slip off the Club in its entirety.

As the saying goes, "If you can't dazzle them with brilliance . . ."

If you don't maintain part of the rural native's survival ability in today's lunatic urban jungle, you have a pretty good chance of becoming one more statistic on Mrs. Roosevelt's "There are no victims, only volunteers" list.

If you think switching traffic lanes without checking your rearview mirror isn't bright, you might consider not sitting at a restaurant with your back facing a window, visible to the entire world driving by and with no hope of seeing approaching trouble. You might consider not buying your merchandise at a store that broadcasts that its employees are not allowed to be armed. You might consider not staying at a seedy motel when you notice the reception office's windows are covered by jail-cell-style burglar bars and every car in the parking lot is painted with gray primer. You might not assume that the door between your garage and home interior is locked merely because the outer garage door was locked when you cruised up the driveway. Just when you thought you'd reached the safe womb of your house, guess who comes barreling through the inner door after you've closed the garage door from the inside? You might not want to throw an iced beverage in Charles Barkley's face when you're 5 foot 2 and have no martial arts ability. You might not want to use a gas pump for cover during a gunfight. You might want to use your car's brakes instead of crude hand gestures when somebody accidentally cuts you off in traffic. It's not worth potentially instigating a gunfight over something that's not worth dying for. Let it go. There're a thousand "you might not want to's," but you might decide to ignore all or some of them—it's your roulette wheel.

Unfortunately life—especially in today's urban jungle—consists of one frustration after another, much like legendary King Sisyphus' existence in Hades. If you choose to have a running chance at reaching your three score and ten, you are almost obligated to formulate some kind of battle plan that will allow you to enjoy life by employing a common-sense balance between tactics, fighting ability, and paranoia.

There are no guarantees, but you can be careful without driving yourself crazy. And being crazy may not be the worst-case scenario—it depends on who you think is running the asylum.

Are You the Hunter or the Hunted?

*I*t's better to be the hunter than the hunted.

The intriguing question is: What is the defining mental approach that establishes whether you're hunter or prey? Obviously, there are physical differences—such as force of numbers, firepower, or simply being out of your element—that will predominantly sway the outcome of a fight. But these physical absolutes excepted, what is the deciding mind-set factor between a winner and loser?

On a daily basis for thousands of years, what should have been the prey turns out to be the victor. Admittedly, these results are the exception to the rule, but they occur on such a regular basis that there has to be a common denominator somewhere. The hyena turns on the lion; the cocker spaniel whips the German shepherd; the 5-foot, 6-inch, 100-pound woman transforms a mugger into a Double Whopper.

Anger is the obvious common thread, but something has to trip this trigger or you wouldn't have definitive words such as *hero* and *coward* describing soldiers' actions in battle; you wouldn't have the school bully running rampant for months on end; and the hyena would always run from the lion. But while anger, maternal instincts, and the so-called adrenaline rush are undeniable elements in the switch from prey to predator in midfight, there are those who have the ability to maintain the fire as a permanent part of their psychological makeup.

Weapons and tactics, and the proficient use of both, are prime essentials in the Fighting Man's toolbox—stupidity and rash behavior aren't. If you're swimming in the ocean a mile offshore and notice you're being tailed by two big black fins, here's some news for you: it's probably not a half-submerged '58 Chevy. It might be time to pull out the bang sticks.

One of the major contributing aspects of losing life-threatening confrontations in Western society is, to this author's mind, a somewhat surprising reluctance, even revulsion, at the thought of having to deliver violence when it is required to survive. This revulsion, however, seems to occur only when one is confronted by the destruction of a fellow human. It doesn't seem to bother most people when it comes to putting a bullet into Bambi or inserting one's hand into the orifice of the nether region of a turkey prior to giving him the 110-volt Ted Bundy treatment for Thanksgiving dinner.

It also doesn't seem to be much of a factor when the dirty deed needs to be executed on an "impersonal" basis, such as long-range artillery fire—as opposed to popping out the eyeballs of a rapist. So why are some people so reluctant to inflict violence on a human who is hell-bent on raping, brutalizing, or killing them? Probably because of "dial-a-cop" convenience resulting from modern, so-called civilization—the "someone else must do the dirty work; I don't want to get my own hands bloody" syndrome. The only problem is that Mr. Police Officer is responding to a dozen other 911 calls and probably won't be able to intervene until after it's over and done. Too little, too late.

Even though modern society has bred a huge element of ivory-tower pseudo-altruists who are as fake as rocking horse droppings, we have only ourselves to blame for the current situation of lack of personal intestinal fortitude, morals, and acceptance of responsibility for one's own actions. As Red Skelton said, "I don't hate my enemies, because I made them."

Unless you are a genuine pacifist, you have no excuse for not fighting for your own survival. If the thought of tearing somebody apart disgusts you, lie down and die—it's as simple as that. Carrying guns, knives, or other weaponry—even if you are mechanically profi-

This is the ideal perspective the homeowner should have. Any intruder will have to approach the potential victim through the proverbial "fatal funnel."

cient in their use—all comes to naught if you aren't truly prepared to use them for real and suffer the consequences, legal or otherwise.

This, by no means, is to suggest that you should disembowel a prankster kid who swats your mailbox with a baseball bat and then string his entrails over the gatepost as a warning to others. But if your life is threatened, you have to push the survival button and fight—viciously and with no quarter given. And it would probably be a good idea if you find out beforehand where your personal survival button is located—and also to confirm that you have said button. Some people don't or won't use it for personal reasons, be they theological or whatever. And that is naturally their prerogative.

On the other hand, if you cannot look into the eyes of your enemy at contact distance while you dispatch him, you're not going to make it through the next decade. In a world gone mad, only the insane can survive.

The current rash of ludicrous gun laws, legal loopholes, and sanctimonious "thousand points of light new millennium" rhetoric is espoused by ivory-tower politicians and benefits only ivory-tower politicians—and criminals. It hasn't stopped crime and the pillaging of the common man for 5,000 years, and it

isn't going to stop it now. It's called history repeating itself.

If animal viscera lying on the cutting board in your kitchen don't bother you, there's no reason why you should toss a load of carrots after being forced to gut out a savage criminal in self-defense. An animal is an animal, and meat is meat. When the snow is deep, you eat at the Donner Pass steak house to survive.

While tactical withdrawal and evasion of violence is obviously the most desirable and intelligent course of action, a predator often won't allow it. And if push comes to shove and you don't stand up to the school bully, you won't stand up to his reincarnation 20 years later when his wolf pack attacks your spouse and kids.

You have the God-given right and choice to be the hunter or the hunted.

Let us prey.

The Difference Between IQ and Battle Smarts

The time is fast approaching when we need to take the *bull* out of bullets and the *tic* out of tactics.

F. Scott Fitzgerald once commented that a test of first-rate intelligence is the ability to simultaneously hold two opposed ideas in one's mind and still retain the ability to function. While he wasn't discussing gunfighting, to a greater or lesser extent the same principle applies during a deadly-force encounter. Unfortunately, when under time, pressure, and fear constraints, it's not your numerical IQ that will get you through the day—it's a matter of whether you can concentrate on the subject at hand and apply intelligent tactics and sufficient battle marksmanship to get the job done.

There's a subtle difference between possessing a high IQ and displaying intelligence in a fight. There are many highly intelligent people who are incapable of exhibiting one shred of common sense under duress—and that's the crux of this article. If you are indeed blessed with an IQ in the multihundreds and spend most of your spare time analyzing the latest fashionable bullets or weapons to determine which will win the day on a battlefield, that's fair enough—but your gray cells might well be better put to use in a research laboratory than on the front lines. Leave the fighting to the "dogs of war"—they know how to use their teeth.

On the other hand, the everyday "canine of conflict" usually doesn't have Mr. Fitzgerald's "first-rate intelligence," and very rarely can he concentrate on two opposing ideas at once and still function well enough to win a fight. That ability is usually "reserved" for the likes of Tibetan monks and others of their ilk who spend their lives from cradle to grave studying the mind and inner self.

Lesser mortals like yours truly have enough problems working out which digit will fit in a nasal cavity during a quiet moment of meditation, let alone trying to simultaneously deliberate over two different courses of action while bullets are flying in the wrong compass direction.

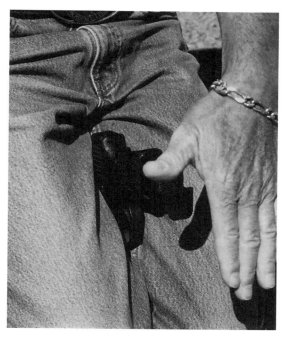

If you're physically incapacitated, you'd better have a gameplan to keep the wheels turning.

There are two major midstream quick-think problems to conquer: tactics and weapon manipulation.

The tactical instant mind switch is easier to achieve when things go bad in midfight than the plethora of variables to be immediately considered when a firearm suddenly becomes a useless lump of metal due to malfunction or total depletion of ammo. In both cases, the first thing that occurs is an instantaneous delay in your actions while your sub-Mensa IQ recovers from the realization that all is not going as planned. This is invariably closely followed by a statement like, "Goodness me, I appear to be in a spot of trouble"—or words to that effect.

Then, and only then, do the afterburners kick in. The tactical quick fix is usually more easily attainable than the mechanical, because at close quarters, one's brain has time to think of only one backup plan—if you're lucky. And this backup plan often succeeds because one usually carries it out quickly—before your worst enemy (your own brain) tries to consider alternatives. And no matter what you do, whether it's withdrawing, attacking, or diving for cover, your action now leads to your enemy losing valuable time because he has to react to your initiation. Thousands of years of ingrained animal survival instincts make this tactical move almost subconscious, and that's why it's so often successful. At least it gives you a second chance—unless you freeze under the burden of indecision.

The mechanical quick fix is a Pandora's box from hell. While the "beware of the man with only one gun" statement has held true for a long time, if the gun doesn't work, the plan doesn't work. While most malfunctions these days are more often than not caused by the operator either not checking the firearm's condition of readiness prior to battle, not maintaining the weapon or components, or (in the case of many of the modern, polymer-framed pistols) "limp-wristing" while firing, malfunctions occur for other reasons. And if it's a heavy fight you can also run out of ammo extremely quickly.

Most instructors drill their trainees mercilessly until malfunction clearances become second nature, and rightly so, in this author's opinion. However, even if the training staff plays "mind games"" and sets up unpredetermined malfunctions, the trainee still knows in advance that he's undergoing a malfunction-clearance training session and doesn't have the brain-freezing, reactionary pause encountered in the street when he expects the weapon to work.

Even the worst-case pistol malfunction nightmare, a double-feed, can be cleared in just over a second in weapons like the Glock, Para-Ordnance, and Heckler & Koch USP, once you've established the problem. But one second, sans the additional Murphy's Law street reaction time, is still not enough when you're at average room distances. It's over. Forget it and revert to your tactical plan B because there isn't enough time to achieve a mechanical plan B. Add on time frames to identify the malfunction, and with most handguns, like Colts, SIGs, etc., you're looking at five seconds instead of 1 1/2 to clear a double-feed.

You'd better be 50 years old and have spent the last 49 in a Tibetan monastery if you think that your Fitzgeraldian brain is going to get you out of this one. When's the last time you practiced malfunction clearances during dim-light/flashlight training sessions? Have you tried it with a remote flashlight and a shoulder weapon? Have you tried it one-handed, or do you think the department rangemaster should be "fair" and give you extra time on the range for one-handed clearances? Your enemy won't. You'll have less time once he realizes you're crippled—and he'll be on your buttocks like feces on a wet blanket.

If you're a proponent of the two-gun-carry school of thought, things become easier but are still extremely hazardous. The good news is you don't even bother with a reload or malfunction clearance, but you still have a reaction time problem. The bad news is, as opposed to a switch in tactics where you have only one decision to make, here you have to decide whether you have time to pull your second firearm or to resort to a fistfight/foot fight—two decisions. It's better than trying to fix a malfunction but still presents a problem with a flashlight, and during training you have to practice a system until it's second nature.

Techniques need to be considered, such as whether you will fire your back-up weapon weak-handed only, whether you will holster an inoperative primary handgun and then fire the alternate weapon strong-handed, whether you will transfer a "dead" handgun to the weak hand, what technique you will use to transition a shoulder weapon, etc. Pandora's box is a kindergarten joyride compared to this.

Obviously, much of the above paragraph's decisions will be predetermined by where on your person you elect to carry your reserve weapon(s), but you'd better work it out long before it cold-cocks you in the street. And equally as obvious for the purposes of this text is that you're on your own and have no manpower for backup to cover your rear end until you can dig yourself out of the mess.

You have a left brain and a right brain—until things start sliding downhill. Then both sides desert you, and all that's left are automatic responses and luck. Undoubtedly, a percentage of readers of this article will assume that this author's porch light burned out a long time ago, and you're probably right.

But as Charles Manson once said, "When I was crazy, it meant something."

Consider the Source—
Not All Information
Is Created Equally

When it comes to modern technology, I'm a self-confessed dinosaur. Basically the only Web site that interests me is one that has to be removed from the ceiling by means of a feather duster. This having been said, I was induced to watch someone plug into a computer "cobweb" site to see how the other half lives—never again.

Naturally, the cyber-whatever-it-was that was selected concerned firearms and tactics. It took only 20 minutes to reaffirm my Neanderthal outlook. Initially, I was mesmerized and stupefied by the technology, but this was fast replaced by disgust at the contents of the subject matter.

Of the computer operator's 101 e-mail messages, there were maybe half a dozen inserted by people who were trying to hold intelligent conversation, ask questions, or discuss weapons and tactics. The remainder ran the gamut from crude jokes about President Clinton to some self-proclaimed expert on everything firearms-related who apparently spends his life attempting to impress the world with his omniscience via his "ego-mail."

The two main subjects supposedly under discussion (supposedly, because it became apparent that most contributors were merely venting their "my way is the only way" statements) were knife fighting and projectile distribution in a gunfight. The answer to the knife-fighting debate is easy: proficient use of a blade is a martial art and, as such, requires years of dedicated training. While there are some good short-course knife instructors, to attain the dizzy heights of a blademaster is a decades-long study. No matter how adept your instructor, trying to use a week's worth of knowledge to beat even a 12-year-old street knife fighter who's grown up with a blade in his hand is not going to increase your longevity. You'll look like a Cuisinart commercial in five seconds—because he won't make the "right" dojo moves.

This is not to presume to suggest that one shouldn't take courses to gain possibly life-saving basic techniques. But if someone claims he can teach you to fight like a SEAL in five days, logic dictates that the SEALs

An easy frontal torso shot.

Same photographic subject, same distance, showing the huge percentage reduction of torso-hit availability when turned side-on.

need spend only five days on the same subject—and I find that hard to believe, even with my limited knowledge and the noncomputerized cabbage that keeps my ears apart.

The second subject on the "new millennium TV" was the here-we-go-again "two to the body and one to the head" dialogue. Not one of the proponents took into account anything but the "if he's at 21 feet and charges you" syndrome. No discussion of two or more assailants; nothing on the possibility of the lone crook being in any body position other than vertical and facing straight on to Sir Galahad; no possibility of the bad guy starting proceedings from a 5-, 12-, or 16-foot distance; no contact distance conversation; no carjacking. Nothing, nada, zip.

Here's how it works.

To stop somebody, you have to hit him. To hit him with bullets, you need a gun. If you are unexpectedly jumped from 7 to 10 feet, you won't even get a handgun out of a holster because of reaction time. If it's a shoulder weapon and you extend the muzzle, he'll take the weapon and insert it where the monkey puts his peanuts. And the last of the good news—you may very well kill somebody without immediately incapacitating him. Being killed by a dead man means you still have to step down to the bottom of the food chain—you're maggot cereal, same as if a live man nails your carcass to the wall.

Someone did bring up the subject of pelvic strikes and for the most part was shouted down. His detractors miss the point. The pelvic girdle is always relatively easy to hit—from the front, rear, or side-on. While the obvious idea is to break the bad guy's gearbox, the main

CONSIDER THE SOURCE—NOT ALL INFORMATION IS CREATED EQUALLY

premise is to impact the target in the easiest, biggest part of meat and bone that will do the most instantaneous damage and end hostilities as quickly as possible. If his forward progress is halted by a broken transmission, take it as a bonus. The bottom line is that the upper torso curves away from the front-on shooter, while the pelvis is concave and is a wider and slower moving impact area. A fast-twisting torso, such as when someone reaches for a knife, can shrink from wide to narrow in zero flat—the pelvis doesn't shrink to anywhere near as much percentagewise.

Try an automatic failure drill on somebody bending down to pick up a weapon stashed underneath a bed and you may have to shoot him 14 times in the butt.

Try two fast body shots while some cretin is cranking off rounds at you, descending a stairwell, and using your 4-year-old daughter for cheap body armor. Good range drills are utopian in nature. If they're offered to you for real, they're the best in the business. If they're not offered, unless you vary your targets and range drills every time dur-

ing practice, your brain will freeze during a confrontation when an "unfamiliar" target presents itself. People can survive perfect brain hits long enough to do serious damage.

For those who think rifle or shotgun projectiles are guarantees, I and a half-dozen trainees witnessed a 12-gauge slug deflect off a baseball hat's bill when fired from 15 feet. It left nothing but a scratched cheek on a humanoid moving-target system we use during training. I've seen it with handguns and rifles enough times that it's getting old. Surprise, surprise when this happens on the street.

There are, among others, three important components in a gunfight—a gun, a brain, and a sphincter muscle. If you have (or can access) a gun, that's a start. If your brain doesn't go to pieces and you can keep your feces coagulated, that helps. If, however, your mind is racing and your rear end has the emergency brake applied, you're in trouble—gun or no gun.

I've been led to believe that computers can get a virus. For my part, they can all contract pneumonia and die.

No Margin for Error for Reliability in Firearms

A malfunctioning firearm is like kissing your own sister—it simply doesn't cut the mustard.

On almost a daily basis one hears the comment, "Well, my pistol is extremely reliable—it experiences a failure to function only two or three times out of 500 rounds fired." Exactly how ecstatic would you be if your car failed to start "only two or three times" out of 500? The average person starts and shuts down the motor of a personal-transport vehicle about half a dozen times a day, or 40-plus times a week; this is about 170 times a month.

If your car died on you twice a month, every month, when would you like it to occur—in your driveway, when you're moving it 10 feet to open the garage door, or when you need it to lay rubber en route to an emergency medical facility? While the answer may be obvious, it does have a corollary. If the above-mentioned pistol malfunctions "only" a couple of times in several hundred firing attempts, would you prefer it to be numbers 199 and 200 on a firing range or numbers two and three in a gunfight?

And while the latter answer may seem equally as obvious as the former, it doesn't seem to occur to some that a consistent reliability problem can occur at any given time. Unless your specific problem is caused by a weapon that hiccups only after many fired rounds have gummed up the works, the gods have a succinct way of throwing rolled dice back in your face in a life-or-death encounter.

There is no degree of reliability when it comes to a firearm that may have to be used for personal defense. Either it's 100-percent reliable or it isn't, and neither the twain shall meet. In international bicycle racing there used to be a two-man, man-on-man time-trial race called "Devil Take the Hindmost." Hoping to make up for a known, potentially malfunctioning pistol by carrying 117 spare magazines is called (guess what?) "Devil Take the Hindmost."

Get the problem fixed and carry two reliable guns.

All of which leads up to several mystifying, at least to this author, problems—that were eventually solved by people with more intelligence than me. If the reader has encountered the same peculiarities, I apologize for wasting printer's ink. If not, the following few incidents may save you some blood, sweat, tears, and foul language in the future.

My first personal incident occurred with a reliable (remember the 100 percent) Colt .45 auto about 30 years ago. All of a sudden, from one day to the next there were intermittent failures to feed. After replacing virtually every possible internal part—including literally trashing about half a dozen Colt factory magazines—I resorted to checking my reloads. Finally I found one that wouldn't rotate freely in the shell holder on my reloading press. In those days, "tuning" and beveling Colt extractors wasn't a common gunsmithing practice, and the sharp edge on the two extractors I'd tried had nicked the much-hoarded and reloaded cartridge-case rims each time the case fed up the bolt face. Once the "nicks" were polished off, that was the end of the problem. Apparently, when the cases were in the exact position where the protuberance on the reloaded case lined up with the unbeveled underside of the extractor claw, the next time it was fed from the magazine, the pistol would fail to function.

And, yes, I did root through the filth and rotten food in the garbage for my magazines, and, no, I never found them.

Fifteen years later a friend from Tennessee was having problems, also with a Colt .45 auto; rounds were nose-diving into the magazine well below the feed ramp on his pistol. After the rest of us know-it-alls and

two very competent armorers had failed to diagnose the problem, Colonel Cooper walked onto the range and inquired as to the nature of the problem. Without deigning to even look at the weapon, he flatly stated that the inside of the slide stop was touching the side of the bullet of the top cartridge in the magazine. He suggested that Alfred either stone the inside of the slide stop or change bullet shape to a longer ogive and calmly walked away. There is no substitute for experience!

The last three cases to be mentioned here all occurred in Tennessee—it must have something to do with country music or Jack Daniels.

Number one was an AK-47, competent marksman, perfect battle zero from prone at 25 yards, first day out. As the day progressed we proceeded with the training ritual of shooting for group at 25 yards to cement the basic shooting positions. Group starts drifting to 10 o'clock. No problem, we'll diagnose the shooter's problem and move on.

Part of the instructional process is diagnosing shooter problems—and when you find the solution it's the thrill of victory. When you struggle to find the answer and you're pacing up and down that's called the "agony of de feet."

After 15 minutes of calluses and bunions on my hind paws, having checked every aspect of the shooter's physique except for resorting to proctology, I decided in my brilliance to recheck the shooter's prone position, figuring I'd be doing the Archimedes bathroom Eureka dance three rounds later.

Okay, we resort to plan B. Rezero him at 25 from prone. There must be something wrong with his prone position; after all, what can mechanically shift on an iron-sighted AK? Nothing.

Group still at 10 o'clock. Rezero the rifle. Sixty rounds later, the group's back at 10 o'clock. Fast approaching a higher level of insanity than normal, I give the shooters a break, asking them to rack the rifles. Staring with hatred at the one Kalashnikov in the world with which my life has now been blessed, I notice a shaft of sunlight strike the muzzle—and about a quarter inch of one barrel land missing.

By the end of the day we'd rezeroed one more time and had the impact shift again, by which time another eighth-inch of the same land had broken off. I understand the rifle was headed for an upcoming gun show to be sold at an extremely attractive price.

Case number two was an M4, resplendent with a supersecret scope from hell. The shooter attended with several sidekicks, similarly armed. They said they'd had success with the other scopes, but this particular one had been giving them trouble. They asked if I would mind if the rifle was used for the class to diagnose the problem. Assuring them that I didn't have a mind, we proceeded to battle zero from 25 yards, prone. Competent shooter, perfect battle zero. Sound familiar? Except this time there's no problem until day three, working from barricade positions. Five inches high at 30 yards. No dead rest, dead-on. And no, it wasn't deflecting because of the barrel or fore-end "kicking" off a hard surface rest. Surprise—nothing wrong with the scope, just a loose barrel nut from the factory.

Number three was an iron-sighted AR-15. Competent marksman, perfect battle zero from 25, first day out, but front and rear sights are set on maximum to attain the zero. That should have been a clue, but it was a parts gun—nothing to stir the senses so far. Day one runs well, apart from lousy weather. We climb into the quick-and-dirty work. Later on day two we traipse back to about 70 yards—and John shoots 10 inches high. Analysis time. Being omniscient, of course, I know what it is—either a loose barrel nut or problems at the muzzle crown. Wrong.

Bullet weight makes no difference. Good marksman. No sunlight on sights. Got to be the shooter. Pass me the rifle, John, let Mr. Big Deal shoot it. Eight inches high. No longer Mr. Big Deal, apparently. Hand it over to a third shooter. Eight inches high.

Back to 25 yards for rezero; something must have shifted in the sights. Dead-on. Thirty-two yards from the target, two inches high. Thirty-seven yards from the target, five inches high. A black rage begins to consume my soul. "Why me, Lord?"

"Because I just don't like you, my son."

"Aha," says a trainee. "Let's check the bolt—I've seen this before on long-range bolt guns." Sho 'nuff, a slight radius on two adjacent locking lugs. Switch bolts, problem solved. The longer I live, the less I know.

Maybe kissing your sister doesn't cut the mustard, but I'm starting to feel like something grey that's been "Pouped on."

The Magnificent Seven
of Pistol Marksmanship

*T*here have always been imponderables in life—the Egyptian pyramids, Mr. Leedskalnin's Coral Castle, and how the bumblebee defies the laws of aeronautics, to list but a few. Some will probably be solved sooner or later; some may never be.

Then there's the Current Reform and Preposterous Society (CRAP for short) that insists on putting a warning label on almost every mechanical device that man has managed to successfully mass-produce—the "don't use this electric hair dryer in the shower" genre. And in the last several years, the final insult—the "objects in mirror may be closer than they appear" legend emblazoned on every vehicle's passenger-side rearview mirror in North America.

First off, I'd like something more definitive than "may be," and secondly I assume that any dented vehicles or flattened pedestrians are normal size when they're on the left rear-side of the truck but have the potential to swell up if they're on the right-side rear. Amazing. And extremely confusing on a five-lane freeway in dense traffic. Of course, one could resort to the last-ditch principle of using one's brain and common sense, but that's apparently out of the question.

The upshot of the foregoing tirade is that while most pistol priests advocate the KISS gospel of simplicity, there are few people who don't roll their eyes or become bored when somebody starts preaching about basics. Inevitably the preacher's sermon is met with looks of "been there, done that, when are we going to get some rounds downrange?" Returning to our analogy, rearview mirrors are a mechanical bonus; they are not a substitute for intelligent driving. All the mirrors give you is a wider field of vision with less head movement. All that fancy shooting techniques do is allow you to perform circus tricks on a firing range. You can try them in a gunfight and you may get lucky, and you can try driving drunk in fast-moving traffic and you may get lucky. But luck's not going to last long. Basics, on the other hand, last forever.

No fancy building will stand on a rotten foundation, and no amount of reinventing the wheel can supplant solid basics in a projectile swap meet. While most pistol fights include less-than-ideal ambient light and terrain, and three-dimensional moving "targets," it's almost imperative that one learn the basics of static marksmanship and then apply them in a confrontation. You may get lucky if you don't—but it's probably just not worth the gamble.

The seven elements of basic pistol marksmanship run thus:

1. *Sight alignment*. This is the relationship of the front to the rear sight. The more precise the required shot placement, the more precise the alignment. On conventional Patridge-type sights this would entail leveling the top of the front-sight blade with the top of the two rear-sight blades. The front should be laterally centered between the rear posts.
2. *Sight picture*. Sight picture is the superimposition of sight alignment on the target, with the top of the front post placed on the desired point of bullet impact. Once sight picture is obtained, the shooter's focal plane should remain at front-sight focal length before, during, and after the firing cycle is completed. Since the human eye can only focus on one plane at any given moment, during firing the front sight should remain in focus while the rear sight and target are blurred.
3. *Firing grip*. Because individual hand size varies, the firing grip differs greatly from person to person. The main requirements, however, include a grip high on the backstrap to counteract muzzle jump, a firm grip

with the middle finger on semiautos, and, if possible, the positioning of the barrel in a straight line with the forearm to avoid wrist flex. Squeezing tightly with the two bottom fingers of the shooting hand on most everything but a revolver will lead to nothing but low shot placement on "conventional" semiautos or the traditional left-side drift for a right-handed shooter shooting the ubiquitous Glock pistol.

Geometrically, the preferred position for the support hand during two-handed shooting is to place all four finger knuckles approximately in a vertical line below the trigger guard. While some excellent shooters choose to extend the index finger around the front of the trigger guard, very few can control a full-powered, heavy-duty pistol using this technique.

4. *Shooting stance*. There are three basic shooting stances: the Weaver (akin to the classic boxing or long-bow stance), the isosceles (shooter faces straight toward a target with both arms extended), and the name-it-after-yourself-to-dazzle-the-world-with-your-omniscience technique. Stay with whatever works for you under all conditions and spit out anything else that isn't applicable to your physique. Probably the sole caveat is to be sure you don't choose a position based on the assumption that the target(s) will be directly in front of you, or that you will have the lee-way to move your feet during a confrontation. If you can deliver accurate, sustained surgical hits in a 180-degree arc of fire without

Classic two-handed firing grip for a semiauto pistol when fired from the Weaver stance.

moving your feet, you've found your personal shooting platform.

5. *Breathing*. Unless it's a "sniper" shot, such as a slow-fire, one-round, one-hit precision shot, forget about breathing—it'll take care of itself.

Scenario: you're aboard a commercial airliner and the flight attendant informs you with a straight face that if you lose cabin pressure a "magic mask" will drop from the ceiling. The idea is that you then calmly place the oxygen provider over your face and supposedly "breathe normally." Truth to tell, you'll be hyperventilating through enough other orifices in your body that you won't need any additional oxygen.

Solution: if you're taking incoming, forget about breathing, lock your abdominal muscles, and get it over with quickly and decisively—

otherwise objects in your sphincter mirror may begin to seem larger than they appear.

6. *Trigger operation*. This is often defined as "pressing the trigger straight to the rear until the pistol discharges without disturbing sight alignment." In actuality, the secret to trigger operation is to follow through after stroking the trigger. This entails maintaining contact with the trigger finger, releasing the trigger only enough to reset the internal sear/hammer/striker mechanism, and then immediately taking up any free play (slack) if it's in single-action mode for potential repeat shots.

You will lose more rounds with poor reset technique than with bad trigger snatching. So many people have been programmed to immedi-

217

ately remove their finger from the trigger because of a supposed range or potential street safety problem that they tend to "fly" their finger off the trigger before the weapon has discharged. (Chalk up more left-drifting hits for the Glock shooters.)

Here's where the anomaly creeps in. If you're undecided about whether or not deadly force is required, don't point the gun at your suspect and don't put your finger anywhere near the trigger.

If, however, the gun is pointed at your enemy it's for only one reason—you are unequivocally going to shoot him—and to achieve that you need your finger on the trigger during and after trigger operation for potential follow-up rounds. Even with perfectly placed hits you may have to continue firing to neutralize a threat. Apart from the fact that trigger reset will improve your paper-punching marksmanship, it can also save you from being flattened by a dead man. There's no future (literally) in whipping your finger off the trigger, coming off target, and then realizing that your bullets were ineffectual.

If the blurred target is still in front of your sights after firing, you're going to have to deliver more projectiles to survive. There's no magic oxygen mask dropping from the ceiling now—unless you keep on trucking, the aircraft's going down.

7. *Follow-through.* This encompasses the trigger reset and a continuum of sight picture, especially if your enemy is moving. It may entail shifting your aiming point to a different part of your target's carcass, but ceasing defensive action at this stage is obviously out of the question if you want to see your next birthday. Follow-through is one of the most important facets of defensive fighting and definitely critical with regard to operating firearms.

Are these basics boring and monotonous? Of course they are. Basics are always boring—but they are also essential. Everybody wants to perform aerobatics, but you can't get off the ground without wings, and you can't land safely without wheels and landing gear.

It's all a matter of perspective. A gunfight's not a big deal; the worst that can happen is that you are killed. It's not a serious problem, such as worrying about whether the mattress police are going to arrest you for cutting off the label or getting an ulcer wondering if the sports car you passed in the right lane is about to become a Boeing in your rearview mirror.

Women's Handgun Drawstrokes

*T*his chapter is directed toward women who believe that a pistol carried on their person is not only a viable option to deter or counter physical violence but also an inalienable right. If we ever reach the stage where a politician has the power—and the unmitigated gall—to decide whether or not a woman has the right to protect herself from physical assault, we are lost as a civilization. While usually proportionately more powerful in leg strength than their male counterparts, women are invariably finer boned, less powerful, and less capable of withstanding brute force that is inflicted on their upper bodies and heads than are average-sized males.

Like it or not, the Boadiceas (ancient British warrior queen) and Kathy Longs (ace kickboxer) of the world are few and far between. Much as many females would like to believe it, the television Xenas are but wishful thinking. This comment has nothing to do with condescending chauvinism—it's an unfortunate statement of fact based on physique, fine bone structure, hand-striking power, and realistic analysis.

Enter the handgun—Sam Colt's great equalizer.

With the increasing proliferation of concealed-weapon permit legislation in the United States has come an attendant increase in the marketing of holsters and "carry" equipment for pistols. And while many males can carry a pistol on a belt holster—either inside or outside the waistband—with extreme concealment, most women cannot. More predominant hip curvature, a shorter upper torso relative to overall height, and clothing styles lead to a large percentage of females carrying concealed handguns in "unconventional" equipment. For the most part, this equipment comprises three major systems: the handbag, the fanny pack, and containers such as the Safepacker.

In all three cases, the holster itself is open to view, but it is supposedly designed to look innocuous to the untrained or predatorial eye.

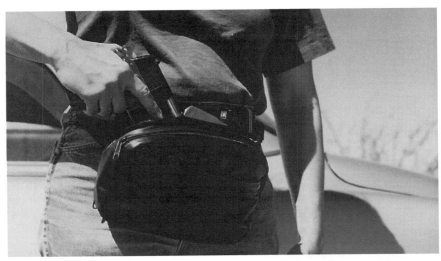

Pistol halfway through a draw-stroke from a fanny pack. Note that the left arm, hand, and wrist are already to the rear of the muzzle line of fire.

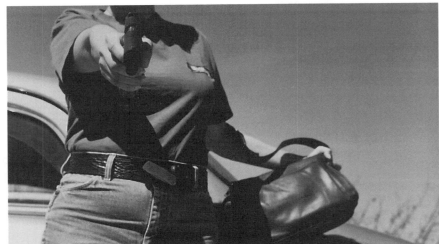

Pistol on target, about to be fired, while the handbag is in the throes of being flung to the rear.

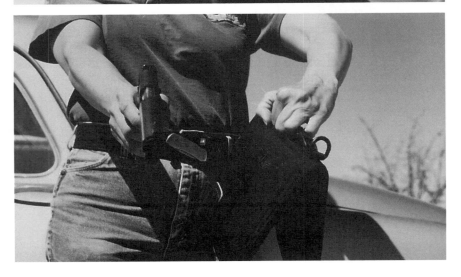

Pistol aligned for pelvis shots, with the shooter simultaneously about to fling the SafePacker into her assailant's face for a diversion. The pelvic area has been chosen as a target area in this instance so that the left arm has no chance of crossing the pistol's boreline while using the distraction technique.

Here's where the pistol pariah rears his ugly head. While he may be lower than shark feces, it doesn't necessarily follow that a scofflaw is stupid. Much of the time criminals are highly intelligent and very proficient at their vocation. Ergo, if he recognizes your supposedly innocent-looking handgun container for what it is, it could spur him on to even more violence than he may have initially considered.

One of the big "tricks" to defensive survival is the element of reactive, explosive surprise. If you look like a lame duck but react like a hawk on steroids when attacked, you're in with a chance. The criminal wants one of two things from women victims—physical violation or their valuables—both of which obviously entail close-quarters contact. If you don't have steel cable sewn into the shoulder straps of your handbag, stand by for Mr. Badbuttocks to razor-slash through the straps from behind. Then he grabs your free-falling bag, beats or kills you, and departs with your handbag and its contents (which include a pistol). The next step is obvious: a third party is shot with the gun you failed to protect or train properly to use.

A gun is no more a security blanket than an abacus is a computer. If you can't, or won't, learn to use it proficiently, don't carry it. Pistol carry systems such as the three described above are undoubtedly slightly slower in allowing access to the pistol, but with a little more training than is required with conventional holsters, one can become fast enough to get the job done. Split times on the drawstroke with a proficient operator are usually only about a quarter-second slower than from a belt holster. That is not enough to matter in the street, if judicious tactics are applied—and tactics are invariably the predominant and ultimate determinant in the outcome of a fight.

If, however, you have to draw the pistol before being in a position whereby you can defend yourself (as opposed to having the weapon in hand and ready to go), the drawstroke must be performed to perfection, or all is lost.

It is said that a picture tells a thousand words. The suggested presentation of a handgun from the three aforementioned holster systems is therefore covered in this article by means of photographs and captions both for clarification and to minimize verbiage. And while this chapter is naturally intended to help women defend themselves against physical attack, there are three caveats attached: (1) The techniques are not cast in stone—there's more than one way to skin a catfish. (2) Drawing a pistol from a holster is an inherently dangerous action and must be performed with safety as a predominant consideration, whatever technique you decide upon. (3) Crooks are, for the most part, neither stupid nor ignorant in the field of fighting—they often know more than the good guys about techniques such as these and the countermeasures to them. There's no free lunch!

There's not much that makes this author froth at the mouth more than an advertisement inserted in a magazine by a holster maker depicting a half-naked bimbo leering at the camera lens, finger on the trigger, and muzzle pointed down at one of her own body parts. It's insulting, it's stupid, and it's downright dangerous.

Unfortunately, women's holster systems are way behind the power curve in design, save for one or two. None of us needs insults, stupidity, and unnecessary danger added to the already-fueled fire of battle.

Predators prey only on the weak—weakness is but a state of mind. If you don't have a mind, move out of the state.

Using a High-Intensity Flashlight

You can't fight if you can't breathe. You can't fight if you're physically or mentally paralyzed. And last but not least, unless you've trained for years in techniques or were born blind, you can't fight if you can't see.

Heat sensors, infrared, and other 21st-century equipment excepted, the common tool of the trade for improving visibility in poor ambient light is a high-intensity flashlight. While this may be overstating the obvious, the attendant tactics required to operate a flashlight safely in a mano-a-mano urban gunfight may not be as straightforward as they might seem initially.

Much dim-light range training is conducted from two perspectives. Initially, one of many mechanical techniques is taught to enable a trainee to manipulate both a weapon and flashlight simultaneously, the objective being to allow said trainee to shoot under circumstances where it would normally be too dark to identify or allow a sight picture superimposed on an enemy.

The second stage usually entails an exercise where a lone shooter is directed to enter the ubiquitous "kill house" and proceed through the mock dwelling like a herd of turtles, hell-bent on butchering anywhere up to half-a-dozen simulated armed baddies. Works great in the movies and in a cemetery— doesn't pan out too well for-real. Nobody but an imbecile would consider doing this unless it's totally unavoidable, such as when quickly approaching an area where family members are being massacred.

And here is where range training so often diverges from reality. There has to be one underlying principle with weapons and tactics training and practice—uniformity.

Most of the time in urban defensive situations there is enough ambient illumination to make the use of a flashlight unnecessary. If, however, a scenario does develop—day or night—where man-made light is required, one's dexterity has to be equal to that achievable in clear visibility conditions. While the tactical solution to a problem will probably change, the mechanical operation of a firearm/flashlight combination must be uniform with good light techniques. Poor illumination, if you have applicable and efficient equipment, is neither a reason to reduce your normal marksmanship capability nor an excuse in a court of law.

To digress, as with most everything else, technology has improved with leaps and bounds in the flashlight industry, but attendant fighting brain power has often retrogressed inversely proportionate to the progress in technology. Vision is a brain function, not something achieved by means of a physical organ (the eye), unless there is definitive organ failure such as glaucoma. There's a reason why a forest dweller can see a candle with peripheral vision from 10 miles on a dark night and a city slicker will pull on a door marked "push to open" till hell freezes over—civilization has reduced our powers of observation.

Back to training. First you have to find a technique that will allow you to fire a pistol or shoulder weapon compatible with your physique and tactical requirements. And part of tactical training has to take into consideration where gunfire is not required, as when the force level in a situation de-escalates. In several years' time if society finally collapses in toto, any defensive situation will be construed as a potential kill mission, and nobody will get their bowels in an uproar if you shoot and kill a miscreant. Until such time we have to—at least in so-called civilized society—play the relative escalation-of-force lawyer game.

What this entails is that half-baked techniques using a shoulder weapon in conjunction with a remotely held flashlight in your support hand will enable you to shoot someone, but not control him if you don't shoot, as you now need three hands. Ultimately, you'll shoot him anyway, because you have no other physical way of controlling him. This displays about as much intelligence as printing an expiration date on a carton of sour cream.

Which probably means if you transition to a less efficient weapon (e.g., a pistol) you might want to consider drawing a flashlight simultaneously with the handgun. If this appears ridiculous and you're of the "judged by twelve, carried by six" persuasion, either you can discuss the problem later with your boyfriend in jail, manage not to get into this situation in the current litigant society, or put a dedicated light on your firearms.

If you rigorously practice reloads and malfunction clearances during daylight conditions, you have to do it in dim light as well; otherwise there's no uniformity to the training. If you're used to working on a practice range firing line where the instructors conveniently give you time to stash your flashlight, reload, reacquire the flashlight in your hand, and then—and only then—re-illuminate the target(s) prior to shooting again, you might want to think how you're going to do this when you're on your own with a shoulder weapon for real. Carry two guns!

If you think turning off the light and stepping laterally will give you automatic concealment, it might. We have, however, already established that in most situations you don't have complete dark. Which means your noisy, gross weapon recharging motor movements had better be completed before your enemy regains the night vision he temporarily lost while blinded by your flashlight. This assumes, of course, that he's alone—you're not going to night-blind two or three enemies with one flashlight.

If you use available cover, as anyone in his right mind probably should, you might want to ensure that your flashlight technique works from behind said cover. It's not as easy as it might seem, even with a solidly attached shoulder weapon flashlight. (Try rolling out a left-side barricade with a 6 o'clock-mounted rifle or shotgun light—or using the Harries pistol technique under the same circumstances, for that matter.)

"No problem," you say. "I have a cover partner. I'll use his illumination to shoot." Sure you will. Until you and your partner split wide to get bet-ter angles of fire at the bad guy and your partner's zillion-candlepower light reflects off a hostage's face and casts the hostage taker's head—and the background—into pitch-black shadow. So now you can't identify to shoot in a thread-the-needle situation. In a scenario like this both partners need a light.

Is the situation always this desperate? Of course not. But after religiously training during daylight conditions, a for-real dim-light incident is a hell of a time to find out that half of your techniques work only under controlled firing-range scenarios.

The name of the game is *zanshin*, the continuing mind. Work out your devil's advocate techniques before you might need them—and before somebody else turns out your lights permanently.

Fighting Skills Aren't the Same as Shooting Skills

You can fool some of the people some of the time. You can fool all of the people some of the time. You can even fool some of the people all of the time. But you can't fool all of the people all of the time.

What is amazing is how often we try to fool ourselves—albeit unwittingly—when it comes to marksmanship training for battle.

First come the basics of weapon manipulation and marksmanship. Eventually, by rote of repetition, a reasonable modicum of ability is attained. This is invariably followed by the "gadget gargoyle"—usually of the "what junk can I bolt on to make up for poor performance" variety.

Then comes the "big secret," surreptitiously discovered like a diamond in gangue. So you sell your Smith & Wesson and buy a Colt, so you can have a reverse barrel twist which will counteract the torque set up by the vicious recoil of a .45-caliber bullet. This in turn naturally reduces your target group size from a 10-inch diameter to one inch—until you find out you're wistfully looking downrange through rose-colored shooting glasses.

That's when the real never-ending learning experience begins. As Benjamin Disraeli said, "To be conscious that you are ignorant is a great step towards knowledge." The intriguing question is what constitutes adequate fighting marksmanship?

Unless you have a 100-percent-safe backstop, or it is on the rare occasion where bystanders can be regarded as expendable, you are morally, ethically, legally—and for reasons of self-preservation—bound to stay within strict parameters of surgical projectile delivery for successful battle marksmanship. If you don't hit the target, you lose. And even if you do strike the designated target area(s), there's no guarantee that the bullets will get the job done.

There can be few things more disconcerting than smacking a buffalo—two-legged or four—with perfect hits and then having him glare at you with a quizzical "Is that all you've got?" look.

Oops. Not a good time to find out that dedicated range drills don't always produce the required result.

Trainee opts for military squat to get a balance between speed and stability for a precision shot.

Nothing should come as a surprise in battle. You can't predict everything that will occur, but an absolute guarantee is that something will not go as planned—assuming you have the luxury of preplanning. With this as a basic premise, the obvious next step after basic marksmanship and manipulation principles have been achieved is to coordinate range training to approximate street/battlefield reality as closely as possible.

To this author's mind there are two major aspects that often aren't taken into consideration during weapons and tactics training: target systems and reaction time. Let it, however, be clearly stated here that this is a personal opinion only, which automatically means that any comments contained herein may very well be incorrect.

This having been said, there are two absolutes:

1. People are not rectangular, 18 inches wide, or one-dimensional.
2. If you are attacked without prior warning, you're starting off behind the power curve with retaliatory reaction on a time clock—by at least two-fifths of a second.

To have a quick pistol drawstroke is essential, but the samurai perfected this *nukitsuke* 400 years ago—it's nothing new. To have marksmanship ability is also essential, but the Swiss had this down 400 years ago—that's also nothing new. Firearm targets of three-dimensional configuration and capable of erratic movement have been in existence for—you guessed it—more than 400 years. So we're back to the same old song. This gives you the basics but is useless if not tied in to a fighting brain that can instantaneously adapt tactics in a reactionary situation.

Experiment: give somebody a prior walk-through for a tactical scenario before he shoots the exercise. Then run the same person through a similar exercise without a preparatory walk-through.

Result: the shooter invariably performs better in the known-in-advance exercise. And while this obviously doesn't require scientific brilliance to deduce, what are you gaining other than marksmanship and weapon manipulation expertise if all your training is conducted on the same targets, at the same distances on a regimented time clock?

Ask the average trained shooter how long and how many rounds it should require to take care of three hostiles positioned 10 to 15 feet to his rear. He'll almost immediately rattle off an answer. The master will first inquire as to target configuration, height, and spacing before he'll venture an approximate answer. He's been there before, he'll always look for the edge in a rencounter, and he knows it'll be different every time. He doesn't assume you've conveniently placed three flat paper targets evenly spaced behind him. He's taken different heights, target shapes, and angles into consideration, even before you've finished posing the unre-hearsed, unexpected question. That's why he's the weapon warrior and the others are mouth mercenaries—and he also knows somewhere out there there's always someone who's faster, luckier, or better. There are no guarantees, but there's no harm in checking to ensure that the blade is sharp if needed.

Static range drills under a time constraint are mandatory to perfect and maintain mechanical skills. Fighting skills are the decider when you're in a trash-strewn alley on a rain-soaked dark night and the heavens drop a dung duel on your cranium.

If you hurl a couple of thousand rounds downrange in a week at non-street-representative targets placed at the Olympus-ordained 3, 7, 10, 15, and 25 firing distances, you need 2,000 hits to have gained any semblance of fighting benefit. If you have 1,800 hits, forget it. All you've "achieved" is 200 misses. Quantity is nothing without quality. If your one-handed shooting—left or right—is not as strong as your two-handed pistol results, work on the problem. No predator will cut you slack when you're floundering on the battlefield—that's when he redoubles his efforts. I haven't noticed sharks lining up at the dentist's office downtown when the surf's up on the beach.

If you want to believe that the bottled water comes from a French mountain stream and is named after a town in France, you're probably right. Me, I can't seem to get rid of a rodent aroma when I notice the product name reads *naive* when spelled backward.

The Golden Rules
of Tactics

I thought I had a problem because I had no shoes—until somebody stole my socks.

You get into a fight, start to take incoming rounds, and figure you're about to lose your shoes. Then the sun appears from behind a dark cloud because you realize there's available hard cover and/or concealment. Utilizing the cover, you figure you can transform the sock thief into the proverbial man who has no feet—until your carcass is perforated with bullets. What went wrong?

There are two schools of thought on the use of cover/concealment. The first is the inevitable "hero" who spurns the use of cover and insists on standing out in the open to "look like a man" in the middle of a gunfight. If required, he can be contacted via any funeral director's agency—his address won't be changing. The epitome of this line of tactical thinking was the classic case last century of the general who took a rifle ball in the head from 600 yards while cockily announcing: "They couldn't hit an elephant from ther . . ."

The second line of thought presumes that anybody with a complete mental ZIP Code will use whatever cover and/or concealment is available—to this author's mind a much more intelligent approach. As with most everything else connected with tactics, however, there's a correct and an incorrect way to get the ultimate benefit from cover. Broken down simply, the two golden rules of tactics apply:

1. There are no golden rules.
2. If you exit a gunfight with the same amount of body orifices as when you entered, you used the correct tactics.

If you leave the fight in a body bag, no matter how perfect the tactics might have seemed according to a textbook, either you ran out of luck or, more likely, you used the incorrect tactics relative to that specific encounter.

Basically defined, hard cover will stop penetration of most bullets; concealment hides your position from an enemy's optics but will not stop incoming projectiles.

The intriguing aspect of the successful use of cover is that many people will learn and employ the requisite techniques, presuming that their body parts are concealed from the enemy, but never ask a friend to assume the same physical position behind a barricade and observe the situation *from the bad guy's downrange perspective.*

From a subjective observation point (e.g., from behind a trainee or from the trainee's own optical perspective), one is invariably convinced that one is protected as best as possible from incoming rounds. Unfortunately, geometry is often based on inversely proportionate angles. In other words, for every degree further outboard of a barricade one's body is extended—dependent on the shape of the barricade, the enemy's position, and the number of hostiles— the proportionate angle of visibility and ballistic access from downrange to your location is magnified at a ratio much larger than one to one.

Obviously, if you're on your own, you'll be scanning or shooting from an apex of a vertical and horizontal triangle of danger. While this supposedly safely opens up your field of view and arc of fire, it conversely pinpoints the enemy's aiming point like a manna-from-heaven homing pigeon. This naturally means that the more of your person that you are unaware is extended past concealment, the more is inversely proportionately available to your opponent as a target.

Does this mean that you either ignore the use of cover or intentionally extend your outline outboard of cover? Of course not. The trick is to know *how much* of your extremities are being offered to hostile fire at any given time— and it's extremely difficult to get a read on this without a lot of practice using barricades of varying shapes and sizes in conjunction with a "hostile" training partner downrange. Needless to say, elevation and distance from a potential enemy must also be taken into account.

The truth is that barricades are often unwittingly not used to their full potential during training, which could potentially lead to a false sense of security in a for-real fight. Almost universally, lone tacticians will back off from a corner and "slice the pie" optically before having to finally commit to entering an unobserved area. When it comes down to using stationary cover, however, the same tactician stays as close as possible to the barricade, thinking he is almost unexposed to a downrange enemy. Unfortunately, this is often not necessarily true.

Barricades are a Pandora's box. There is a razor-edge distance from cover where you are safer from hostile fire *and less visible* to a lone opponent than if you maintain close proximity to the protective structure. Withdraw any further from this safe zone and you're worse off than if you maintain the normally used proximity to the cover. Here's where you need religious observation practice with a partner downrange, because the geometrics of the situation dramatically change with barricade shape, angle, and elevation relative to the lone enemy. Again, the aforementioned is discussed primarily for a scenario where you are stranded without a backup partner and are faced by a single

Too much exposure from behind concealment.

Even though this subject can still be hit by projectiles penetrating the plastic trash can, he has maximized concealment by the simple expedient of withdrawing from the barricade to the best affordable position—in this case a matter of 24-inches' distance has made all the difference.

opponent. Most anything else is an entirely different ball game.

In summation, there are three "distance zones" of safety from cover:

1. Close proximity: relatively safe.
2. Perfect distance: has to be perfect but affords extreme safety and a wide field. of visibility, especially in a flashlight-required situation. To attain success at this art—and it is an art—one has to be able to index on a target and acquire the exact safe distance from the barricade required, relative to the target.
3. Too far back from cover: self-inflicted turkey shoot.

An important aspect in the use of barricades that must be remembered is that incoming ricochets/skip-fire deflect within only a 12-degree angle from the last hard object with which they come into contact. If the object is level and unblemished with dents (such as a car hood), your enemy doesn't have to have the marksmanship ability to tack-drive a bullet into your head. All he has to do is skip rounds into your to head off a horizontal car hood if you're dumb enough to shoot over the top of cover when you can return fire around the side of a protective barrier. Or he can bounce rounds off a smooth, vertical brick wall or regularly surfaced terrain, like a linoleum-tiled floor. He isn't concerned about the niceties of responsibility for the terminal resting place of his projectiles. One round of the indiscriminately launched dozen that he skip-fires can put cement or wooden shards into your eyes, which effectively ends the fight—and your life.

Yes, one should always be aware in advance of what potential cover and/or concealment is available if it's needed when things go bad in midfight. Yes, one should always use said cover/con-cealment when entering a potential danger zone. No, like so many other facets of tactics, safe barricade use is not easy to understand until you've stood in your enemy's shoes downrange and seen how stupid you look when you thought you were cunningly concealed.

I thought I had a problem because I had no shoes—until I met a man who'd had his feet shot off.

Condition White:

*How Being Unaware of
Your Surroundings Can
Get You Killed*

When I was fired as head of security from the Bates Motel after a few *minor* incidents had occurred, I realized there might be a small problem with my powers of observation.

Seeking to fine-hone my skills in this field, it seemed the solution was to take example from my peers and study how they were overcoming the mental state of what is now commonly known in the fighting fraternity as "condition white." For the uninitiated, condition white is the first in a progressive series of "colors" of mental awareness à la the U.S. Marine Corps/Jeff Cooper color code, and in essence it indicates at this particular stage one's mind is in neutral. In condition white the only things going through your mind are some blood, oxygen, and a couple of bugs that bypassed your motorcycle's windshield.

No rational thought processes are in evidence relative to your surroundings at this stage, because you are not exercising your latent powers of observation—much like the father of a newborn son who thinks his wife has just hatched the only boy-child in history who doesn't look like a miniature Winston Churchill sans cigar.

Once we've attained adulthood in modern society, we tend to see only that which we wish (or would prefer not) to see. In other words, if it's new or potentially exciting, or if there's potential danger—be it a rogue lion, the enemy on a battlefield, or even rush-hour traffic—one tends to concentrate one's senses on one's surroundings. Whether it's vision, smell, touch, or whatever, the senses are all in essence usable for observation.

An infant child doesn't have this capability, as his entire world is concentrated two feet in front of his countenance for the first 18 months. Big surprise when his first intelligible words are "mama" and "dada." What did you think he'd do on his first birthday, point to the heavens and say. "Look, Boeing's just brought out a new swept-wing jet"? After all he's seen and smelled for a year was mama, dada, and kaka?

As we approach adolescence, our horizons expand and we look for—and SEE—new and interesting objects and environments. Then along comes adulthood, and unless you make a conscious effort, it becomes mostly a blasé "been there, done that" existence, with an attendant lack of attention to—and appraisal of—your surroundings. We become creatures of habit—and unless you're a nun, habits can get you killed.

Much as life imitates art—and vice versa—the three stages of growing up are emulated by three comparable stages of tactical awareness. The only difference is once we're old enough to think tactically, in theory we possess the IQ to have the wide-eyed sensory perception of the adolescent, the adult's caution and awareness of action and responsibility—and hopefully more brains than an infant to know that if you have to dump in the diapers, dump in your enemy's and not in your own.

Unfortunately, often for reasons beyond his control, much of the time of an urbanite is spent in "forced" condition white, and he is an easy mark. It's hard to catch a jungle native napping because he never loses his animal instincts—he can't afford to. His very survival depends on his animal-like senses, while the city slicker has partially lost these attributes to so-called civilization and predominantly believes that predators will select everybody but him for a victim. Most of the time he never even sees it coming.

That doesn't mean you have to be paranoid, nor does it mean that you use your brain solely as a spacer shim to keep your ears apart—there's moderation in most everything. The bottom line, however, is that no matter how well you shoot, punch, or kick, if you don't smell the trouble coming, you probably won't

be capable of handling it successfully.

And that requires alertness and observation of your surroundings. As Mark Twain said, you can't depend on your judgment when your reasoning power is weak.

As the above-mentioned slight problem with Norm Bates' mommy indicates, my résumé doesn't exactly resonate with tactical observational brilliance, but if you ever want to observe imbecilic behavior—and the apparent lack of understanding of physics in urban society—spend a couple of hours eating a meal at a restaurant.

Naturally, you opt for a back-to-the-wall booth that's in a dimmer illuminated area than the outside parking lot, to always look for "the edge," but maximum benefit will be derived from the exercise if you can observe the approach to the entrance.

Man approaches front door, lit cigarette in hand. Attempts to push open entrance door clearly marked "pull." Surprise—door won't open. What does Einstein do? He pushes the door harder. Amazingly, door still won't open. Step two is to peer through a side window to see if the restaurant is open for business. Yes sir, it is—that's why you had to push through a dozen people waiting in line for an available table.

Several deep drags on cigarette, then Archimedes smacks him on the head with a bathtub. He performs the secret "pull" maneuver with the door and *it opens.* Walks up to maitre d' trailing a cloud of tobacco smog. You know what's coming—restaurateur inquires as to his smoking preference. While you're wondering if you'll be the first person to commit suicide by intentionally inhaling cream of broccoli soup, you cast an anguished glance at the entrance—only to see Man Number Two, who was glued to Einstein's back during the tactical entry, attempting ingress by pushing on the front door. Unbelievably, the door won't open.

Wishing you'd been killed in your last fight, you swivel your head—only to see the never-ending ketchup bottle routine being enacted at the adjacent table. Slim damsel up-ends opened bottle, slaps bottom of bottle. Ketchup slides to rear of bottle. "Here," says accompanying Conan, "I'll get it out." Slaps bottom of bottle with mighty palm. Ketchup slides at supersonic rate of knots—to rear of bottle. After the

inevitable fruitless pounding on the rear of the bottle comes the inevitable messy conclusion. One mighty fist grabs the bottle, up-ends it like a strangled chicken, and the notorious vertical ketchup bottle shake begins—and ends as it always does, with the usual three-way split: one-third of the ketchup on the floor, one-third on the tablecloth, one-third anointing the damsel's décolletage.

Maybe it's just not worth it. Maybe it's better just to walk around in condition white. Oscar Wilde claimed that a dreamer's punishment is seeing the dawn before others. Maybe I'm just Psycho or merely in need of a shower at a nice quiet motel.

The Gunfighting Mind-Set
A Color-Coded Guide to Mental Awareness

Discussions, techniques, and operations manuals on the combat mind-set have been put forth since Methuselah was in diapers. But it takes a simple question from the likes of actor/comedian Martin Mull to elucidate the bottom line: "What's the point in cleaning up your act if you don't have an act?"

In the context of this article, if you don't realize that mental conditioning is an absolute prerequisite for the battlefield, you don't have an "act." In other words, if you don't do all you can to prepare for battle, the only time the truth will dawn on you is when the feces impact the oscillator—and that's usually a day late and a dollar short for laundering your act.

The bible of tactics, Sun Tzu's *Art of War*, is age-old and battle-proven. The curious aspect of this literary work is that little mention is made of specific weapons and/or their application, manipulation, or operating techniques. The primary focus of the text is to cover tactics and mental awareness.

For the past four decades of the 20th century, Jeff Cooper—a rifleman par excellence, but who is primarily renowned for his instigation of the modern technique of the pistol—has expounded on the essentials of mental conditioning as part of the firearms fighting triad. Modifying the Marine Corps system of awareness levels, Cooper's succinct and condensed color code has been adopted, adapted, modified, plagiarized, and bastardized until it often bears little resemblance to the original—with a resultant loss of knowledge and impact being imparted to the recipient.

The Cooper color code, with humble poetic license, runs as follows:

White: Oblivious to surroundings.
Yellow: Relaxed but aware of your overall surroundings.
Orange: Specific alert, such as, for example, somebody wearing a topcoat in a bank in 100-degree weather. He may be a completely innocent party, but your level of awareness has

now been relegated to a specific area or scenario.

Red: This level does *not* mean there is a fight. What it *does* mean is a mental line drawn in the sand—an "if this happens, I will react thus" syndrome.

The Marine Corps did have an additional level—*black*—which denotes "fight," and is included in some current instructional programs.

Having discussed the color code, it is obvious that condition yellow is the logical level to maintain in normal everyday life. Yellow is an easy level to learn and maintain without reaching the depths of paranoia. Unlike condition white, where you are oblivious to anything and/or everything, yellow allows you to subconsciously pick up on something that is amiss and to then mentally zero in on it.

Paranoia, on the other hand, is a mental state diametrically opposed to white. Condition white occurs when you are more interested in the dead brain cells you have just removed from your nasal cavity with your pinkie when you should be observing the road, traffic, and your rearview mirror.

Paranoia occurs when you think the whole world is out to nail your epidermis to the wall. Let's face it, if the little green monsters want your hide, they'll get it sooner or later. And if you spend your entire life trying to find a bandit behind every bush, one day you'll be right—except he'll be behind the one bush you weren't watching because a lone operator can't maintain 360-degree surveillance (unless he is a fly or a chameleon). And even though a fly has a 360-degree vision, it extends only

18 inches—so the chameleon slurps him down anyway. That's called Murphy's Law.

So how do you maintain condition yellow for self-defense purposes? The same way you do for all the other mundane daily activities. You see what you're looking at and identify what you're hearing. If it looks like a duck and walks like a duck, there's the remotest possibility that it might actually be a duck. Ergo, if you notice something out of the ordinary, it's time to shift to condition orange. An old-timer's technique for training yourself to observe what you're looking at is to lay out a variety of objects in a vertical line on a table top. Look at them for several seconds, close your eyes, and attempt to remember the objects in chronological order.

Verify the results and then reverse the visual image in order of sequence, check the results, and then scramble the sequential visual list. This simple technique improves your powers of observation dramatically with very little effort required.

"If you don't see the threat, it's probably too late to retaliate," John Doe, famous dead man. Use store-front windows, unpowered TV screens, car mirrors, etc., to see what's occurring behind you. If you're approaching your car in a parking lot, for example—unless it's sprayed primer gray—cast a glance at the paint work. Mirrored reflections are easy to pick up without skulking around looking like Jack the Ripper. Usually one is most easily taken from behind—there's a reason fighter pilots maintain a "check 6" as a priority. They too, like a fly, normally maintain an extremely short focal plane distance ahead of the cockpit (usually about 18 inches)—until condition orange.

Condition white. If money is all that this woman loses, she can count herself lucky.

Condition yellow, already merging into orange. Heavy topcoat in hot weather, close quarters, and alms-seeker's right hand is hidden from view.

Condition red! Bullet-swapping time.

Remember that mirror images will be reversed if you turn around.

If you aren't prepared to get your hands dirty, don't jump into a cesspool. If you honestly can't bring yourself to gouge out a rapist's eyes, you can't blame the rest of the world for not coming to your aid. It's nothing to be ashamed of, but you have to know your limitations. Rambo may have looked good on the silver screen, but with all due respect to Mr. Stallone, he was never in a real war. Could the real-life Stallone gut out an adversary? If the answer is no, he must accept that a tactical withdrawal is required and get out of the danger zone. Don't fight if you aren't prepared to go 10 rounds.

Most people expect a miracle to occur or the cavalry to arrive from a black hole in space. It ain't goin' to happen. "The mass of men lead lives of quiet desperation," observed Henry David Thoreau.

And last, but certainly not least, the subject of unrealistic training. Carry on punching bullet holes in a flat piece of paper imprinted with an eight-inch bull's-eye, and you'd better pray that if you're ever attacked it's going to be by a flat piece of paper imprinted with an eight-inch bull's-eye.

The sword is more important than the shield and skill is more important than either. The final weapon is the brain. All else is supplemental.

—John Steinbeck

12-Gauge Options

*T*here seems to be no middle-of-the-road attitude toward shotguns—people either like them or dislike them. The latter is usually because of ignorance of how to manipulate the weapon, coupled with a lack of knowledge of ammunition capability and performance.

The shotgun has two advantages over most other shoulder-fired weapons—it delivers tremendous close-up power and has the ability to fire a wide variety of ammunition to suit varying tactical conditions. The basis of effective shotgun operation is a thorough knowledge of the ballistic capability of the many different loads available—and knowing what the weapon will *not* do in certain situations.

There are pros and cons to shotguns for defensive use, but there is no "one gun fits all situations" firearm. And while training with any gun is essential, it is absolutely mandatory with a shotgun. Knowledge of specific shot pattern sizes and slug trajectories at varying distances is a must, and each shotgun barrel will pattern differently than the next, irrespective of the nominal choke size. This, coupled with the shooter's responsibility for the terminal resting place of every projectile, is what makes training and knowledge of the shotgun's external and terminal ballistics so important.

There is a difference between wing or skeet shooting and the shooting of a human being, and the oft-misunderstood patterning data commonly leads to confusion in the mind of a self-defense shooter as to the potential—or lack thereof—of his specific barrel combined with a specific shot load.

Conventional patterning is done at 40 yards. One round is fired at a large piece of paper (usually about four feet square). A 30-inch circle is then circumscribed around the *densest* part of the pattern. The pellet holes contained therein are then counted and a fraction taken of the total amount of pellets in that given load.

For example, if a nine-pellet 00 buckshot load were used, and six of the pellets were in the 30-inch circle, you have just under 70 percent of

A trio of deadly beauties. Top to bottom: Remington 11-87; Robar-modified Remington 870; and the illustrious Mr. Browning's A5.

the pellets hitting the target. This would conveniently give you the information that you have a full-choke barrel with that manufacturer's brand and shot size of ammunition. Unfortunately, this is, in essence, "cheating" the data. The only information you can achieve from this test is that you have full choke density in one area of the overall pattern where you have chosen to draw the circle.

Unless you have totally even pellet dispersal throughout the pattern (extremely rare), you could have a so-called full-choke pattern containing a gap large enough for a jet to fly through.

In defensive shooting you need *all* of the pellets to impact your adversary; otherwise you will have stray pellets flying down the street—plus you may not have enough of the initial payload striking the target to get the job done. To reiterate, each and every shotgun barrel patterns differently at different distances, with different shot sizes and different brands of ammunition—guaranteed!

Winchester 00 will not pattern the same as Federal 00 in your barrel, and

Remington 00 will not pattern the same as Winchester, etc. By the same token, X brand of 00 will not pattern the same as X brand of No. 1 buck, 000—or any other shot size, for that matter. You must pattern your own barrel yard by yard with specific brands and shot sizes of ammunition before considering serious social work with your shotgun. Anything less is a liability both to yourself and others.

That's the bad news. The good news is that the 12-gauge shotgun has a plethora of different ammunition types available for mission-specific situations, such as buckshot, gas, rubber pellets and slugs, lead slugs, string shot, "Avon" rounds for blowing door locks, and on and on, ad nauseam. Obviously, you can't hump two tons of ammunition around with you, so you select the ammunition most likely to be required, considering your lifestyle or imminent mission.

A good example of the variety available in special-purpose 12-gauge rounds is the SPLLAT (Special-Purpose, Low Lethality Anti-Terrorist)

selection by Accuracy Systems Ordnance Corp. (Box 41454, Phoenix, AZ 85080). Special-purpose rounds available from Accuracy Systems include the following:

- Shok Lock—frangible metal/ceramic slug in a plastic obturator jacket for blasting locks and hinges from doors
- Dust Off—as above but without ceramic binder, for increased safety
- Starflash Muzzle Blast—a diversion/distraction round producing a brilliant blast of sparklets from the muzzle to beyond 30 meters
- Thunderflash—a nonfragmenting, exploding projectile available in ranges of 50, 75, 100, and 150 meters
- Starflash—similar to Thunderflash but includes brilliant white sparklets
- Tear Gas Muzzle Blast—produces a cloud of tear gas from the muzzle out to 5 to 10 meters
- Bursting Tear Gas—fires a CS-1 projectile to approximately 50 meters, which ejects a cloud of tear gas and may be used indoors
- Slingshot—soft rubber projectiles available as "00" (18 .32-caliber pellets)
- "Triple Ball" (three .69-caliber round balls)
- Rubber Rocket—with a single-finned projectile
- Stingbag—a cloth bag filled with small lead shot for applications requiring less-than-lethal force
- Obscurant Smoke—muzzle-blast-type rounds producing a thick cloud of opaque white smoke to approximately five meters, providing instant concealment in tactical operations.

Buckshot gets the popular vote in 00 and—for some obscure reason—No. 4s. While No. 4s generally have a reasonably regular pattern density (and overall pattern size seems to open almost predictably and consistently relative to target distance), they have a poor track record for penetration from 15 yards out. Although 00 buck is extremely popular and generally gets the job done, its selection seems to be based more on the "I use it because everybody else does" syndrome than anything else. There are many other loads available, such as 0 (12 pellets, similar caliber) and 000 (8 pellets, slightly larger caliber).

The bottom line, again, is to pattern your barrel until you find the heaviest shot that will stay in the tightest overall pattern diameter. Magnum rounds have more pellets, usually don't pattern well, and are *slower* than a standard round but are popular with law enforcement special teams.

Birdshot is popular for indoor use but may as well be a slug at six feet if you're concerned about overpenetration—it merely dissipates in a shorter distance compared to buckshot. Shotgun projectiles, even though ballistically impressive, are less of an overpenetration threat than a handgun, submachine gun, or rifle bullet. Although one heavy buckshot pellet can kill at 60 yards if the victim is hit in a vital area such as an eye or through an open mouth, it does not compare in lethality to even a .22 bullet, which is dangerous for more than a mile.

One final advantage to the shotgun is its inherent capability—in able hands—to shoot inside five inches at 100 yards with slugs through a smoothbore barrel. While rifle shooters may scoff at this "mundane" grouping potential, most people can't shoot that tight with a scoped rifle using match ammo—and bear in mind that with "generic" .72-caliber bullets you can shoot a five-inch "cloverleaf" with six rounds.

Home Defense

Handguns or Scatter-Guns

No matter how well versed you may be in the martial arts, a rolled-up copy of the Brady Bill is no match for an armed intruder. Some politicians may not like it, but one of the few means accessible to the law-abiding citizen for defending his life and limb is the "great equalizer"—a firearm.

The two most commonly selected guns for home defense are the handgun and the shotgun. Assuming the homeowner is adequately trained in the manipulation, marksmanship, and tactical use of his weapon of choice—because without operator skill a gun varies from being useless to being a liability —it becomes a matter of deciding which weapon is more suitable for a specific scenario.

Both have salient features, and both have liabilities. The obvious advantage of the handgun is its portability and relative simplicity of operation. It is, however, an extremely difficult weapon to shoot accurately in real-world stress situations, and its terminal ballistics fall short of satisfactory, irrespective of caliber.

Using the shotgun, on the other hand, gives tremendous close-up power, and it is easier to hit your mark under fighting conditions—but more manipulation training and a more thorough understanding of the weapon and its ammunition are required than with the pistol.

On this latter subject, one big plus for the shotgun these days is that it is much more difficult for children to accidentally operate a shotgun as opposed to a handgun.

While this is a sign of the times and not a safety feature inherent in the weapons, it could be a deciding factor in the choice of home defense weapons for the concerned parent. A shotgun could be stored within reach, for example, with an empty chamber, safety on, action locked, and a fully loaded tubular magazine. This would make it instantly available for use by the homeowner, but safe from accidental discharge by a child, as the safety would have to be depressed and the action racked before the weapon could fire—difficult combined mechanical operations to perform for anyone but a trained adult. Naturally, this "safety" feature

While some are stupid enough to argue with this end of a big-bore pistol . . .

. . . only an idiot will try mouth-to-mouth with a 12-gauge.

does not apply to a conventional double-barreled shotgun.

Handguns, on the other hand, are more susceptible to the "child accident" problem and thus have to be left in a condition of lesser readiness when intended for home defense. The obvious solution is to train the child and not the weapon, as was the case for 200 years, but this subject, nevertheless, has to be taken into consideration.

This problem excepted, which of the two guns is better for home defense? The first question is that of overpenetration—the "What if I miss?" problem. And the answer is that a pistol bullet will penetrate more apartment walls than will buckshot—a much-misunderstood fact. By the same token, using birdshot instead of buckshot to counteract the same potential problem is not the answer either because if the intruder/rapist/mugger is at any distance farther than five or six yards it probably won't do the job, and if he's close and situated next to a wall, a load of birdshot will penetrate the wall like a slug before the pellets disperse. An ounce of lead is an ounce of lead, and if birdshot hits drywall in a two-inch pattern you may as well be shooting slugs. Overpenetration is a big consideration in a home defense situation, as family members can often be in the line of fire in rooms behind the intruder.

Question two asks, "Is the shotgun too long for gunfighting at home?" And the answer to that one is "no," as long as intelligent "ready" positions are used relative to the situation at hand. Weapon retention should, of course, be practiced with both the shotgun and the pistol. Neither protrudes more than the other if employed intelligently.

And no, using a pistol-gripped, stockless shotgun is not the answer, because even at close quarters you will miss if you don't use the sights, and a stockless shotgun actually projects farther from your body than does a fully stocked model.

"So why shouldn't I just use the shotgun every time and blow that sucker to Kingdom Come when he puts one toenail past my front door?" Because there's a thing called the law, even to the extent that in some states you have to prove that you couldn't have escaped from your own house, irrespective of the intruder's intentions—or actions. And secondarily it ain't over till it's over, which means either help has arrived or you have personally bound his hands together—an extremely difficult thing to do when you're carrying a shotgun.

This final problem is the biggest decision maker of them all. If there is anything but good ambient light, you will need flashlight illumination to be used in conjunction with either weapon. This means either a flashlight mounted on the weapon, which can be operated by the firing hand or, in the case of the shotgun, an on/off override switch in addition to the conventional fore-end pressure switch.

It's all very well to have a pump shotgun with a pressure switch mounted on the fore-end—but if you have to use your support hand to open doors, tie up Mr. Baddie, etc., all you have is one shot and no vision. This may affect your decision whether to buy a pump gun or semiauto or even opt for a handgun.

The bottom line in a home defense situation is that you are attempting to stop a deadly-force threat—this does not necessarily mean killing. And even if your intruder is dead (which is the exception to the rule), you still have to control the situation. This isn't a matter of shooting steel or paper targets! You have to finish the job tactically—you can't just walk away. With either weapon you will need a flashlight (and with the shotgun a carry strap) to transition the weapon out of the downed intruder's reach and to leave your hands free for other duties.

Bear in mind, too, that often you won't shoot, which also leads to tactical problems with either weapon. And if you do shoot, you are responsible for every single projectile you sling downrange.

So what's the perfect answer? There isn't one.

This author's personal preference is to stabilize close to a telephone with a shotgun (a) because of the weapon's inherent power, (b) the fact that it's easier to hit the target with a shotgun than with a handgun, and (c) I will wait for the intruder to come to me, as opposed to hunting him down, unless I have manpower for backup. There is no material possession I own that would warrant my running headlong into someone else's battlefield of choice, irrespective of weaponry.

As stated above, both weapons have pros and cons. The shotgun wins the ballistics-and-marksmanship contest, as long as you understand the vagaries of shotgun ballistics and patterning. The handgun wins in the portability department, plus possibly some extremely close-quarters tactical points.

The best answer is to have both weapons at hand, but, bucknaked at 0300, this is highly unlikely.

Gentlemen, choose your weapons.

Belly Gun Basics

*I*t is not mere conventional wisdom that one's person is increasingly in jeopardy from violent attack. Crime statistics prove it beyond reasonable debate.

It is also patently obvious that law enforcement resources are stretched to the limit, both logistically and judicially. Prudent preparation for active self-defense is often the only protection against being mugged, raped, murdered, or carjacked.

The simplest precaution to enable the good guy to defend against deadly force is a firearm and attendant training in his weapon of choice. This article will not cover the training aspect, but it will offer some rationale for carrying more than one sidearm.

While this suggestion often raises eyebrows and elicits comments seasoned with terms like *paranoia* and *cowboy*, the idea is not as ludicrous as it might appear at first glance. If you cannot access your one and only handgun instantly with either hand while standing, kneeling, prostrate, or seated in your car at a traffic light, all you are doing is carrying a "security blanket," as opposed to a security device.

Likewise, it doesn't help to have a second gun in such deep concealment that it, too, is inaccessible. The base reasoning for having more than one gun available is to allow instant access to either one of the guns, depending on the tactical defensive scenario of the moment. And the operative word is *defensive*. If the scenario is of your choosing, and thus essentially offensive in nature, the basic problem discussed in this article is not relevant.

It is interesting to note that while many people tote a high-capacity semiauto pistol and abundant spare magazines, the mere mention of two or more guns on or near one's person often raises doubts about your sanity. What situations could arise to warrant the consideration of multiple sidearms?

The first—and most obvious—is when the primary weapon is out of commission. This can be the result of numerous causes, ranging from running out of ammo to mechanical malfunction.

While there have been horrific, extended fights where shootists have run their weapons down to zero ammunition, the usual bland reply to this possibility is, "Well, I always carry enough spare mags to cover that eventuality." The only prob-

A typical customized belly gun. Note the "trick" pants clip attachment by Tussey Custom of Santa Ana, California.

lem is that no matter how proficient you become at speed-loading you cannot count expended rounds in a hot-and-heavy, rapid-fire confrontation; you don't always have the luxury of cover and concealment, and it will take at least a second to work out the reason your weapon has ceased to function. In other words, the man hasn't been born who can perform a one-second shot-to-shot reload in a contact-distance fight, because of the reaction time that will pass before the actual process of reloading can begin.

So don't be beguiled by that one—or the premise of a split-second malfunction clearance

either—for the same reason. This is a real war we're talking about, not some trumped-up, predetermined firing-range exercise. Pulling a second gun is invariably faster than trying to fix a mechanical problem.

Additionally, while weapon-retention techniques should be rigorously practiced, anybody can be overpowered and have a weapon either snatched from his possession or deflected off target for long enough to effectively put him out of commission.

A second tactical consideration is that of injury. Again, while you should practice accessing your primary weapon with either hand, this may be too slow for a specific scenario, not feasible on a given day, or simply impossible because you take a hit before you can clear leather with the hand of your choice. The smug thought that you're tactically aware and will always see trouble building in advance has filled many a coffin.

Take a round through your car window into your strong-side arm and your normal sub-one-second drawstroke becomes a nightmare of eternity. Correlated to this situation is the relatively new to America fad of carjacking, which is essentially a new version of a tried-and-true terrorist assassination technique. Tactics need to be modified in consideration of the ever-changing avenues and techniques of criminal attack, but there is one inviolable answer to a carjacking: either react with explosive, instantaneous force of your own, or be prepared to beg mercy from a barbarian—and we all know how *that* story ends.

If you choose the former option and elect to use a firearm, you will probably need to carry a second or even a third handgun. And, again, if words like *paranoia* or *lunacy* leap to mind, ask yourself, "Can I bypass a seat belt and access my handgun *without* delay while seated behind the wheel at a traffic light?"

If the answer is negative, your current mode of carry won't help you one whit in a jacking situation: you need either an additional gun or an alternative mode of carry.

There is neither a middle-of-the-road answer nor a perfect solution. But you don't have to be a rocket scientist to figure out that you're probably not going to win a gunfight without a gun. And that you had better put your hand on one fast if you have a gun muzzle shoved in your face through your car window because you have only about three-fifths of a second to react before you're dog meat.

So what's the golden answer to how many guns you carry and how you carry them?

There isn't one.

It will depend on your lifestyle and clothing, and legal considerations; and most everybody's needs are different. But if you're carrying a backup gun in the ubiquitous ol' ankle rig, don't wear skintight jeans. It doesn't matter how sexy you look if you're dead.

Don't Snub the Snubbie

Buried deep in the cemetery of firearms design and evolution lies the "forgotten soldier"—the snub-nosed revolver.

Often the butt of derision, the snubbie has been, and will be, around for a long time. In fact, demand is so heavy that Colt is reintroducing its Detective Special. The "usual" objections to this weapon are its relatively low ammunition capacity, complexity in loading and reloading, and its supposed "inaccuracy."

As the snubbie is usually encountered in .36-caliber (inevitably as .38 Special or .357 Magnum) and in its most common form contains either five or six rounds, it does indeed have a much lower cartridge capacity than a high-capacity semiauto of comparable caliber, such as a P-35 Browning or Glock. The advantages of the short-barreled, small-framed revolver, however, are in its inherent concealability and the availability of ammunition to feed it almost anywhere in the Free World. Thus, reasons for carrying this weapon are concealability, portability, and its usefulness as an "ambidextrous" backup gun.

As for the supposed inaccuracy of this weapon type, it's more the singer than the song—if you can shoot accurately you will hit just as accurately at normal close-quarters confrontational distances with a snubbie as you will with any other handgun. The only limitation is the typically crude sights mounted on this breed of pistol.

Most problems encountered with the snub-nosed revolver can be attributed to the operator's lack of knowledge, ham-fistedness, or lack of maintenance. The revolver, contrary to popular belief, is not as reliable as a semiauto if it is not regularly maintained. The weapon must be kept scrupulously clean, especially underneath the extractor star and in the barrel-forcing cone area. Regular checks must also be made to ensure that the ejector rod is tight and hasn't come unscrewed during repeated operation.

The focus of this article is loading, reloading, and general revolver manipulation techniques. The first rule of thumb is to know in which direction your revolver cylinder rotates when the weapon is fired. Smith & Wessons and Rugers, for example, rotate opposite to Colts. This one fact is the master key to all revolver loading and reloading functions.

If, for example, you have only enough time to load two or three rounds, ideally you want them to cycle under the firing pin before the empty chambers do.

Thus, in a Colt revolver, while manually rotating the cylinder in a counterclockwise direction during loading, you should insert individual cartridges in a clockwise sequence in the chambers. Smiths and Rugers are manipulated exactly the opposite. This ensures that the first chamber to line up underneath the hammer will contain a live cartridge if a half-loaded cylinder is hastily shut during an emergency.

Even though, by its very nomenclature, a cylinder is round in shape, two adjacent chambers are always in a straight line. This is another basic fact that simplifies the loading/reloading process and cuts down the overall time required to complete the sequence. Two individual rounds can be easily chambered simultaneously with very little practice; based on this knowledge, it becomes even easier and faster using the Speed Strip manufactured by Bianchi International (100 Calle Cortez, Temecula, CA 92590).

One of the few firearms accouterments for which you get more than your money's worth, the Speed Strip is a straight rubber container that holds six rimmed cartridges in a secure, long-lasting, concealable package. Rounds can be loaded either singly or in pairs, based on the aforementioned "straight-line" principle.

While most firing-range reloading practice is conducted using speed-loaders, these items have two serious drawbacks: they are bulky and difficult to conceal (probably the primary reason why most people resort to carrying a snubbie in the first place) and using a speed-loader necessitates dumping *all* the rounds from the initial cylinder load, irrespective of whether some of the rounds are live cartridges. In other words, live ammo is often sacrificed in a revolver speed-load when using a cylindrical speed-loader, whereas a tactical loader with or without a Speed Strip requires the replacement of only the fired brass.

The latter process is almost as fast and requires less manual dexterity—but it does not ordinarily have the mind-bending pressure tactically dictated by a speed load.

Again, if the speed-loader is used, the "straight-line" theory is applied. First, contact the mouth of two adjacent chambers with the bullet noses and then rotate the remaining three or four cartridges into their respective chambers. For a right-handed shooter, the speed load sequence runs as described below.

SPEED LOAD

Step 1: The cylinder is swung open, the revolver is transferred to the left hand, and the muzzle is elevated to full vertical to avoid any possibility of brass becoming entangled behind the extractor star. The cylinder is controlled by the left thumb and middle fingers.

Step 2: The ejector rod is firmly "pumped" with the right-hand palm to aid in positive brass/cartridge ejection.

Step 3: The gun muzzle is now pointed straight down, and the speed-loader is employed as described above.

Step 4: The release mechanism on the loader is operated, and the loader is flipped over the top of the revolver as the cylinder is swung shut.

TACTICAL LOAD

Step 1: The cylinder is swung open with the gun muzzle pointed straight down.

Step 2: The ejector rod is pushed up about a quarter of an inch by the left-hand index finger or thumb.

Step 3: Fired brass is plucked out and thrown away right-handed.

Step 4: Emptied chambers are refilled individually or in pairs, either inserted by finger or by using a Speed Strip.

Step 5: The cylinder is swung shut and the Speed Strip, if used, is pocketed.

No, the revolver is not as prolific as it once was, but neither are honest men, courage, or responsibility for one's actions. That doesn't make any of them less admirable—nor is there any reason to relegate them to the fate of the dinosaur.

The Drawstroke:
Key to Keeping the Tactical Advantage

*T*o have any chance of winning a gunfight, there is one piece of mechanical equipment that is essential—a gun.

And if you're caught flat-footed and a holstered handgun is all you have, your drawstroke had better work. If you blow the drawstroke, it doesn't matter how well you shoot because you won't have a chance to test your marksmanship prowess.

Handguns are carried in a variety of receptacles, most predominant of which is the strong-side belt holster. For purposes of simplicity, this article is written from a right-handed shooter's perspective; thus the strong side denotes right and the weak side the left throughout the ensuing discussion.

Because federal and state laws vary as to when and where handguns may be carried on one's person, and because occupations and specific missions may require differing carry positions, this text covers several different drawstroke techniques. It should be borne in mind, however, that the KISS principle should be seriously considered. Whenever possible, carry the same handgun in the same position on the body and in the same rig, be it a holster, fanny pack, "trick" or altered clothing, etc.

There's nothing so disconcerting as to reach for Old Betsy in your shoulder holster only to realize too late that you switched guns and placed a PPK into your coat pocket on that given day.

Each sequential step of the drawstroke should be practiced by the numbers until the steps become reflexive. This ensures that no tactical advantage is given away and also prevents any safety problems.

In all cases, *the trigger finger does not contact the trigger until the sights are aligned with the target.*

THE STRONG-SIDE BELT HOLSTER

Step One

The right hand obtains a firing grip on the pistol in the holster while releasing any holster retaining device such as a thumb snap. The left hand is simultaneously placed flush against the body at approximately belt level. If you are drawing from concealment (i.e., from under a coat) the right-hand fingertips are initially lightly placed against the abdomen. The gun hand is then swept rearward, maintaining contact with your body until placement on the pistol can be achieved.

This automatically sweeps the coat clear of the weapon. Don't rely on such "tricks" as putting a bunch of keys in the coat pocket to provide added "swing"—tricks have a habit of failing at the worst possible time.

To access a pistol from beneath a sweater or Hawaiian-style shirt, the left hand reaches across and raises the right side of the shirt to give the gun hand clear access to the holster. While this last technique works well, the assumption is that you will have the left hand free to operate—which is often not the case in extremely close-quarters situations. This is also a big downside to fanny packs and handbags—these carry systems assume availability of a two-handed drawstroke.

With the handbag and fanny pack, practicing should be rigorously conducted one-handed. While this may be fractionally slower, you won't be caught flat-footed if the need arises for real.

Step Two
The handgun is brought to the "rock-and-lock" position, which entails muzzle alignment with the target (achieved by rotating the barrel to a horizontal position, once clear of the holster, and locking the wrist *tight* against the pectoral muscle). The gun should also be canted slightly outboard of the body to avoid malfunctioning of the semiauto, which can be caused by the rear of the slide slamming into the shooter's chest, body armor, or clothing. This is a weapon-retention firing position.

It is essential not to "limp-wrist" the gun when firing from this position—especially with Glocks—as otherwise the weapon will often short-cycle. As this technique is accurate out to only about four to six feet in a for real situation, it is definitely not the time to cause a self-induced malfunction!

At this stage of the fight you may be able to settle the problem by using your left hand instead of bullets. If this eventuality is to be considered (bearing in mind that this technique is for arm's-length circumstances only), the left hand is whipped up as the firing grip is obtained in the holster. The left forearm should face your opponent at this stage, unless you have a penchant for having your wrist slashed by a knife blade.

Step Three
The left hand overlaps the right in your normal two-handed firing grip. The gun has not moved from the rock-and-lock position at this stage. If the left hand is raised (as in the preceding paragraph) and you are not going to fire from the above-mentioned weapon-retention position, the support hand must be lowered to achieve a two-handed firing grip. This is done by physically contacting your chest and abdomen as you sweep the hand down.

If this is not done it will result in the left hand being covered by the gun muzzle. The same undesirable result will occur if step three is eliminated from the drawstroke sequence, especially as you start going for speed.

Step Four
The pistol is punched out, either to a low ready (or "guard") position or onto the target. In low ready the trigger finger remains straight and outside the

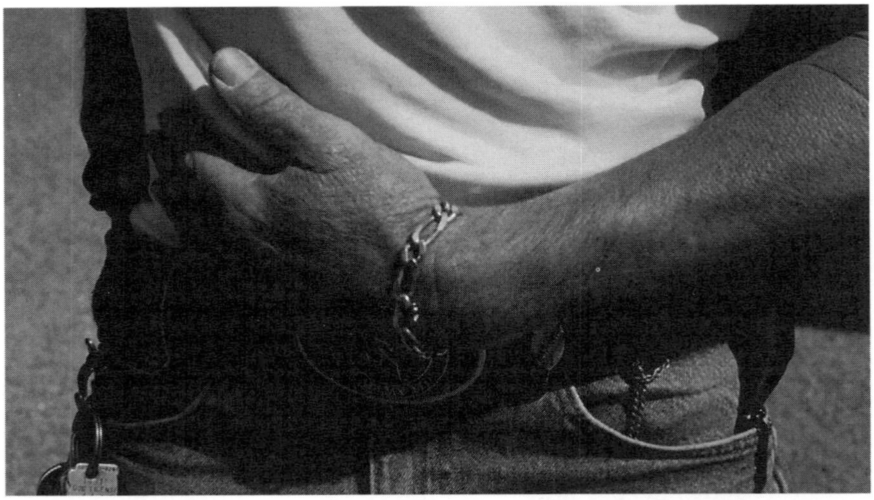

The firing grip is obtained, and the support hand palms the abdomen. The drawstroke from a strong-side belt holster.

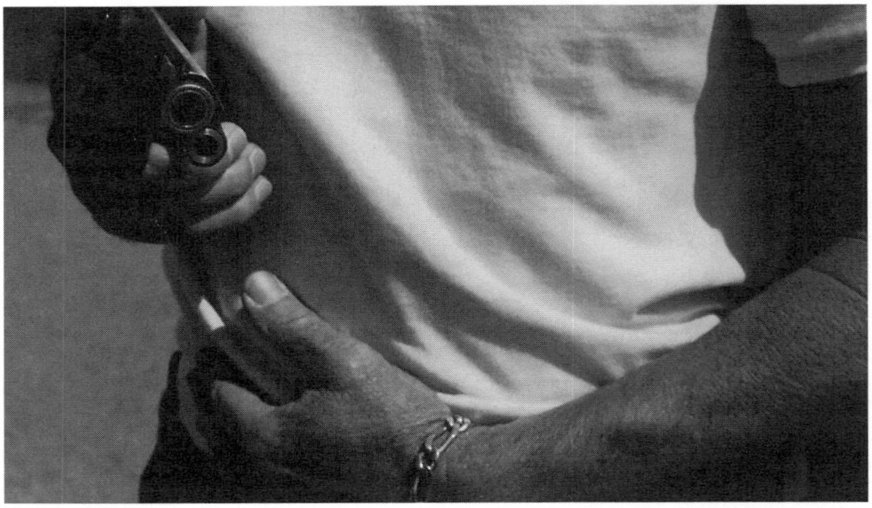

The rock-and-lock position. The full drawstroke would be stopped at this position if extremely close-quarters live fire was required to avoid a potential gun takeaway.

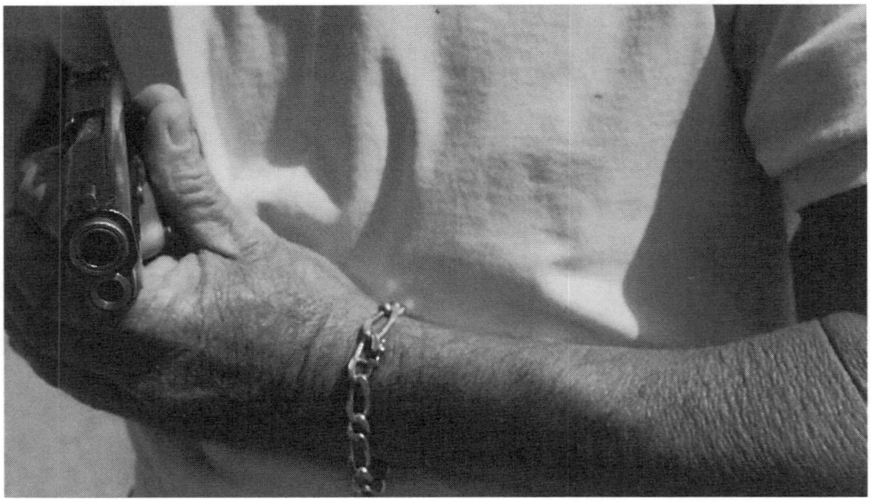

Both hands meet at this stage, partially to obtain a two-handed firing grip as soon as possible but also to keep the support hand out of the line of fire.

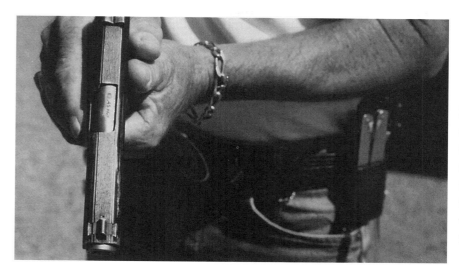

In this case, ths shooter has elected to go to low ready, maintaining control but assessing the situation as not warranting shooting . . . yet.

trigger guard. If you are on target the finger contacts the trigger *only* once the sights are aligned. If you are undecided as to whether or not you are going to fire, you have no business pointing the weapon at someone. Pointing the weapon at your enemy means that you are unequivocally going to shoot, and your finger is therefore on the trigger immediately *after* sight alignment and sight picture are obtained.

If you are unsure of the threat, maintain a low ready where you can see the threat, with a straight trigger finger. Obviously, if you use the step two weapon-retention position for firing, the finger contacts the trigger only *after* the rock-and-lock position has been attained and the sights are aligned with the target.

Holster

These systems are usually employed for concealed carry, and for this reason—concealed or not—the left hand should be placed high on the chest to physically grab and pull the coat (if any) clear of the weapon. A low grasp will not clear a jacket from a shoulder hol-

ster, but the primary problem is to avoid sweeping across the left arm with the gun muzzle when the postol clears leather. Once the left-hand arm position is achieved, it remains there all the way through step two until the rock-and-lock stage is completed. Steps three and four for a crossdraw or shoulder holster drawstroke are the same as above.

While it may be economy of motion to skip the weapon-retention phase, it is too easy for your enemy to divert your gun hand off target if you bring the latter straight out onto target or low ready. This, again, will be disastrous at extreme close quarters. Though it's nice to think that you will have the time to complete the drawstroke at relative distance from the threat, most of the time you are reduced to last-second, last-ditch scenarios in the real world because either you don't smell the trouble brewing, you are not justified in drawing the pistol until the last minute, or—in the case of law enforcement—you have to react to the threat progressively as it escalates. This last situation means, as a law enforcement officer, your department may not allow you to draw the gun until the 11th hour. Unfortunately, "fair" is just another four-letter "F" word.

The Fanny Pack

The fanny pack drawstroke is esssentially the same as the strong-side belt holster, but, as mentioned above, should often (or preferably) be practiced with the gun hand only. Again, economy of motion rears its ugly head. But if your're used to pulling the zipper, Velcro, or whatever with your left hand and for real you find a 220-pound Cookie Monster attached to your left hand—good luck and good-bye.

The Handbag

Most women's holdster-handbags currently available necessitate a two-handed drawstroke. For a right-hander the shoulder bag is best carried slung over the left shoulder, Velcro or zippered enclosure forward. The drawstroke is the same as for crossdraw, except that the weapon has to be rendered accessible by initially opening the bag with both hands. Once the pistol clears the bag, the bag is pulled to the ground. In

effect, the "holster" is pulled and thrown away from the gun once a firing grip is obtained, as opposed to the gun's actually being drawn from a holster.

THE ANKLE HOLSTER

Most of the time, the ubiquitous ankle holster is about as much use as a rodent's anal orifice. This carry method also invariably necessitates a two-handed drawstroke but in addition usually requires calisthenics with trouser legs to gain access.

In a quarter of a century in the game, I have met only one man who could access a pistol in an ankle rig under all situations—and to do that, he had to Velcro the inseam of his pants from crotch to ankle.

The moral of the story is as follows: If you cannot access a carry pistol one-handed—right or left—in any body position, under all situations, you have one of two choices. Either carry an additional pistol or face the fact that you're walking around with nothing but a three-pound security blanket. "Peanuts" is a comic strip—a gunfight isn't a joke.